The Marketization of Religion

The Marketization of Religion provides a novel theoretical understanding of the relationship between religion and economy of today's world.

A major feature of today's capitalism is 'marketization'. While the importance that economics and economics-related phenomena have acquired in modern societies has increased since the consumer and neoliberal revolutions and their shock waves worldwide, social sciences of religion are still lagging behind acknowledging the consequences of these changes and incorporating them in their analysis of contemporary religion.

Religion, as many other social realities, has been traditionally understood as being of a completely different nature than the market. Like oil and water, religion and market have been mainly cast as indissoluble into one another. Even if notions such as the marketization, commoditization or branding of religion and images such as the religious and spiritual marketplace have become popular, some of the contributions aligned in this volume show how this usage is mostly metaphorical, and at the very least problematic. What does the marketization of religion mean?

The chapters provide both theoretical and empirical discussion of the changing dynamics of economy and religion in today's world. Through the lenses of marketization, the volume discusses the multiple, at times surprising, connections of a global religious reformation. Furthermore, in its use of empirical examples, it shows how different religions in various social contexts are reformed due to growing importance of a neoliberal and consumerist logic.

This book was originally published as a special issue of the journal *Religion*.

François Gauthier, PhD, is a Professor *ordinarius* in Religious Studies at the Social Sciences Department of the Université de Fribourg, Switzerland. He is the author of *Religion, Modernity, Globalisation. Nation-State to Market* (Routledge 2020), and has worked together with Tuomas Martikainen since 2009 on a framework for understanding religion in a globalised, neoliberal world. Together they will be co-editors of the forthcoming publication, *Routledge International Handbook of Religion in Global Society* (Routledge, 2021).

Tuomas Martikainen, PhD, is the Director of the Migration Institute of Finland. His research has focussed on international migration, immigrant congregations, governance of religion and contemporary religion.

The Marketization of Religion

Edited by
François Gauthier and Tuomas Martikainen

LONDON AND NEW YORK

First published 2020
by Routledge
2 Park Square, Milton Park, Abingdon, Oxon, OX14 4RN

and by Routledge
52 Vanderbilt Avenue, New York, NY 10017

Routledge is an imprint of the Taylor & Francis Group, an informa business

© 2020 Taylor & Francis

All rights reserved. No part of this book may be reprinted or reproduced or utilised in any form or by any electronic, mechanical, or other means, now known or hereafter invented, including photocopying and recording, or in any information storage or retrieval system, without permission in writing from the publishers.

Trademark notice: Product or corporate names may be trademarks or registered trademarks, and are used only for identification and explanation without intent to infringe.

British Library Cataloguing-in-Publication Data
A catalogue record for this book is available from the British Library

ISBN13: 978-0-367-47438-6

Typeset in Minion Pro
by codeMantra

Publisher's Note
The publisher accepts responsibility for any inconsistencies that may have arisen during the conversion of this book from journal articles to book chapters, namely the inclusion of journal terminology.

Disclaimer
Every effort has been made to contact copyright holders for their permission to reprint material in this book. The publishers would be grateful to hear from any copyright holder who is not here acknowledged and will undertake to rectify any errors or omissions in future editions of this book.

Contents

Citation Information		vi
Notes on Contributors		viii
	Introduction: the marketization of religion *François Gauthier and Tuomas Martikainen*	1
1	Christmas fairs in Danish churches abroad: a resource mobilisation perspective *Margit Warburg*	7
2	From nation-state to market: The transformations of religion in the global era, as illustrated by Islam *François Gauthier*	22
3	Religious change in market and consumer society: the current state of the field and new ways forward *Marcus Moberg and Tuomas Martikainen*	58
4	Governing religious identities: law and legibility in neoliberalism *Marian Burchardt*	76
5	Religion and the marketplace: constructing the 'new' Muslim consumer *Özlem Sandıkcı*	93
6	The marketization of church closures *Jes Heise Rasmussen*	114
	Index	127

Citation Information

The chapters in this book were originally published in *Religion*, volume 48, issue 3 (June 2018). When citing this material, please use the original page numbering for each article, as follows:

Introduction
The marketization of religion
François Gauthier and Tuomas Martikainen
Religion, volume 48, issue 3 (June 2018) pp. 361–366

Chapter 1
Christmas fairs in Danish churches abroad: a resource mobilisation perspective
Margit Warburg
Religion, volume 48, issue 3 (June 2018) pp. 367–381

Chapter 2
From nation-state to market: The transformations of religion in the global era, as illustrated by Islam
François Gauthier
Religion, volume 48, issue 3 (June 2018) pp. 382–417

Chapter 3
Religious change in market and consumer society: the current state of the field and new ways forward
Marcus Moberg and Tuomas Martikainen
Religion, volume 48, issue 3 (June 2018) pp. 418–435

Chapter 4
Governing religious identities: law and legibility in neoliberalism
Marian Burchardt
Religion, volume 48, issue 3 (June 2018) pp. 436–452

Chapter 5
Religion and the marketplace: constructing the 'new' Muslim consumer
Özlem Sandıkcı
Religion, volume 48, issue 3 (June 2018) pp. 453–473

Chapter 6

The marketization of church closures
Jes Heise Rasmussen
Religion, volume 48, issue 3 (June 2018) pp. 474–486

For any permission-related enquiries please visit:
http://www.tandfonline.com/page/help/permissions

Contributors

Marian Burchardt Institute of Sociology and Center for Area Studies, University of Leipzig, Germany.

François Gauthier Department of Social Sciences, Faculty of Arts, Université de Fribourg, Switzerland.

Tuomas Martikainen Migration Institute of Finland, Turku, Finland.

Marcus Moberg Study of Religion, University of Turku, Finland.

Jes Heise Rasmussen, Faculty of Teacher Education, University College Copenhagen, Denmark.

Özlem Sandıkcı Adam Smith Business School, University of Glasgow, UK.

Margit Warburg Department of Cross-Cultural and Regional Studies, University of Copenhagen, Denmark.

Introduction: the marketization of religion

François Gauthier and Tuomas Martikainen

ABSTRACT

The contributions in this volume show a balanced ratio between – highly needed – theoretical discussions and analysis of empirical material. They also more or less equally distribute according to prevalence awarded to either consumerism or neoliberalism as a driving force for religious change. Far from being exhaustive or even representative, it is a worthy and timely addition to the discussion on the rapports between marketization and religion.

Where we are and where we have been

While the importance that economics and economics-related phenomena have acquired in modern societies has increased since the consumer and neoliberal revolutions and their shock waves worldwide, social sciences of religion are still lagging behind acknowledging the consequences of these changes and incorporating them in their analysis of contemporary religion. This does not mean that the theme is absent from our academic field. Back in 1967, already, Berger wrote that:

> As a result [of pluralization, and therefore the end of religious monopolies in favour of voluntary adhesions], the religious tradition has to be *marketed*. It must be "sold" to a clientele that is no longer constrained to "buy". The pluralistic situation is, above all, a *market situation*. In it, the religious institutions become marketing agencies, and the religious tradition become consumer commodities. And at any rate a good deal of religious activity in this situation comes to be dominated by the logic of market economics. (1990, 138; italics in original)

Yet this lead was only given continuation as of the mid-1980s in the so-called new paradigm of the Economy of Religion or Rational Choice Theory (RCT) applied to religion current which has been massively popular, especially in the US. Some years later, Roof (1999) was among the first non-RCT analysts to speak of a religious/spiritual market to characterize the contemporary religious landscape. Since, liberal economics terminology has been widespread. Yet this trend has been accompanied by very little critical, theoretical, and analytical considerations. While RCT authors and, to a perhaps lesser extent, sociologists such as Roof overtly celebrate the virtues of 'choice' as dynamizing religion (versus the fundamentally 'bad' intervention of the state in matters of regulation of religion), others have taken the symmetrically opposed standpoint and have lamented, as Carrette and King (2005), the 'corporate takeover' and de-naturalization of religion by market forces. Rare are the authors, unfortunately, who have denounced the profoundly normative and ideological nature of these opposed positions which only replay the classical opposition between liberal and Marx-inspired epistemologies that has structured a whole continent of social scientific production over the last century and a half.

In the midst of this polarization, what has been lost is how the present situation, in which economic terminology has become so natural, came to be, and what is meant by such notions as the commodification/commoditization, branding, and marketization of religion. With a bit of hindsight, it is not hard to see how religion and economics seemed completely heterogeneous not very long ago, and that this insolubility seemed to reach very far back in time. Until very recently, no one would even have thought that religion could even remotely be thought of in terms of 'offer and demand', that believers could be understood as consumers of religious products, and that religious institutions could be advantageously cast as 'private firms'. What happened? Is it religion that has changed, or our gaze? Unless it is something like a mix of both. But what, then? Was it not the state and politics whose terminologies, concerns, and concepts that used to irrigate the bulk of the studies of religion? And what about today? Is religion to be considered as a product or a good like any other, as the proponents of RCT believe (this assumption is foundational to the very exercise of RCT), or is commoditization supposed to mean some kind of reification serving 'corporate' interests in the end?

The aim of this ensemble of articles is to contribute to the clarification and complexification of these questions outside of any blatantly normative stance. While if notions such as the marketization/commoditization/branding of religion and images such as 'the religious/spiritual market/marketplace' have become popular, some of the contributions aligned here show how this usage is mostly metaphorical, and at the very least quite problematic. What does the marketization of religion mean, then? And what does it mean to make the reverse analytical claim that thinking about religion in market terms is anything but metaphorical (RCT) and that the supposedly 'natural law of offer and demand' apply to one of society's most complex and elusive manifestation of the 'symbolic consistency of human societies' (Mauss)? It is hard not to agree with Mauss when he wrote that humans are not calculating machines, as neoclassical economics assumes: '*Homo oeconomicus* is not behind us, he is before us' (Mauss 1950, 273, my translation). A century later, can we not affirm that Mauss was right? Is not the fact that neoclassical economics have captured even the study of religion the proof that *homo oeconomicus* has deployed itself fully across our societies in a way that has no historical precedence? And what does this mean for sociology – and the sociology of religion in particular? Does this not indicate that some important transformations have affected the very morphology of modern societies, their very dynamics, even perhaps their foundations?

Providing insights with respect to these questions is the aim and objective of these collected essays. This thematic issue furthers the work we started almost a decade ago, in 2009, when we first joined to coordinate a panel at the ISSR conference in Santiago de Compostella on the effects of consumerism and neoliberalism on religion. Our focus was Western at first, but the amazing success of that first panel and the conferences that followed have led us to consider things globally. These endeavours have resulted in a series of co-edited publications (Gauthier, Martikainen, and Woodhead 2011; Gauthier and Martikainen 2013; Martikainen and Gauthier 2013; Nynäs, Illmann, and Martikainen 2015; Caillé, Chanial, and Gauthier 2017; as well as our forthcoming *Routledge Handbook on Religion in Global*

Society, edited by Cornelio, Gauthier, Martikainen and Woodhead) that can be read as 'cousins' of the present, which is itself the by-product of a panel that we coordinated at the 2015 ISSR Conference in Louvain-la-Neuve.[1] We are very happy of having been able to accept *Religion*'s invitation to publish these essays in this fine and respected journal, and hope that it will give impulse to further investigations and debates. It is only fair to recognize that the last few years have seen a number of serious publications on issues related to religion and marketization, of which Rinallo, Scott, and Maclaren (2013), Usunier and Stolz (2014), Koch (2014), Jafari and Sandicki (2016), Moberg (2017) and Possamai (2018) are particularly noteworthy. While no consensus emerges from these works taken together, they do significantly refresh the ways in which issues of marketization and religion are approached, beyond the limitations and the heavily normative dimensions of the aforementioned liberal and Marxist perspectives.

Where we are going

There is no better way to begin this issue than with the 'classical' perspective adopted by Margit Warburg on the rapports that Danish churches abroad entertain with market economics. In this account, the distinction between *Gesellschaft* – associated to functional relations typical of the modern state and modern economics – and *Gemeinschaft* – associated to personalized relations and pre-modern forms of communities – are clear: church religion offers a space apart from the functional relationships of the market and market society, one in which community – and in this case the national community of Danish expatriates – is cared for. Yet it is not Sunday mass which is the most important moment in the Danish churches' abroad lives, but the Christmas fairs, which are also essential events for fundraising. The fairs illustrate how voluntary work is essential in producing the event and binding the community but also inefficient in terms of market rationality. This example shows how things were not so long ago in the era when churches and nations were intimately bound. Yet the article also shows how the fair must operate increasingly under 'pure market conditions', as the rupture of the link between religion and nation signifies a sharpening decline in donations by Danish businesses abroad, who are becoming increasingly globalized and no longer identify as serving a national purpose which entails symbolic gestures such as funding churches.

Against this classical example, the rest of the contributions are concerned with the world that Warburg's article announces. François Gauthier proposes a radical elevation of perspective towards the macro-level. In order to better understand the present neoliberal and consumerism-structured situation, this contribution sketches a narrative in which the advent of modernity first saw a profound remodelling of religion's location and significance through the rise of the nation-state as the main social structuring force. The argument stresses how religion was formatted within a 'national-statist frame'. An important aspect of the argument is to stress how this construction, which was naturalized within the secularization paradigm and modernization theories, was the result of colonial and imperial relations and was therefore not solely a Western phenomenon, but a global one. It is in

---

[1]To be honest, only Marburg, Gauthier and Rasmussen's contributions originate from that panel. Burchardt and Moberg's are issued from presentations at the same conference but in different panels, and Sandikci's is the result of a later invitation.

contrast to this national-statist 'regime' that the present, 'global-market' regime can best be apprehended in its characteristics and importance. This heuristic frame ('from nation-state to global-market') is illustrated by the global transformations of Islam from the end of the nineteenth century to today's 're-islamisation' through the rise of Islamic fashion, Islamic sportswear, halal goods, Islamic banking, and Sharia-friendly vacation packages.

Marcus Moberg and Tuomas Martikainen's contribution offers a welcome theoretical discussion on the meaning of marketization through a systematic review of literature on religion and market economics. Complementary to both the introduction to this volume and Gauthier's contribution, the authors note the ambiguous nature of the 'market' in most work to date, showing how what is meant by 'the market', 'capitalism', and notions borrowed from neoclassical economics are fuzzy at best, while the question of the rapports between economics and religion remain for the most part non-thematized and kept in the background. Engaging in such a necessary discussion as to what the market signifies – whether one considers the history of social sciences or RCT – the article sketches the lineaments of how to better understand the influence of the rise of neoliberalism and consumerism on religion in a way that avoids reducing religious phenomena to neoclassical economic categories while showing how these categories have come to impose themselves on 'religion' as well as to its study.

While neoclassical economics stresses autonomous and undetermined, value-free individual choices, a major area of study consists precisely in shedding light on the normative dynamics of market societies. Outside of the study of religion, a privileged means of addressing this question has been to mobilize Michel Foucault's work on liberal governmentality. Foucault showed how liberalism (of which liberal economics are the backbone) proceeds to govern modern individuals' behaviour by empowering them in a specific way. Marian Burchardt makes a significant contribution to this scholarship by showing how 'diversity', which has become a powerful normative ideal and political buzzword under neoliberal conditions, participates in practices of classification that have diverted objectives of social justice and equality into 'diversity as an end in itself' that supports the dissemination of free-market practices and ideologies. He furthermore maps out the variegations of the concrete actualizations, appropriations, and mobilizations of this normative frame by drawing onto two case studies: Quebec and Catalonia, two nations embedded in larger federations with active independence movements. The analysis shows how the level of integration within globalized capitalism (in economic factuality and cultural imaginary) is directly correlated with the normative pull of 'diversity'.

Özlem Sandikci, who is an influential author in Marketing Research and has published widely on topics dealing with marketization and Islam, presents a significant contribution that turns our attention back to consumerism. The opening theoretical discussion argues that the emergence of the consumer 'as a dominant mode of identity' and 'subjectivity' is a process in which 'marketing plays an important role'. In a rich and sweeping account, she discusses 'three phases through which the view of Muslims as modern consumers in search of distinction and propriety comes to dominate the view of Muslims as non- or anti-consumers: exclusion, identification, and stylization'. Echoing Gauthier's analysis of the transformation of Islam within a marketized form, Sandikci stresses how the impact of neoliberalism and consumerism are a global phenomenon that follows a coherent yet variegated and locally determined set of characteristics. The article offers precious tools for understanding how the new generations of Muslims, from Jakarta to Lahore, Cairo, and the Gulf countries, not to mention in Western diasporas, 'have grown up with a model of identity through consumption that was not previously available in any substantial way' (Lewis 2015, 87).

Finally, Jes Heise Rasmussen's contribution brings us full circle back to Denmark, as he analyses the impact of neoliberal ideologies and management practices on the Danish Evangelical Lutheran Church. Echoing Marcus Moberg's (2016, 2017) analysis of these processes in the case of Finland and Sweden, Rasmussen shows how the language used by Church officials, commissions, and committees evolved in two distinct phases: the first, stemming from the 1970s to the 1990s, modulated discourse and administrative Church reforms along the lines of state bureaucracy. The second, which starts in 1996 with the establishment of a consultative think tank, largely adopted the language and precepts of New Public Management (NPM), of which the article gives a precious synthesis. The analysis, which is a non-choreographed yet perfect illustration of Gauthier's nation-state to global-market model, shows how the NPM categories progressively come to dominate Church discourse, even when the official policies of such traditional religious institutions attest to a certain resistance with regards to fully enacting neoliberal-type reforms, for example, as concerns church closures and parish merges for economic reasons.

All in all, the contributions in this volume show a balanced ratio between – highly needed – theoretical discussions and analysis of empirical material. They also more or less equally distribute according to prevalence awarded to either consumerism or neoliberalism as a driving force for religious change. Far from being exhaustive or even representative, it is the editors' conviction that this issue is a worthy and timely addition to the discussion on the rapports between marketization and religion.

Disclosure statement

No potential conflict of interest was reported by the authors.

References

Berger, Peter L. 1990. *The Sacred Canopy. Elements of a Sociological Theory of Religion*. New York: Anchor Books.

Caillé, Alain, Philippe Chanial, and François Gauthier, eds. 2017. Religion. Le retour? Entre violence, marché et politique." *Revue du MAUSS Semestrielle* 49: 1–292.

Carrette, Jeremy, and Richard King. 2005. *Selling Spirituality: The Silent Takeover of Religion*. Abingdon: Routledge.

Cornelio, Jayeel Serrano, François Gauthier, Tuomas Martikainen, and Linda Woodhead, eds. Forthcoming. *Routledge Handbook on Religion in Global Society*. London: Routledge.

Gauthier, François, and Tuomas Martikainen. 2013. *Religion in Consumer Society. Brands, Consumers and Markets*. Farnham: Ashgate.

Gauthier, François, Tuomas Martikainen, and Linda Woodhead, eds. 2011. "Religion in Consumer Society. Special Issue." *Social Compass* 58 (3): 291–483.

Jafari, Aliakbar, and Özlem Sandicki, eds. 2016. *Islam, Marketing and Consumption. Critical Perspectives on the Intersections*. London: Routledge.

Koch, Anne. 2014. *Religions-ökonomie. Eine Einführung*. Stuttgart: Kohlhammer.

Lewis, Reina. 2015. *Muslim Fashion. Contemporary Style Cultures*. Durham, NC: Duke University Press.

Martikainen, Tuomas, and François Gauthier, eds. 2013. *Religion in the Neoliberal Age. Political Economy and Modes of Governance*. Farnham: Ashgate.

Mauss, Marcel. 1950. *Sociologie et anthropologie*. Paris: Presses universitaires de France.

Moberg, Marcus. 2016. "Exploring the Spread of Marketization Discourse in the Nordic Folk Church Context." In *Making Religion. Theory and Practice in the Discursive Study of Religion*, edited by Frans Wijsen, and Kocku von Stuckrad, 239–259. Leiden: Brill.

Moberg, Marcus. 2017. *Church, Market, and Media. A Discursive Approach to Institutional Religious Change*. London: Bloomesbury.

Nynäs, Peter, Ruth Illmann, and Tuomas Martikainen, eds. 2015. *On the Outskirts of 'the Church'. Diversities, Fluidities and New Spaces of Religion in Finland*. Zürich: Lit.

Possamai, Adam. 2018. *The I-zation of Society, Religion, and Neoliberal Post-Secularism*. Singapore: Palgrave Macmillan.

Rinallo, Diego, Linda Scott, and Pauline Maclaren, eds. 2013. *Consumption and Spirituality*. London: Routledge.

Roof, Wade Clark. 1999. *Spiritual Marketplace. Baby Boomers and the Remaking of American Religion*. Princeton, NJ: Princeton University Press.

Usunier, Jean-Claude, and Jörg Stolz, eds. 2014. *Religion as Brands. New Perspectives on the Marketization of Religion and Spirituality*. Farnham: Ashgate.

Christmas fairs in Danish churches abroad: a resource mobilisation perspective

Margit Warburg

ABSTRACT

An important source of income for Danish churches abroad is the profit from the traditional Christmas fairs. Arranging a successful Christmas fair requires that the church engages in a resource mobilisation effort to get donations of goods and free services for the fair and to raise voluntary labour among the local expatriate Danes. This requires a concern for both *Gemeinschaft* and *Gesellschaft*. Data on economy and number of person-hours spent on Christmas fairs at five Danish churches abroad showed that the profitability of the fairs could be questioned in some cases. During field studies at three of these Christmas fairs, I investigated many volunteers' motives for spending their time and efforts on the Christmas fair. I also tested their willingness-to-accept (hypothetically) to substitute the Christmas fair with an annual lump sum. The answers showed that the Christmas fairs are highly valued for their strengthening of *Gemeinschaft* in the expatriate milieu.

The Danish Folk Church has a special constitutional status as the national church of Denmark. The domestic church activities are largely financed through a special income-dependent church tax (levy) paid by the members of the Danish Folk Church. By 1 January 2017 about 76 per cent of the Danish population were members (*StatBank Denmark*). It is, therefore, unfamiliar to most Danes to finance church life by direct contributions from the congregation. However, this becomes an issue for Danish emigrants when they seek religious services in one of the about 50 Danish churches and congregations abroad (Warburg 2012). The emigrants are here encountered with the fact that the Danish churches abroad by and large must operate on market conditions. However, as will be shown in this article, important limitations to the market thinking are also prevailing among the expatriates participating in fund-raising activities for the church.

The legal and organisational position of the Danish churches abroad

A Danish church abroad is an independent legal entity in the host country managed by a board of trustees, usually called the church committee. The church committee is responsible for all practical affairs of the church, except when it comes to the position of the pastor. The decision to fill a vacant position is taken – in conjunction with the church committee – by the umbrella organisation of the church, the Danish Church Abroad/ Danish Seamen's Church. In theological matters, the pastor is supervised by one of the bishops of the Danish Folk Church (Warburg 2012). The Danish state is also more directly involved in many of the Danish churches abroad; for example, in the Danish churches in Berlin, Brussels, London, New York, Paris and Singapore, the local Danish embassy or consulate is or has been represented in the church committee (Warburg 2012). Conversely, a pastor in the Danish churches abroad sometimes serves as social attaché at the embassy and enjoys diplomatic status.

The Danish churches abroad are also in other contexts more than providers of Evangelical-Lutheran Sunday services and pastoral care for the religiously active expatriate Danes who are members of the church. My studies of the Danish churches abroad have demonstrated that they resemble other immigrant religious institutions by playing a much wider role as social and cultural centres for the local Danish immigrant communities (Warburg 2013). Not the least because of its tight connection with the Danish state, a Danish church abroad offers a professional, blue-stamped organisational frame for the expatriate Danish community life.

The number-one resource mobilisation event: the Christmas fair

Although the Danish churches abroad receive some state support in varying degree, a substantial part of their expenses must be covered by private means. This exposes the churches to market conditions to a degree unparalleled to the conditions facing any ordinary parish church in Denmark. Such a challenge forces the Danish churches abroad to engage in systematic resource mobilisation activities in order to acquire the means for upholding congregational life.

Among the most important income-generating activities are the traditional Christmas fairs arranged by many of the Danish churches abroad (Jacobsen and Warburg 2013). The Christmas fairs mobilise and attract a wider circle of Danish expatriates than any other church activity. In fact, in most Danish churches abroad the Christmas fair is advertised as the highlight of the year and the most important yearly event in the church:

> The Christmas fair is the biggest event in *Frederikskirken* [The Danish church in Paris]. With stalls abounding with pork roast [flæskesteg], pixies [nisser] and doughnuts [æbleskiver] there is a genuine Danish Yuletide spirit for every penny. (www.frederikskirkenparis.dk. Accessed 10 October 2014. Translated from the Danish)

> The Christmas fair is the biggest event in the church [in Rotterdam], and it is the only thing that people talk about all the year round. It has great social significance for all the volunteers, but for the church it also contributes to secure the economy. (*Nyt fra danske sømands- og udlandskirker*, no. 4: 15 November 2013. Translated from the Danish)

The Christmas fairs in Danish churches abroad are shaped over the same traditional mould wherever they are held, and in many big cities, the Danish congregations have successfully organised profitable Christmas fairs for decades. The second quotation above indicates that arranging a Christmas fair is not just a way of providing important income to the church – apparently, this form of resource mobilisation has a sustainable resonance among the volunteers, and it has positive social implications for the congregation and for the local expatriate community. To investigate this assumption, the present paper analyses in more detail the mobilisation of resources at a number of Christmas fairs in Danish churches abroad.

An intriguing aspect which arose from my field trips to Christmas fairs in Danish churches abroad was that many of the volunteers whom I interviewed definitely declared that they were not interested in the Sunday services and never attended them. This leads to the question: Why is it possible for the church to mobilise these non-users to support the church by volunteering at the Christmas fair?

Sources

The present work is part of my study of the Danish churches abroad (Warburg 2012, 2013). The sources were acquired through my field trips to Christmas fairs at three Danish churches in the late autumn 2013 (Berlin) and 2014 (South France and Paris). In addition, the paper draws upon my pilot study of the Christmas fair in Rotterdam in 2010 and from field trips to the Danish churches in Hong Kong, Sydney and Zürich in 2015.

Theory

Resource mobilisation is a traditional and widely applied term among economists who have analysed as diverse issues as improving agriculture in India, why the allied won the Second World War, and devising more effective taxation systems in less-developed countries (Khan 1963; Harrison 1988; Di John 2008). In the study of social movements, the resource mobilisation approach was pioneered by John McCarthy and Mayer Zald, and it quickly gained a position in this field as a more satisfactory alternative to earlier theories based on shared discontents among people (McCarthy and Zald 1977; Klandermans 1984; della Porta and Diani 2006, 11–16). The resource mobilisation approach seeks to direct attention to the less conspicuous, but no less significant, economic and organisational aspects of social movements (Gamson 1987; McCarthy and Zald 2001).

The resource mobilisation approach was soon applied in the sociology of religion in order to understand how some new religions were able to accumulate large fortunes through fund-raising among their followers (Bromley and Shupe 1980; Hall 1988). Conversely, resource mobilisation has been applied to argue why other religious movements fail after some time and disintegrate (Balch 2006). In the same vein, the rise and decline of the anti-cult movements in the USA can be linked to their ability of mobilising people and money in a sustainable way (Shupe 2011). It is also commonly proposed that one of the reasons why Muslims in Western Europe has a disproportionate low political influence is that they have not proven the ability to mobilise the resources to effectively promote their causes within the political system. The argument certainly has merit, but it is hardly the sole explanation (Soper and Fetzer 2003; Tatari 2009).

The resource mobilisation approach is pragmatic and seeks to identify and analyse the resources that a group can raise and has at its disposal. These resources are not just pecuniary in nature; apart from the members' money, a voluntary organisation such as a congregation in a Danish church abroad can also draw upon the members' willingness to invest their time in congregational life, and when financial resources are scant, paid labour may to a certain extent be substituted with voluntary labour. Not all kind of labour is equally useful, however; inexperienced volunteers working for Christmas fairs cannot, for example, take responsibility for decisions on purchasing goods for sale, for accountancy, or for organising and supervising the preparation of food to be served. In a resource mobilisation analysis, it is, therefore, often necessary to distinguish between the human resources of specialists, including leaders, and the unspecialised supporters (Jenkins 1983). This is well known among the religious organisations themselves; for example, a practical handbook of church fund-raising written by a Baptist pastor from Houston spells this issue out: 'The number one priority in your church budget should be quality staff' (Bisagno 2002, 9).

Critics of the resource mobilisation approach have targeted its inherent assumption of rationality, stating that the resource mobilisation approach overdoes the rationality of collective action (della Porta and Diani 2006, 14–16). Factors such as ideology, group solidarity and individual expectations as to the value and effect of participating or not cannot be overlooked (Klandermans 1984; Buechler 1993). However, there is a big step from questioning individual cost–benefit considerations to assuming that religious organisations, including the Danish churches abroad, in general, do not act rationally in their mobilisation and management of resources.

In my earlier study of the Baha'i religion (Warburg 2006), I have found it analytically rewarding to combine a resource mobilisation analysis with the use of *Gemeinschaft* and *Gesellschaft* (Warburg 2006, 374–376). A few introductory comments are needed though (see also Warburg 2006, 111–118 for a more detailed discussion of *Gemeinschaft* and *Gesellschaft*).

The concepts of *Gemeinschaft* and *Gesellschaft* were originally proposed by the German sociologist Ferdinand Tönnies (1970, 1974). Unfortunately, in much of the literature referring to Tönnies, *Gemeinschaft* and *Gesellschaft* has been seen primarily as an evolutionist historical transformation of human relations from the rural close community to the modern impersonal society, not as the general and time-independent ideal types, which they ultimately were meant to be (Tönnies 1931; Heberle 1973; Schachinger 1991). The evolutionist understanding of *Gemeinschaft* and *Gesellschaft* can be traced both to ambiguities in Tönnies' early writings and to Émile Durkheim's biased reading of Tönnies, and it has been perpetuated in later literature (Tribe 2004).

However, by reading Tönnies carefully it is clear that he goes beyond an idealisation of European societal development and conceives of *Gemeinschaft* and *Gesellschaft* as general ideal types (*Normalbegriffe*, Tönnies 1931; Heberle 1973; Schachinger 1991). The paired concepts of *Gemeinschaft* and *Gesellschaft* must thus be seen as ideal types of structural relations between people within a given social entity (a business, a religious group, a nation, etc.) (Tönnies 1931; Heberle 1973).

Gemeinschaft relations are unspecific and rest on sentiments of kinship, neighbourhood and friendship; *Gesellschaft* relations are limited and specified and are based on rationality and calculation (Tönnies 1931; Heberle 1973). This, however, should not lead to mistaking *Gemeinschaft* with informal groups and *Gesellschaft* with formal groups (Cahnman 1973). Nor is *Gemeinschaft* the characteristic social order of the village, and *Gesellschaft* that of the city – a misconception that can be traced to influential American sociologists, in particular, Talcott Parsons (Schachinger 1991). As Tönnies emphasised: 'the essence of both Gemeinschaft and Gesellschaft is found interwoven in all kinds of associations' (Tönnies

2001, 17–18). The fact that a group of people know each other well and are bound together by sentiments of loyalty does not exclude that formal rules play a role. On the contrary, *Gemeinschaft* relations are often best served when people in a group also obey formal rules and where the practical needs of the group are managed in a rational way.

Both activities that strengthen *Gemeinschaft* and activities that strengthen *Gesellschaft* are important for any kind of group or community – at least all those based on voluntary participation (Warburg 2006, 374–420). There must be activities that fulfil the members' expectations of *Gemeinschaft* – otherwise, they may become disinterested in participating in community life. However, proper functioning of the organisational backbone of the community, in this case, a Danish church abroad, requires administrative efficiency and rational management of resources, which are *Gesellschaft*-oriented activities. Any voluntary group embarking on a specific project – in this case arranging a Christmas fair – therefore, face the strategic issue of how to mobilise resources most effectively, and at the same time find a satisfactory balance between activities that strengthen *Gemeinschaft* and those that strengthen *Gesellschaft* (Warburg 2006, 376).

In the present study of resource mobilisation at the Christmas fairs in Danish churches abroad, I shall show that the Christmas fair is the foremost event that serves both *Gesellschaft* and *Gemeinschaft* purposes – *Gesellschaft* through the provision of money, and *Gemeinschaft* through creating a space where Danish expatriates nurture their Danish belonging. I shall further apply a resource mobilisation approach investigating the significance of the two purposes for arranging the Christmas fairs, year after year.

Christmas fairs in three Danish churches abroad

Christmas fairs in Danish churches abroad are very much like each other wherever they are held, as mentioned above. There are local variations, of course, but these are expressions of a pragmatic adaption to the available resources in the form of people and premises.

The Danish church in South France does not have its own church building, and the Christmas fair takes place in a small hotel rented for the purpose. Likewise, in Zürich, the congregation borrows the school of a local Reformed Church for the fair. However, in those Danish churches abroad that have their own building, such as Berlin, Paris and Rotterdam, the church premises are used for the fair. The church room is utterly transformed during the weekend in November when the fair is held. The altar and the furniture are set aside, the cross above the altar is covered (in Paris for example with the Danish flag), and the church room and the adjacent space, both inside and outside, is one large Christmas fair area.

The many stalls are decorated in red, green and gold, and volunteers man the stalls and sell Danish food items, Danish Christmas decorations, Danish knitwear, second-hand books, second-hand children's clothes and other items according to individual stall entrepreneurs' interests and access to supplies of goods. Food and drinks are offered for sale, and tradition dictates that this always includes hot sausages, Danish Christmas doughnuts (*æbleskiver*), freshly prepared Danish open sandwiches (*smørrebrød*), hot spicy red wine (*glögg*), beer and Danish *schnapps*.

The core customers in the fairs are expatriate Danes, of course. A survey study from 2009, *Religion Among Danes Abroad*, showed that the respondents' Danish identity was particularly expressed at Christmas, where Danish Christmas traditions are held in esteem (Jacobsen and Warburg 2013). Thus, 64 pct. declared that they perceived themselves to be most Danish at Christmas time. The Christmas fair offers the special foods and items which characterise a 'real' Danish family Christmas, and it, therefore, supports the customers' sense of their belonging to the imagined community of Danes.

However, the fairs also attract many people with no particular relation to Denmark; in Berlin, where there is a great tradition for Christmas fairs, there were between 4000 and 5000 visitors in 2013, and the far majority of them were Germans. This segment of customers is rather important for the *Gesellschaft* purpose of the Christmas fair, namely to generate income to the Danish church in Berlin. The pastor and her husband clearly expressed this in my interview with them on 3 December 2013: 'This is cool business. We sell to the Germans to make money, but it is also a promotion of Denmark.'

Tradition also dictates that the Christmas fair is officially opened by a Danish ambassador or consul. This little ceremony where a red ribbon is cut is a very strong signal to visitors that the arrangement enjoys the support of the Danish state.

Organisational embedment of the Christmas fairs

During the Christmas fair period, all other churchly activities are suspended. In most of the Danish churches abroad, the pastor is essentially the director of the Christmas fair and assisted in this capacity by a few key persons, usually present or former members of the church committee. A competent accountant is essential, for example. The pastor's function is not a question of voluntary work – the duty of organising the Christmas fair is part of the employment interview with a new pastor. I was informed by the chairman of the church committee in Paris that they would dismiss a pastor who, rather hypothetically though, turned out not to take this responsibility seriously.

There are some differences in the way the organisation work is carried out. In South France where the congregation is relatively small, the pastor is not only the top manager of the Christmas fair but also takes care of many of its practical details, such as renting and transporting extra frost cabinets for the food to be sold. In Rotterdam, in Berlin and in Paris, the pastor has an important managerial role in relation to the paid church assistants who take care of much of the practical work. In Paris, which is the biggest of the Christmas fairs, experienced volunteers run the different stalls as separate businesses, which include that the stall managers have the responsibility for buying the goods to their stall. This flat organisation was introduced in the Paris church in 1972 and has functioned well since then (Grosbøll 2003, 172).

In all cases, the workload on the pastor is considerable, and from my interviews with the pastors, I estimate that at least 15–25 pct. of the work of a pastor in a Danish church abroad is associated with the Christmas fair.

The anchoring of the Christmas fair in an established organisation and the fact that it aims at generating a substantial and predictable profit for the church spur a professionalisation of the key persons involved and a routinisation of the activities. At the same time, the Christmas fair is dependent on a large number of other volunteers who have the interest but are inexperienced in Christmas fairs, and many have signed up for this voluntary work for the first time. There are plenty of tasks that these inexperienced volunteers can take care of after a little instruction. For example, arranging the Christmas fair in Berlin required the assistance of about 80 volunteers who primarily manned the many stalls that were temporarily erected inside and outside the church. Many of these volunteers were young people who did manual work, such as baking Danish Christmas doughnuts.

In Paris, the youth secretary arranges a get-together evening every Tuesday for the many Danish students and au-pairs who live in Paris. These young people are informed that in return for these free evenings they are expected to work for the Christmas fair. Typically, they are asked to man the different stalls, help in the kitchen, and to assist with unpacking before the fair and tidying up afterwards. When I interviewed the au-pairs they told that very few of them attended Sunday service, neither in Paris nor in Denmark. The used the church for social reasons; as one of them said: 'The reason why I chose to go to Paris [as an au-pair] was because of the Danish church. Then I knew that I could always go there if I wanted to meet other au-pairs.'

So in November, these young people are enrolled in the rank and files of unskilled helpers. In Paris, I saw five to six young men, all busy making open sandwiches for the kitchen. There are established traditions in the making and decoration of different types of open sandwiches, and in Danish restaurants, these sandwiches are prepared by professionals having three years of training and education in this trade. Such a professional lady was, of course, in charge of the kitchen, while the young men obviously were not trained. They were therefore provided with photos of standard types of open sandwiches. Working tongue-in-cheek, they prepared the sandwiches, although hardly at a competitive pace!

The management structure of the Christmas fair is not static, but bound to change in response to the changing possibilities for resource mobilisation. During my interviews with stall managers at the two Christmas fairs in France, it became quite clear that donations from businesses are a dwindling resource. It seems as if more and more Danish companies are not as generous as they used to be some years ago supporting the Christmas fairs with donations – they are probably more focused on calculations of return on investments than of supporting activities just because they are Danish. Another trend affecting resource mobilisation is a demographic transition among the volunteers, where the present cadres of housewives or women working part-time are growing older and approaching retirement without apparently being released by other, younger women with a surplus of time for voluntary work.

There is little doubt that these trends will affect the resource mobilisation negatively in the future. For example, I learned from the Christmas fair in Paris that the turnover from the fair has risen during the last years, but the profit has stagnated, indicating a decline in the mobilisation of resources in the form of donations of goods, either for free or at reduced prices. It could also be formulated so that the Christmas fair in Paris seems to be losing some traditional income-generating social capital among Danish companies, and the fair, therefore, has to operate more and more on pure market conditions.

Resource mobilisation in quantitative terms

Through interviews with key persons and use of other sources such as written manning plans I was able to estimate the person-hours spent on the different tasks for arranging the Christmas fairs in Berlin 2013, and in South France, Hong Kong and Sydney in

Table 1. Person-hours spent on four Christmas fairs.

Task	Berlin (2013)	South France (2014)	Hong Kong (2014)	Sydney (2014)	Category
Contact sponsors, ordering, organise manning, receive and store goods, economy control[a]	1100	350	420[b]	380[b]	Gesellschaft
Set up stalls and tables, cleaning, re-organise church room, tidying up[c]	150	50	40	80	Gesellschaft
	150	50	40	80	Gemeinschaft
Make open sandwiches, bake cakes, cook soup (Berlin only)[c]	50	20	50	20	Gesellschaft
	250	50	100	40	Gemeinschaft
Manning of stalls, jazz band (Berlin only)[d]	700	350	400	300	Gemeinschaft
Sum of person-hours	2400	870	1050	950	
Additional voluntary resources[e]	1600	50			Gemeinschaft

[a]Interviews with the pastors.
[b]Estimated as proportional to the manning distribution in South France.
[c]Interviews, written manning plan.
[d]Participant observations, interviews.
[e]Needlework (Berlin) and Christmas decorations (South France) prepared at home and sold at the fairs. Data from interviews.

2014.[1] These estimates are given in Table 1, where I have categorised the different tasks as mainly *Gesellschaft*-oriented, mainly *Gemeinschaft*-oriented or intermediates of both. *Gesellschaft*-oriented tasks are primarily tasks carried out by one or a few people working alone, such as planning work, ordering of goods, contacting potential sponsors and similar administrative work. Such work is mostly the pastor's responsibility, though with the support from the paid assistants in the larger churches. *Gemeinschaft*-oriented tasks typically include manning of the stalls by the large number of people who volunteered for these tasks and evidently enjoyed the company of each other. This is obviously a popular task; for example, I was told at the Christmas fair in South France in 2014, that there even was a waiting list for serving as a volunteer!

As appears from Table 1, the Christmas fair in Berlin needed to mobilise 2400 person-hours, which is equivalent to one-and-a-half years of full-time work for one person working typically about 1600 hours per year. Of these, 2400 person-hours, 1300 hours are mainly *Gesellschaft*-oriented and 1100 hours are mainly *Gemeinschaft*-oriented. The additional hours spent on preparing items at home for sale are not included in the total sum of person-hours, as they should rather be regarded as donations on par with the many other donations from individuals or commercial suppliers.

The turnover from the Christmas fair in Berlin is typically about 28,000 EUR, and the profit is around 18,000 EUR, according to information from the pastor and her husband. This is a profit rate of about 64 pct., which should be an attractive business. However, it required an investment of 2400 person-hours to obtain this profit, which means a return of only 7.5 EUR (= 18 000/2400) per hour. This is on a par with the minimum wage of 8.5 EUR per hour in Germany introduced in 2015, and this indicates that if the Berlin Christmas fair was run on a strictly commercial basis, it would be a rather poor business.

Similar brief economic analyses are given in Table 2 for all five Christmas fairs, and the figures will be briefly commented upon.

---

[1]The available data on the personnel resources at the Christmas fair in Paris were too incomplete to allow the same specification as for the other fairs. This is partly due to the decentralised organisation of the fair, as discussed above. My own rough estimate from participation observations is that the fair, which runs over three days, requires at least about the double of the person-hours as the fair in Berlin (2400 person-hours, cf. Table 1). This gives an estimate of at least 4800 person-hours for the Christmas fair in Paris.

Table 2. Economic analysis of five Christmas fairs.

	Berlin (2013)	South France (2014)	Paris (2014)	Hong Kong (2014)	Sydney (2014)
Turnover (EUR)[a]	28 000	46 000	150 000	83 900	56 500
Profit (EUR)[a]	18 000	25 400	87 000	50 300[b]	35 600
Profit rate	64 pct.	55 pct.	58 pct.	60 pct.	63 pct.
Person-hours	2400	870	4800[c]	1050	950
Profit per hour (EUR)	7.5	29	18	48	37

[a]Turnover and profit (rounded figures) are taken from the balance sheets from the fairs.
[b]Estimated from assumed average profit rate of 60 pct.
[c]Estimated from observations and interviews during field trip, cf. note 1.

The person-hours spent in South France are 870 person-hours in total, which is equivalent to 6½ month of full-time work for one person. Four hundred and twenty person-hours, or a little less than half of the total hours, are mainly *Gesellschaft*-oriented. The profit is higher than in Berlin, and this is obtained by investing less than half of the person-hours. This corresponds to a return of 29 EUR per hour, which is a decent but not impressive profit. The better profitability of the Christmas fair in South France compared with that of the fair in Berlin can probably be ascribed to two factors: the volunteers are nearly all experienced in organising the Christmas fair, and the expatriate community in South France is more well-to-do and is willing to spend more money. For example, the popular open sandwiches were sold in South France at twice the price in Berlin, although they were identical in composition. According to the accountant's data, this price policy made the stall with open sandwiches one of the most profitable at the fair in South France.

The turnover from the Christmas fair in Paris which runs over three days is typically around 150 000 EUR; there are about 3500 visitors and the profit is about 87,000 EUR, placing this fair in a league above the other Christmas fairs. A crude estimate of the return on invested person-hours is 18 EUR per hour.

The data from Hong Kong and Sydney indicate that these two Christmas fairs are rather profitable. The high profitability may to some extent be due to that these fairs only run over one day, which means that less person-hours are invested. However, the Christmas fair in Hong Kong undoubtedly also profits from the many well-to-do expatriate Danes there.

In a comparative light, the Christmas fair in Berlin stands out as having a peculiar low profitability, but I have not been able to pinpoint if there is a bias caused by an underestimate of the total earnings or an overestimate of the input of person-hours.

Valuation of the Christmas fair as a congregational community venture

A Christmas fair shares characteristics with community ventures such as establishing a local festival, which also strengthens local community cohesion besides generating local economic activity (Vestrum and Rasmussen 2013). For a community venture to be successful it is important to be embedded in the community with mutual trust and reciprocity between the actors (Vestrum and Rasmussen 2013). This is clearly the case among those engaged in the Christmas fairs, and the embeddedness even extends beyond the community of Danish expatriates to other resource providers; for example, in Berlin, I was told that a German neighbour to the church who was a professional electrician usually established all the outdoor electric installations for free.

The profit from the Christmas fairs is important – it covers about one-third of the running expenses of the church in Berlin, about one-fourth of the running expenses of the church in South France, and nearly half of the running expenses of the church in Paris. It is evident that the churches cannot do without the income from the Christmas fairs. However, the above calculations demonstrate that the churches must mobilise many person-hours to arrange the Christmas fair, and that the return on invested person-hours is rather modest, at least in the case of the Christmas fairs in Berlin and Paris. So, is it really worth for the expatriate community to have all the trouble arranging the Christmas fair?

In order to probe into this issue, I interviewed many central persons who were involved in arranging the Christmas fairs at the churches in Berlin, South France and Paris. The interviewees included the pastors, the chairpersons and the treasurers of the church committee, the senior staff manning the stalls, and a number of other key persons. I asked them why the Christmas fair was so important to the congregation. Most of them answered that it was really a cosy event, and the labour was meaningful because the money was needed. The fair was also regarded as important for the social coherence of the congregation and for attracting the local Danes to the church. The informants knew that most of the volunteers only came for the Christmas fair.

> The families with children come for the Christmas fair, and the newly arrived come and meet the church and the pastor. It is only the grey- and white-haired who attend the Sunday services, but everybody comes for the Christmas fair. (Interview with the chairman of the church committee in South France, 22 November 2014)

> The church is also known for its Christmas fair. It is part of the Berliner landscape. Many Danes only come to the church once in a year, and that is for the Christmas fair. Here, young and old are together. (Interview with the vice-chairman of the church committee in Berlin, 30 November 2013)

A key question in the interviews was:

> Imagine that I am a millionaire and that I detest Christmas fairs. I even detest Christmas fairs so much that I will pay the congregation an annual sum in ten years for giving up the Christmas fair entirely. How much should I then pay?

Sometimes I added: 'I can inform you that the profit from the fair is about X EUR (X depending on which of the fairs I visited).' This question was answered by about 40 interviewees altogether in Berlin, in South France and in Paris.

The question is basically asking the interviewees to give their valuation of the Christmas fair. Economists here distinguish between willingness-to-pay measures of value and willingness-to-accept measures of value when asking interviewees to engage in deals such as exchanging the Christmas fair for an annual sum (Shogren et al. 1994). Willingness-to-pay typically involves situations where the alternatives are readily exchangeable, for example, asking car drivers how much they will pay to use a new toll road to save some minutes of driving time. In short, willingness-to-pay indicates how much people are willing to pay for gaining something. Willingness-to-accept often concerns a more far-reaching question, such as the acceptance of losing something of immaterial value if an economic compensation is given. An example from the Bible is the story about Esau who accepted to give away his birth right to Jacob for a bowl of lentil stew.[2] In general, the willingness-to-accept value is considerably higher, often many times higher, than the willingness-to-pay value which better reflects a true market value, provided that the market exists (Shogren et al. 1994). Cases of willingness-to-accept rarely involve a real market, however; and the answers are much influenced by individual values because the deal involves items that are not ready substitutes to each other (Shogren et al. 1994).

The answering pattern to the millionaire question, therefore, depended very much on how the interviewees perceived the consequences of the deal offered by my imagined millionaire. The majority were not immediately ready to accept the deal at all, namely to give up arranging the fair – 'it would be like selling your own soul', one answered at the fair in Berlin. About half of the informants gave similar 'protest' answers, such as '10 million Euros'; 'There are things you can't buy for money. We only see each other once in a year, and it is so cosy'; 'I will drag this millionaire type down in the bicycle cellar and beat him up until he begins to think differently.' Several of the informants at the Christmas fair in South France said to me that I would have to ask the pastor about this, demonstrating how central the pastor is in the arrangement of the Christmas fair. However, not only this pastor but all the pastors I asked declined to engage in the millionaire question, arguing that it was the congregation's decision to hold the Christmas fair.

Among the other half who were willing to consider the deal at all, some informants wriggled like a worm on a hook before answering, while others thought it over and then typically asked for an annual sum of between two and five times the profit. Quite a few informants added 'but we will hold the Christmas fair anyway!' which essentially is a protest answer. Only a few, about five of the altogether forty informants were immediately willing to accept the millionaire's deal for an annual sum of less than twice the profit. These few informants apparently regarded the Christmas fair as having its primary function of generating income to the church, because they were willing to seriously consider alternative funding opportunities.

The informants were contacted at random during the fairs and they probably represent the majority of those with vested interests in the Christmas fair. However, the amount of money mentioned is only indicative and not a validated data set which can be used in a quantitative assessment of the valuation of the Christmas fairs. Furthermore, the question is hypothetical and it is known that people do not react in the same way when facing a real choice and not a hypothetical and ironic situation like the offer by the Christmas-fair-hating millionaire (Fitzsimons and Shiv 2001). But the qualitative conclusion that can be drawn is valid: The far majority of informants regarded the Christmas fair as something of much more value than the *Gesellschaft*-oriented purpose of earning money. They either rejected to 'sell' the Christmas fair altogether or they claimed a sum which far exceeded the pecuniary value of holding the fair. They were more steadfast than Esau tempted by his hunger! So, although everybody agreed that the Christmas fair would not give meaning

---

[2]Willingness-to-accept may also involve asking people how much they are willing to pay for reducing the risk of an undesirable event. For example, Shogren et al. (1994) asked people in an experiment how much extra they were willing to pay for food where the risk of *Salmonella* infection and other food-borne diseases was virtually eliminated. Here, the informants are asked to substitute money for a further reduction in the minute risk of catching an illness which may be fatal. If the alternative has a low probability to occur but has drastic consequences if it occurs, as is the case with the example of food poisoning, it is generally observed that people are willing to pay more than probabilities dictate for avoiding severe negative consequences (Kahneman and Tversky 1979). If that were not the case, insurance companies would go out of business.

if it was not profitable, the majority of respondents simply did not regard the Christmas fairs as a classic economic exchange which would be selling individual Christmas items to individual customers with the purpose of maximising the profit of the church.

Like many other markets, a Christmas fair in the Danish churches abroad is only to some extent about 'the meeting of supply and demand between the self-interested, rational, maximising individual of the liberal-utilitarian model' (Gauthier, Woodhead, and Martikainen 2013, 17). Continuing with these authors, the Christmas fairs fit squarely into their characterisation:

> Markets are *marketplaces*: loci for complex social interactions and social re-formations. They are socially instituted and socially embedded institutions that are best described as networked and hyper-mediatised arenas of mutual exposure. They are also opportunities for the dissemination of information that can serve as resources for experimentations and interpretations. With respect to religion today as with the whole of consumer societies, 'markets' are where the complex rapports linking identity and recognition occur. (Gauthier, Woodhead, and Martikainen 2013, 18)

To accept the millionaire's offer would mean to give up all these *Gemeinschaft*-strengthening side-effects of the Christmas fairs as marketplaces.

A space of expatriate *gemeinschaft*

So what kind of *Gemeinschaft* is valued by the volunteers? Some of the volunteers also regularly attended the Sunday services, but as described above, others – the majority of volunteers – never did. Quite a few of the Christmas fair volunteers also supported the church economically without even being registered members of the church. For example, a professional Danish cook donated and personally sliced all the smoked salmon for the sandwich buffet in Paris. His reason for giving this support ran as follows:

> When I came to Paris for the first time and did not know even one person, I went down to see where the church was. I sneaked by because I did not want anybody to see me, and I did not enter. I just wanted to know where it was, because if one day it became really difficult for me, it would be there, and I could get help there. (Interview in Paris, 30 November 2014)

This informant supports the church to be sure that it exists for the sake of all eventualities apart from housing the Christmas fair. In this respect, he is representative of many Danes of today who appreciates the existence of the church but rarely, if ever attend the Sunday services (Gundelach, Iversen, and Warburg 2008, 136–149). When they use the church, they do it in a more selective way, choosing only what fulfils their individual needs, rather than following the conventional practices of active church-goers.

The Christmas fair is the visible, tangible result of the joint mobilisation of labour and money among both religiously active and religiously passive expatriate Danes. When the Christmas fair is arranged by a Danish church abroad it offers the opportunity for the expatriate Danes to gather in an unconditional social space that feels officially Danish, but is owned and controlled by the expatriate community (Warburg 2013). Data from the Danish Seamen's church in Singapore demonstrated that the mobilisation at Christmas-related events involved more expatriates than any other event in the church (Warburg 2013). This was confirmed in the present field studies and reflects the paramount symbolic significance of Christmas for Danish identity. I suggest that this resource mobilisation effort every year creates a temporary but unique space of expatriate Danish *Gemeinschaft*, which is so highly valued by the expatriates that a considerable contingent among them is willing to invest their time, labour and money in the Christmas fair.

Disclosure statement

No potential conflict of interest was reported by the authors.

Funding

This work was supported in part by the Danish Research Council – Culture and Communication through the project *The Danish Model of Religion Under Change – a Comparative Perspective* [grant number 12-127493]. I also wish to thank my colleagues in the research project *What Money Can't Buy. The Dynamics between Market Orientation, Individualization, and Social Capital. The Case of the Danish National Church* [grant number 4001-00173], for their constructive comments to the first draft of this paper.

References

Balch, Robert W. 2006. "The Rise and Fall of the Aryan Nations: A Resource Mobilisation Approach." *Journal of Political and Military Sociology* 34: 81–113.

Bisagno, John R. 2002. *Successful Church Fund-Raising. Capital Campaigns You Can Do Yourself.* Nashville, TN: Broadman & Holman.

Bromley, David G., and Anson D. Shupe. Jr. 1980. "Financing the New Religions: A Resource Mobilization Approach." *Journal for the Scientific Study of Religion* 19: 227–239.

Buechler, Steven M. 1993. "Beyond Resource Mobilization? Emerging Trends in Social Movement Theory." *Sociological Quarterly* 34: 217–235.

Cahnman, Werner J. 1973. "Introduction." In *Ferdinand Tönnies. A New Evaluation. Essays and Documents*, edited by Werner J. Cahnman, 1–27. Leiden: Brill.

della Porta, Donatella, and Mario Diani. 2006. *Social Movements. An Introduction.* London: Blackwell.

Di John, Jonathan. 2008. *Taxation, Resource Mobilisation, and Productive Capacity-Building in LDCs (Background Paper No. 5)*. Prepared for UNCTAD Least Developed Countries Report 2009: The State and Development Governance. Geneva: United Nations Conference on Trade and Development.

Fitzsimons, Gavan J., and Baba Shiv. 2001. "Nonconscious and Contaminative Effects of Hypothetical Questions on Subsequent Decision Making." *Journal of Consumer Research* 28: 224–238.

Gamson, William A. 1987. "Introduction." In *Social Movements in an Organizational Society. Collected Essays*, edited by Mayer N. Zald and John D. McCarthy, 1–7. New Brunswick: Transaction Books.

Gauthier, François, Linda Woodhead, and Tuomas Martikainen. 2013. "Introduction: Consumerism as the Ethos of Consumer Society." In *Religion in Consumer Society. Brands, Consumers and Markets*, edited by François Gauthier and Tuomas Martikainen, 1–24. Farnham: Ashgate.

Grosbøll, Jakob. 2003. "1972–78." In *Historien om den danske menighed i Paris fra 1660–2000* [History of the Danish Congregation in Paris from 1660–2000], edited by Finn Egeris Petersen, 168–177. Paris: Frederikskirken.

Gundelach, Peter, Hans Raun Iversen, and Margit Warburg. 2008. *I hjertet af Danmark. Institutioner og Mentaliteter* [In the Heart of Denmark. Institutions and Mentalities]. Copenhagen: Hans Reitzel.

Hall, John R. 1988. "Collective Welfare as Resource Mobilization in Peoples Temple: A Case of a Poor People's Religious Social Movement." *Sociological Analysis* 49: 64–77.

Harrison, Mark. 1988. "Resource Mobilization for World War II: The U.S.A., U.K., U.S.S.R., and Germany, 1938–1945." *The Economic History Review, New Series* 41 (2): 171–192.

Heberle, Rudolf. 1973. "The Sociological System of Ferdinand Tönnies: An Introduction." In *Ferdinand Tönnies. A New Evaluation. Essays and Documents*, edited by Werner J. Cahnman, 47–69. Leiden: Brill.

Jacobsen, Brian Arly, and Margit Warburg. 2013. "At være dansk i udlandet – en religionssociologisk profil [To be Danish Abroad – A Sociology of Religion Profile]." *Religion. Tidsskrift for Religionslærerforeningen for Gymnasiet og HF* (2): 38–50.

Jenkins, J. Craig. 1983. "Resource Mobilization Theory and the Study of Social Movements." *Annual Review of Sociology* 9: 527–553.

Kahneman, Daniel, and Amos Tversky. 1979. "Prospect Theory: An Analysis of Decision Under Risk." *Econometrica* 47 (2): 263–291.

Khan, N. A. 1963. "Resource Mobilization from Agriculture and Economic Development in India." *Economic Development and Cultural Change* 12 (1): 42–54.

Klandermans, Bert. 1984. "Mobilization and Participation: Social-Psychological Expansion of Resource Mobilization Theory." *American Sociological Review* 49: 583–600.

McCarthy, John D., and Mayer N. Zald. 1977. "Resource Mobilization and Social Movements: A Partial Theory." *American Journal of Sociology* 82: 1212–1241.

McCarthy, John D., and Mayer N. Zald. 2001. "The Enduring Vitality of the Resource Mobilization Theory of Social Movements." In *Handbook of Sociological Theory*, edited by Jonathan H. Turner, 533–565. New York: Kluwer Academic.

Schachinger, Mildred. 1991. "Tönnies in the Literature: The Reductionist Approach of Talcott Parsons." In *Hundert Jahre "Gemeinschaft und Gesellschaft." Ferdinand Tönnies in der internationalen Diskussion*, edited by Lars Clausen and Carsten Schlüter, 527–536. Opladen: Leske and Budrich.

Shogren, J. F., S. Y. Shin, D. J. Hayes, and James B. Kliebenstein. 1994. "Resolving Differences in Willingness to Pay and Willingness to Accept." *The American Economic Review* 84: 255–270.

Shupe, Anson. 2011. "The Modern North American Anti-Cult Movement: Its Rise and Demise According to Resource Mobilization Theory." *Alternative Spirituality and Religion Review* 2: 288–317.

Soper, J. Christopher, and Joel S. Fetzer. 2003. "Explaining the Accommodation of Muslim Religious Practices in France, Britain, and Germany." *French Politics* 1: 39–59.

Tatari, Eren. 2009. "Theories of the State Accommodation of Islamic Religious Practices in Western Europe." *Journal of Ethnic and Migration Studies* 35: 271–288.

Tönnies, Ferdinand. 1931. "Gemeinschaft und Gesellschaft." In *Handwörterbuch der Soziologie*, edited by Alfred Vierkandt, 180–191. Stuttgart: Ferdinand Enke Verlag.

Tönnies, Ferdinand. 1970. *Gemeinschaft und Gesellschaft. Grundbegriffe der reinen Soziologie*. Darmstadt: Wissenschaftliche Buchgesellschaft.

Tönnies, Ferdinand. 1974. *Community and Association* [Gemeinschaft und Gesellschaft], edited and translated by Charles P. Loomis. London: Routledge and Kegan Paul.

Tönnies, Ferdinand. 2001. *Community and Civil Society*, edited by Jose Harris, translated by Jose Harris and Margaret Hollis. Cambridge: Cambridge University Press.

Tribe, Keith. 2004. *Community and Civil Society*. By Ferdinand Tönnies, edited by Jose Harris and translated by Jose Harris and Margaret Hollis. Cambridge: Cambridge University Press 2001" [review]. *German History* 22: 478–479.

Vestrum, Ingebjørg, and Einar Rasmussen. 2013. "How Community Ventures Mobilise Resources. Developing Resource Dependence and Embeddedness." *International Journal of Entrepreneurial Behaviour & Research* 19: 283–302.

Warburg, Margit. 2006. *Citizens of the World. A History and Sociology of the Baha'is from a Globalisation Perspective*. Leiden: E.J. Brill.

Warburg, Margit. 2012. "Den danske religionsmodel i den store vide verden [The Danish Model of Religion in the Big, Wide World]." In *Fremtidens danske religionsmodel* [The Danish Model of Religion of the Future], edited by Christoffersen Lisbet, Hans Raun Iversen, Kærgård Niels, and Warburg Margit, 55–70. Copenhagen: Anis.

Warburg, Margit. 2013. "An Alternative National-Religious Space Abroad: The Danish Seamen's Church in Singapore." In *A Comparative Ethnography of Alternative Spaces*, edited by Jens Dahl and Esther Fihl, 151–174. New York: Palgrave.

From nation-state to market: The transformations of religion in the global era, as illustrated by Islam

François Gauthier

ABSTRACT
This article has three parts. The first analyses how notions of the market and of marketisation have been literally and metaphorically applied to the study of religion. The article argues in favour of thinking consumption as the circulation and exchange of symbols rather than goods, and therefore reintegrates economic phenomena into the fold of history and socio-anthropology. The second part argues that the major transformations of the last half-century are best understood as the shift from a national-statist religious regime to a market regime cast against the backdrop of globalisation. The rise of consumerism as a social and cultural ethos, the spread of neoliberal and managerial ideologies, are the key processes which underlie a major reconfiguration of societies and cultures on a global scale. The third part argues that the important mutations occurring within Islam – as illustrated by Indonesian Islam – demonstrates the heuristic potential of the suggested approach.

What is the marketisation of religion?

Themes related to religion and economics have traditionally been outweighed by those related to religion and politics (Gauthier, Martikainen, and Woodhead 2013a; Koch 2014). This has to do with the overarching importance of politics in modern epistemology, as well as to how the foundations of the Nation-State were erected in many ways *against* 'religion'. In the last decades, the rise to world dominance of a new brand of financialised and consumption-based capitalism in the wake of the latest wave of globalisation characterised by post-Keynesian neoliberal deregulation has reshuffled the cards in such a way that economics now seem to determine to a large extent other social spheres, including politics and religion. Social sciences have been slow to acknowledge this shift and bring it to the fore of its analyses of global religious trends, perhaps thereby neglecting the extent to which religion has been substantially transformed over the course of the last half of the 20th century.

A major feature of today's capitalism is 'marketization', which is the focus of the contributions assembled in this issue. In economics, marketisation is the construction and formatting of a given ensemble of goods, service or any other order of natural or social reality into a marketable product destined to a 'market segment'. A market, in turn, is defined by neoclassical economic theory as an abstract space in which the conflict between self-interests is resolved through the encounter of *supply* and *demand* resulting in the 'natural' or 'spontaneous' fixation of *price*. In this model, individuals are the only consistent reality, and collectives have no other substance than the aggregation of individuals. Furthermore, individuals are cast as pre-social, undetermined autonomous beings with pre-given preferences, motivated by self-interest, and constitutively geared towards acquisition, all the while guided by the rational laws of cost/benefit computing.

Thus conceived, religion, as many other social realities, has been traditionally understood as being of a completely different nature than the market. Like oil and water, religion and the market have been mainly cast as indissoluble into one another. Market-type exchanges, along with the bureaucratic operations of the modern state apparatus, have been cast as partaking in functional types of relations, typical of modernity, in which individuals are interchangeable. In this type of sociality, social bond is not created or maintained, and hence it stands opposed to another type of sociality which is said to have been the lot of traditional, pre-modern societies, and which is in turn said to endure in close-knit familial and friendship relations. This distinction is captured by the classical opposition between *Gesellschaft* (society) and *Gemeinschaft* (community) proposed by Tönnies (1970 [1887]. This set of concepts, be it in the formulation given by Tönnies or its variations in Durkheimian and Weberian sociologies, has structured social sciences since. From this perspective, the core of religion is something 'money can't buy', as Margit Warburg's contribution highlights. Certainly, religion (churches and their communities, for example) exists today in a market environment, and must comply with certain economic necessities (like funding the church's activities), yet it preserves a 'non-marketable' core in so-doing – something increasingly endangered by the surrounding marketisation, as Warburg's article also makes clear.

This classical casting of the religion and market couple has produced a large body of valuable scientific literature and still does. Yet the opposition has been progressively eroded, to the extent that the answers to the questions 'what is marketization' and 'what is the relation between religion and the market' now appear to be blurred. We can point to Peter Berger's chapter six ('Secularization and the Problem of Plausibility') in his classic *The Sacred Canopy* (1967) as the inaugural moment of such a shift. Berger writes:

> As a result [of pluralization, and therefore the end of religious monopolies in favour of voluntary adhesions], the religious tradition has to be *marketed*. It must be 'sold' to a clientele that is no longer constrained to 'buy'. The pluralistic situation is, above all, a *market situation*. In it, the religious institutions become marketing agencies, and the religious tradition become consumer commodities. And at any rate a good deal of religious activity in this situation comes to be dominated by the logic of market economics. (1990, 138; italics in original)

This passage has often been quoted, yet the whole of Berger's chapter as concerns marketisation has not been the object of a thorough discussion to my knowledge. While there is no space to engage in such a discussion here, it is possible to make a few remarks. Put back in the flow of Berger's book, it appears today as both visionary and dated. For Berger (as with Weber), market economics are the *summum* of rationalisation, and are therefore constitutively *secularising* in the sense that they erode the former social function of religion

– providing an unquestionable 'sacred canopy' for pre-modern societies – and contribute to the privatisation of religion. While Berger's version of secularisation has been widely repudiated, including by himself, and while the terms in which he understood privatisation have been contested, he did highlight the ways in which religion was becoming reconfigured according to the moral and therapeutic 'needs' of modern individuals. While he overstated the disappearance of 'supernatural' elements in religion, he did foresee how religion would become increasingly voluntary and guided by the logics of 'choice'. Yet what did he mean by 'marketing', 'selling', and 'buying' religion? Is this to be taken literally or metaphorically? The quotation marks applied to the last two terms seem to introduce a distance with respect to any literal interpretation, but if we read the chapter in its entirety, Berger is undoubtedly literal in his resort to free-market terminologies, such as when he discusses how 'consumer demand' impacts the product being supplied in the 'religious market'.

Following Berger's thread, religion in pre-modern societies, as a monopolistic institution involved in the production of a 'sacred canopy', was not thinkable in economic terms. Secularisation, as a constitutive feature of modernisation, was the result of various rationalisation processes, of which the development of capitalism. Once it's social functions have been sufficiently eroded, religion itself thereby *became* marketable. In Berger's view, casting religion in economic terms is something that is historical: anyone who has read any classics of anthropology knows that this only becomes plausible in modernised societies. Many decades later, another American sociologist of religion, Wade Clark Roof, made a similar argument when he defined the religious landscape of contemporary societies as a 'spiritual marketplace': 'An open, competitive religious economy makes possible an expanded spiritual marketplace which, like any marketplace, *must* be understood in terms both of "demand" and "supply"' (Roof 1999, 78; italics added). The only difference with Berger here is that an analysis in neoclassical terms has become so self-evident as to become a 'must'. Marketisation therefore signifies that the divide between religion and market that existed in classical sociology has been blurred in favour of the market, and that religion has become a product in its own right. It may be a peculiar product, but in the end, it is believed that one can apply a neoclassical calculus to the outcome of the encounter of individual religious 'needs' and suppliers' 'offers'.

The promises and deceptions of economic theory

The most radical offspring of Peter Berger's prophetic chapter is paradoxically the Rational Choice current. It is a paradox since Rational Choice authors' have energetically contested secularisation theory (of which Berger was a tenor) and have sonorously beaten the drum of its death, self-appointing themselves as a 'new paradigm'. Yet they have simply developed Berger's market argument to its full extent. Using the United States as their preferred laboratory, they have celebrated the 'fact' that religious pluralism, i.e., a religious market freed from the 'unnatural' intrusions of state regulation unlike Europe, did not result in the decline of religion but rather its 'vitality'. Rational Choice sociologists endeavoured to apply a rather simplistic version of neoclassical market theory to religion as of the mid-1980s, i.e., a decade after Gary Becker declared that liberal economic theory could explain not only economic but all social phenomena.

That religion is a 'product' here is anything but metaphorical, and the aim of such a theory is even to extend to predictions, as in pure sciences. Some authors, such as Steve Bruce, have voiced a critique by challenging Rational Choice on its own grounds. This strategy might be missing the point. Most sociologists of religion seem to ignore that Durkheim's sociology of religion was elaborated precisely as a radical critique of the pretensions of neoclassical economics in social theory (hence his repeated attacks on the leader of utilitarian sociology of the time, Herbert Spencer). Durkheim, as well as his companions at the Fifth Section of the Sorbonne, composed what is today still the basis of a most radical critique of neoclassical economic theory, one which is still very much applicable today. In fact, it is even safe to say that Durkheim founded sociology in general, and sociology of religion in particular, *against* neoclassical political economy. After critiquing the neoclassical and utilitarian theories on the methodological and epistemological levels in his first sociology (that of the *Division of Labour*, the *Rules of Sociological Method* and *Suicide*), his second sociology (that of the *Elementary Forms of Religious Life*, as well as Marcel Mauss' production) turned to religion in order to explain the workings of human societies, in stark opposition to the self-interest-based individualist model (cf. Steiner 2005). A Durkheim-inspired sociology of religion, therefore, is constitutively in radical opposition to Rational Choice, and provides the basis for a radical critique.

Rational Choice has two major fault lines that are pertinent to our discussion. The first, already elaborated by Durkheim and others more than a century ago, is that economic theory is fatally flawed *on its own turf*. Apart from the Marxian critique of neoclassical economic theory, there is a landmass of critical works that have underlined how the latter is methodologically and empirically false in the analysis of basic economic facts. For instance, neoclassical economics lack a credible theory of currency and does as if all transactions were barter (Caillé 2005; Graeber 2011; Orléan 2011). They are also completely impotent in providing an analysis of the causes of market bubbles and economic crises, as the basic assumptions of the model claim that markets are naturally geared towards equilibrium (Jorion 2008). Causes for depressions can only be attributed to 'outside' factors, most often state policy, even when bubbles and crises, such as in 1929 and 2008, come after stark deregulation of the financial sector. Part of the latest wave of English language 'heterodox' economists, Keen (2011) has compiled a mass of arguments and empirical evidence which combine to undermine *all* of the assumptions of the neoclassical model – which meanwhile remains universally taught today in universities around the world (Keen talks of 'indoctrination') – , and has pledged in favour of a well overdue intellectual aggiornamento. Even a liberal sympathiser such as Robert H. Nelson (Public policy professor at the University of Maryland and former economist at the US Department of the Interior) has denounced the 'theological assumptions' underpinning neoclassical economics (from Keynesianism to neoliberalism) and equated the field of economics to a 'religion' (Nelson [2001] 2014; see Gauthier 2017), as it provides a set of metaphysical 'ultimate values'. If what is left of neoclassical economics, with respect to economic phenomena, is a 'field of ruins' (Keen 2011), importing this model to the study of religion appears utterly problematic. Unfortunately, scholars of religion are illiterate in matters of economic theory and tend to outsource anything that has to do with economics to neoclassical prophets (e.g., Seele and Zapf 2017). Yet if social scientists were as severe in their scrutiny of economists as they are amongst themselves, there is little doubt that most of the economics discipline, in its massively dominant orthodox strand, would be simply discredited.

The second fault line has to do with the shift that Rational Choice operates with respect to Berger's perspective. By negating secularisation, Rational Choice has also set aside theories of modernisation in order to present a completely de-historicised and decontextualised theory that pretends to be valid for all religion, everywhere, at any point in history. Hence religion did not become a marketable product in modernity, it always was one. Rather than providing tools for understanding religious transformations in modern times, Rational Choice simply translates religion (or rather a very conservative, institutional, substantive, and therefore partial definition of religion) into economic language. Rather than shedding light on the effects of the rise to dominance of neoliberalism and consumerism on religious phenomena worldwide, Rational Choice is one of the very ideological products of such dominance. As a consequence, defining and understanding marketisation along neoclassical lines appears highly problematic.

Rational Choice does not do away with the distinction between *Gesellschaft* and *Gemeinschaft per se*. By positing that non-functional – i.e., non-economic and non-bureaucratic – phenomena can be analysed with neoclassical economic theory, it rather stipulates that the distinctiveness of *Gemeinschaft* sociality is negligible in the end and that individuals behave in love, friendships, and religion much like they do in a supermarket and any other market-type exchange, i.e., as self-interested, pre-social, and rational agents seeking to maximise their 'utility' – in other words their pleasure or profit. There is no longer anything that 'money can't buy'. How such a reversal of the classic social scientific perspective can be fruitful to the study of religion is something which should at the very least be seriously doubted.

A whole strand of research has nevertheless emerged within the parameters set by Peter Berger without actually mobilising neoclassical economic theory and Rational Choice. Wade Clark Roof evokes a spiritual marketplace that should – must! – be analysed according to the 'natural law' of supply and demand, yet nowhere does he actually resort to the arcana of utilitarian calculus. The reference to neoclassical economic theory appears therefore more metaphorical than literal. Jörg Stolz and Jean-Claude Usunier (2014) have provided the most thorough examination of the question as to how economic and marketing theory could apply to the study of religion, and their discussion supports a metaphorical more than a literal heuristic. Usunier (2014) has further listed the set of assumptions that run through 'economics of religion' approaches (e.g., economy = market; individuals only seek to maximise utility; commoditisation as non-ideological; etc.), which combine to make any non-metaphorical use rather hazardous.

Mara Einstein's book *Brands of Faith* (2008) illustrates the tension that runs through much research on the marketisation and branding of religion. Through a score of mostly American examples (again …), she brilliantly illustrates how religion is increasingly being marketed and branded, and how religious organisations are now faced with the obligation to think about themselves in market terms. Like Roof, she concludes to the existence of a religious free market that can be largely understood in the terms of neoclassical economics and Rational Choice theory (even if she also refrains from doing so). Yet she also insists on how branding is primarily concerned with creating *identity* and *meaning*. A former marketer herself, she argues that this is where marketing and religion meet rather than oppose themselves: in the creation of identity, meaning, and communities. In so doing, she does not seem to be aware that she is opening a door onto another way of considering the market: not as an abstract space for the encounter of rationalities, but rather as a social institution involved in the circulation of meaning. A symbolic space. One that is best approached from an anthropological rather than an economistic perspective.

Consumption seen from an anthropological lens

In 1978, celebrated anthropologist Mary Douglas linked up with economist Baron Isherwood to publish *The World of Goods*, which inaugurated the anthropology of consumption and whose aim was to contest the validity of neoclassical economic theory and provide an empirically grounded alternative (cf. Heilbrunn 2014). For Douglas, understanding consumption should not start from a self-interested and atomistic, individualistic standpoint, that of neoclassical economics, but rather from a social and relational perspective able to show how consumption involves the dynamics of identity, transmission, community, normativity, belonging, and meaning. Turning the neoclassical assumption on its head (that modern economics can understand all human behaviour, including pre-modern forms), Douglas shows how modern consumption follows the basic functioning of 'primitive' consumption. In other words, that the rupture between modern and pre-modern societies is not as sharp as is usually believed, and that much of what had been classified under *Gesellschaft* sociality can be understood with the tools used in the analysis of *Gemeinschaft* sociality.

Interestingly, the discipline of marketing foreshadowed this cultural turn. Authors had started to shift away from the neoclassical framework long before (as early as the 1950s!) by introducing psychological methods and theory in the study of consumer behaviour (Arvidsson 2006). Strands of marketing theory joined the anthropological perspective inaugurated by Douglas and Isherwood in the 1980s, giving an impulse to Consumer Research and Cultural Studies. The result has been a flourishing field which has produced invaluable material showing how consumption, branding, and marketing work to produce lifestyles, meanings, identities, and communities (see ; Gauthier 2014a, 2014b; Gauthier, Martikainen, and Woodhead 2013b, 2013c). This scholarship has also highlighted the specificities of modern consumptions, from the century of Enlightenment until today, and therefore represents a rich source from which to investigate the combined effects of marketisation on religion. Unfortunately, Consumer Research and Cultural Studies have been all but ignored by most scholars of religion, until recently (see contributions in Gauthier and Martikainen [2013] as well as Sandıkcı 2018; Moberg and Martikainen 2018).

Instead of this, two sets of concurrent theories have attracted scholars' (and the media's) attention. Both maintain the opposition between market-type *Gesellschaft* and *Gemeinschaft* socialities, yet provide opposite interpretations of the recent impact of marketisation on religion. The first perspective denounces the instrumentalisation of the market by religious actors and is widespread in research concerned with the exponential development of halal and 'sharia-friendly' products worldwide. While this point of view is seldom expressed as bluntly, its' narrative runs something like this: the 'halal explosion' is the result of a manipulation of the possibilities of the globalised markets by fundamentalist currents aiming at disseminating their ideology and normativity (e.g., Kepel 2012). The purity of the market (and of the 'secular' in general), in other words, is co-opted by religion.

The second perspective worries about the 'capitalist takeover' and sullying of religion. It is championed by Jeremy Carrette and Richard King (2005), who lament and denounce the dissemination of 'holistic spiritualities' that claim to 'soothe away the angst of modern living' and 'the shallowness of materialism' (a 'fallacy') but which instead legitimates 'corporate interests'. Religion and spirituality appear to have been 'hijacked' and turned into an 'alienating addiction'. Rather than being something new, this perspective simply re-actualises the old Marxian idea of religion as the 'opium of the people' and ideological superstructure serving the domination of capitalism, with the twist that somewhere under the surface lies not class warfare, but rather an authentic and unsullied spirituality with a potential for resistance. In *Brand Islam* (2016), Faegheh Shirazi presents a variation on this theme, as she similarly denounces the instrumentalisation and 'exploitation' of Islam by morality-devoid profit-seeking market actors who promote 'false halal' products and 'hijabi dolls'. Here it is the purity of religion that appears to be threatened by the sullying potential of evil market forces.

The reader will probably have noted how these two perspectives are symmetrical, therefore specular: they are mirror images of one another. Both view economics and religion as exclusive social spheres, yet diverge in their interpretations. The first accuses religion's spoiling of the purity of the market, while the second points the finger at market opportunism and the way that it corrupts religion. Both these interpretations are normative more than they are analytic, as they define what the 'secular' or religion (e.g., halal) *should* be. They therefore fail as heuristic frameworks for understanding marketisation, which is cast as being either a tool for manipulation or a vehicle for corruption of 'authentic' religion.

So what, then, is marketisation? At this stage of our introductory discussion, we can try to advance by adopting the anthropological perspective sketched above. It does run against the thrust of classical stances such as that of Max Weber, for whom the historical process of rationalisation that culminated in modern bureaucracy and capitalism is held to have a disenchanting effect. With respect to the categories used so far, according to Weber, *Gesellschaft* (utilitarian) type sociality is held to erode *Gemeinschaft* type, leading to a meaning and axiological crisis. Without contesting the fecundity of this view – for certainly our societies are under severe pressure to conform to utilitarian modes of functioning – a theory of marketisation can come at a slant and consider that the meeting of consumption and religion does not enslave one or the other to the other's logic, but rather that it produces *a new kind of rapport between religion and economics in which they are profoundly intertwined*, giving way to a set of new social phenomena. An excellent example is that of 'halal', which is an indissociably economic *and* religious phenomenon: its global efflorescence is the product of a novel and non-dissociable assemblage of marketisation and religious dynamics (Bergeaud-Blackler 2017a; see also Gauthier 2018).

Marketisation: a two-sided complex of processes in market societies

If we come back to our initial definition of marketisation and slightly rework it as the formatting of given social realities into commodities, or 'goods', it is not so bad as long as we steer away from a neoclassical definition of market exchange. For it is not religion that has become a merchandise (like any other), whose value could be determined by supply and demand curves following undetermined individual 'preferences'. Rather than boiling down symbols to goods and reducing the qualitative to the quantitative, it is more fruitful and empirically founded to consider consumerism as involving the circulation of *symbols* and therefore operate a reverse movement. Hence the possibility for consumerism to hinge onto religion and give it new shapes. From hunter-gatherer, Siberian shamanism to Aztec sacrificial religion to the 'world's great religions', religion has known innumerable forms, and there is no reason why religion could not transform into novel yet fully religious forms. The marketisation of religion signifies its transformation along the structures and dynamics of consumer capitalism, in which the expression of choice is constitutive of subjectivities, identities, agencies, communities, and so forth. Marketisation thereby refers to a globalisation-specific type of rapport to the self, others, the world, and even nature. Marketisation transforms religion into lifestyles, practices, and voluntary adhesion rather than 'belief and belonging'-oriented forms. Marketisation also profoundly modifies religious organisations and their rapport to tradition, whose former modes can be dismissed, challenged, and/or renewed.

In order to make the notion of marketisation even more operational, I suggest that it can be made to encompass two distinct yet intimately bound processes: consumerism, understood as the dominant social and cultural ethos today, and neoliberalism, which can be defined broadly as the set of free-market ideologies and practices that have come to dominate the arena of world politics and management since the end of the 1970s (Harvey 2005; Saad-Filho and Johnston 2005). Neoliberalism also involves market formatting, although in some ways different from consumerism. To make a short argument, neoliberalism marketises in the sense that it does in fact reduce social realities (e.g., education, health, welfare, labour, subjectivities, etc.) to a utilitarian characterisation and normative standards of valuation (cost-effectiveness, quantity, 'human resources', 'human capital', etc.). In this case, marketisation *does* correspond to a reduction to neoclassical understandings of market dynamics. On the other hand, neoliberalism also purports a worldview as well as a set of values (e.g., mobility, transparency, self-realisation, individual responsibility, seeing difficulties as opportunities to grow, etc.) that provide meaning, thereby exceeding any computing model (Boltanski and Chiappelo 1999; Gaulejac 2005; Gauthier, Martikainen, and Woodhead 2013a). While neoliberalism's free-market ideology claims value neutrality, this is of course far from being the case. Examining the marketisation of religion specifically linked to neoliberalism entails a careful analysis of its normative effects, something to which Marian Burchardt and Jes Heise Rasmussen's contributions in this volume proceed to shed some light.

With respect to marketisation, neoliberalism and consumerism operate in two diverging yet complementary processes. On the one hand, neoliberal practices commoditise non-commodities: e.g., Karl Polanyi's (2001) classical examples of land, labour, and money, a list that can be expanded to include water, knowledge, and life itself (in the case of GMOs), as well as education, healthcare, and welfare more generally. It leads to privileging economic efficiency in societal institutions, including religious ones. On the other, as we have seen, consumerism commoditises in the opposite direction, as the world of consumer goods is a world of meanings and identities competing for choice. As a result, visibility becomes a defining feature of religion. Visibility becomes a politic in a public realm reconfigured into an arena of mutual exposure (Taylor 2002, 85).

Neoliberalism and consumerism are two coextensive yet distinct processes, the first affecting religion mostly via the political and the societal (i.e., on the institutional and organisational level) and the second through culture and the social. Or, in a more imaged fashion, the first acts as if from above, while the second impacts from below. On the level of individuals, two imperatives combine as a consequence: behave as an entrepreneur in all things, act rationally in a way that maximises your utility on the one hand (the 'Adam Smith imperative'), and dare be yourself (and express it via consumption choices) on the other (the 'consumerised Kantian imperative'). This double imperative has a formal, utilitarian side, and a substantive one. In other words, still: individuals are pushed towards being neoliberal in production and idealist (or a Romantic: Campbell 1987) in consumption.

Marketisation is thus a double-sided complex of normative processes through which societal realities at large are made to conform to a neoclassical market model while social imaginaries are geared to think according to a market idea and ideal. Approaching the study of religion through the marketisation approach signifies that 'the market' is identified as the most salient and defining feature of contemporary societies: both the market as a social and societal institution (the actual market), and the market as idea and ideal (Durkheim: a moral ideal) of optimal social regulation and production of meaning. From this perspective, our societies are 'market societies' (Gauthier 2009; Slater and Tonkiss 2001; Slater 1997).

Such an approach to marketisation distances itself from that of Berger and Roof on many counts, the main one being that it does not outsource its analysis to neoclassical economic theory but rather *reintegrates economic phenomena into the fold of history and socio-anthropology*. Furthermore, it is clear in Berger's chapter that the marketisation of religion is part of the secularisation process, and that free-market economies are coextensive to the spread of democracy. The approach adopted here, on the contrary, does not at all entail secularisation (be it privatisation, the loss of social function of religion, religious decline or differentiation of social spheres) nor any essential connection between marketisation and democratisation, on the contrary. If anything, the trends that it highlights are renewed visibility, new political and social functions for religion, profound religious transformation and the blurring and interpenetration of social spheres. In fact, the marketisation approach developed here opens onto a refreshed heuristic that is completely independent not only from secularisation *theories* but also from the *secularisation paradigm* that has been constitutive of modern social sciences.

The consequences have been listed in part in the discussion above: choice as both imperative and means of agency, the life-styling of culture, the consumer as the naturalised form of citizenship, generalised commoditisation (i.e., formatting into a marketable form) and so on. This diagnosis forms the underlying thread of the contributions that have been united here. Of course, such an assemblage can only be partial, yet the hope of the editors is that it will contribute to a shift in the social scientific study of religion towards acknowledging the importance of the rise of economic domination over our societies as a key feature of globalisation.

Moving beyond secularisation: from nation-state to global-market

The secularisation paradigm has long constituted the interpretational frame through which religion has been understood. This framework has favoured a political interpretation of the transformations of religion in modern times, one which continues to endure today still, even as its lacunae appear increasingly manifest. Speaking here of a secularisation paradigm aims at suggesting that 'secularisation' exceeds by far the restricted set of theories which explicitly claim the appellation and continues to underlie work on religion today through the following assumptions: methodological nationalism (Wimmer and Schiller 2002) a political-institutional bias; the opposition between public and private; the differentiation of social spheres; modernisation as rationalisation and individualisation; the marginalisation of religion; the corrosive effects of pluralism; the loss of social function and public relevance of religion. Paradigms, in Alain Caillé's Kuhn-inspired workable definition, are composed of a set of shared theories and explanatory models within a scientific community, by which the realm of legitimate research methods and questions is defined (Caillé 2000, 13). They become explicit in certain models, but their strength lies precisely in that parts of their structure remains hidden, unquestioned and implicit. Paradigms are necessary for scientific knowledge, yet they are rooted in the cultural ideologies of a given time. This is why they are difficult to shed, and why paradigmatic shifts are, as Kuhn's (1962) main argument goes, rather sudden, when the implicit foundations of a given paradigm no longer 'stick' (that Kuhn did not think that his model applied to human and social sciences is not relevant here). The secularisation paradigm favours a political interpretation of the transformations of religion in modern times, one that endures in the recent 'post-secular' and 'multiple secularities' strands of research. While a true alternative to the secularisation paradigm is yet to emerge, the only consensus seems to be that the current religious landscape is fragmented and/or transitory.

In my view, social sciences fail to recognise the coherent and structured nature of religious phenomena because they have been made blind to macro-level socio-economic changes as a result of this political and institutional bias. Starting in the West in the 1960s, religion underwent a profound transformation that flew under the radar of state control and religious institutions. These transformations started to erupt into public visibility in the 1980s and 1990s, challenging the secularisation framework. The hypothesis here is that, prior to this, the embedding power of the political sphere with respect to other social spheres started to erode. As a consequence, religion, which was heretofore shaped within a model provided by the Nation-State, started to spill outside of its institutionalised frontiers and into the social and cultural fabric. Religious institutions, as all other institutions, have been the object of distrust and critique, and religion has accordingly reconfigured in less instituted forms. I would like to argue that the important changes that have marked the religious landscape in the last half-century result from *the shift from a National-Statist to a Global-Market regime of religion*. This perspective suggests that we cast the transformations of religion against the backdrop of wider socio-economic and cultural transformations catalysed by the spread of consumerism and neoliberalism, which are the core of the latest wave of globalisation. Rather than insisting on the 'deregulated' and 'fragmented' nature of contemporary religion, the claim made here is that recent mutations point to a major shift in the foundation and regulation of societies, one in which the following processes are determinant: the massification and globalisation of consumerism, understood as a dominant social and cultural ethos; the rise of neoliberal ideologies and practices (management, marketing) that has accompanied the institutionalisation of supranational regulating bodies (WTO, IMF, World Bank, G7/8/

20, World Economic Forum etc.), the dismantling of the Welfare state and economic deregulation leading to a financialised global-market economy; and the development of communication technologies (television, satellite, digitalisation, Internet), which has contributed in accentuating the effects of the former. While the effects of this shift have been studied with respect to politics (e.g., the critique of institutions, the crisis of the democratic model, the precedence of economic criteria on political decisions, the loss of sovereignty of the nation-state, etc.), broad studies of religion continue to neglect the rise of economics and its incidence on the whole of societies.

This article therefore argues *the shift from a politics-embedded, 'National-Statist regime' of religion to an economics-embedded, 'Global-Market' one.* The historical formations of both constellations (or 'regimes' as I call them) are briefly outlined, as are the main characteristics of each. The sections end by exemplifying the major incidences for religion through an analysis of some the main transformations affecting Islam that remain otherwise overlooked by secularisation-entrenched, political analyses.

The national-statist regime

It has been common, in my formative years, to hear Christian forms of belonging, belief and practice that existed before the second half of the 20th century referred to as 'traditional religion'. This label is mistaken, as this is in fact a very modern brand of religion that dates back to early Modernity and the centuries of unrest which followed the Reformation. These modern forms broke with mediaeval Christianity and its traditions (see, e.g., McGuire 2008). By the 19th century, what we call 'traditional religion' was already of a very peculiar, modern and de-traditionalised type – one intimately tied to the rise of the modern nation-state.

The embedment of society in the nation-state

The *guerres de religions* that plagued Europe in the 16th and 17th centuries made finding practical, political, and philosophical solutions a necessity. The Treaty of Westphalia (1648), which ended the 30 years' war, constitutes a crucial moment in this history, as it consecrated the primacy of politics over religion and laid down the bases for the sovereignty and legitimacy of the modern territory-bound state. The Latin maxim *cujus regio, ejus religio* ('the religion of the ruler is the religion of the land') submitted religion to the exercise of rule, and therefore to the state. Unity over a territory and a people was ensured by the monarch (as head of state), since religion could no longer provide societal cohesion as it had in earlier times. The state was elevated so as to transcend any religious particularism (Portier 2010, 241). As Peter Beyer writes, the solution of the Peace of Westphalia to this problem was 'to coordinate the foundational religions – now plural or, more precisely in the European context, "confessional" – with the foundational polities in the form of the states. [… Hence] each state would be a kind of society of its own' (Beyer 2013, 667), and under one rule. The multiple layers of sovereignty that characterised feudal Europe, with Christianity acting as a unifying force, was replaced by a 'set of plural, contiguous and competing states; not by another Empire' (Beyer 2013). The legacy of Westphalia was the creation of (relatively) religiously homogeneous states or sub-states (e.g., German Ländern, Swiss cantons) with corresponding national churches. Pluralism within this frame was managed according to the classical liberal doctrine of tolerance applied to minority communities (not individuals). From this point on, the Churches in particular and religion in general were submitted to the modern political project carried and enacted by the state (Spickard 2007). As Marcel Mauss wrote in his text on the nation, the modern state is a *nation-state* (Mauss 1969). In other words, the modern political form that is the state is unthinkable without its community of reference, the nation, which provides its legitimacy and its hold on social reality. The sovereign state was the organisational centre and principal actor in the project of rationalisation and reform of society according to the utopian cultural programme of modernity and its governing idea of progress. The autonomisation of the political sphere and its institutionalisation in the state was the basis from which other social spheres such as economics, law, education, and healthcare were differentiated, albeit within the regulating framework of the state. This is how one must understand the idea according to which society and its social spheres became 'embedded' (Polanyi 1944) in the political. In this sense, the political sphere, through the foundational and regulative function incarnated by the state, became far more than strictly political. The state was the carrier of a moral mission to forward society on rational principles and accomplish the utopian ideals of the Enlightenment and the emancipatory project of modernity: the creation of a utopian society and of a new 'Man', freed from the bonds of traditional culture and feudal hierarchy. This normative frame warranted the extension of the state's outreach into the whole of social and individual lives through the organisation of health, wealth, and welfare, supported by the development of scientific, bureaucratised, and rationalised projects of documentation, statistics, and planning (Mauss 1969; Rosanvallon 1990; Veer 2001, 53). The modern state was invested in such a way that it reconstructed and shaped the other social spheres, including – and perhaps especially – religion: 'With the rise of the nation-state comes an enormous shift in what religion means' (Veer 2001, 20) as well as what religion is. The overarching regulation of the nation-state, in other words, impacted the very localisation and signification of religion – its form as well as its substance. The various degrees of separation of Church and state among European powers, for example, acted to co-create the categories of religion as well as the secular (Asad 1993, 2003), parallel to the modern distinction between the public and the private (Weintraub 1997). Depending on the country, religion was either privatised (in strict separation regimes) or publicised (cooperation regimes with institutional recognition and financing of the national Church: Scandinavian countries, Greece, etc.) (Portier 2010, 243). Such developments occurred in the various countries forming the 'Western world' (i.e., including North America and Oceania) at unequal rates and with variegated results, although typologies are not only possible but tremendously useful (see, e.g., Koenig 2005; Portier 2010). Beyond these variegated pathways of modernisation, the nation-state regime signified both the 'statisation' and the 'nationalisation' of religion. Authors have remarked how the pre-modern Catholic Church's structure provided a model for the burgeoning state (e.g., Beyer 2006). By the 19th century, things turned around: it is the modern bureaucratic state that provided the model for the establishment of Churches as interlocutors for the state. At the same time, religion was nationalised: it became a defining feature of the 'national character' (Mauss), alongside race and language (Veer 2001, 33). Religion from then on was required to serve national unity and bow to the legitimacy of the state. Minority religions were tolerated to the extent that they did not question the social contract through excessive communitarianism. Churches were integrated in state projects for rationalisation and modernisation, in many cases rather willingly (as in Germany, the UK, and later in Quebec), through the administration of health care and education by networks of bureaucratised institutions. In other cases, as in France, the resistance of the Catholic Church to the formation of the Republic was only partial, limited to certain aspects, and paradoxically only strengthened the reformatory and salvific mission of the state. The 19th century post-Revolution *'conflit des deux France'*, between monarchist Catholics and Republicans, was a divide that opposed two conceptions of the state in a fight over political power *within* the frame of the totalising and embedding state. In all cases, Churches became bound to the construction and service of national identity.

The globalisation of the national-statist regime

The rise to structural dominance of the political sphere through the processes of formation of the nation-state was not a solely European affair (Beyer 2013, 668). By the end of World War I, the nation-state was institutionalised as the natural political form of modernity in all regions across the globe (Eisenstadt 2000). This is not to say that its global dissemination was a one-way process. Shmuel Eisenstadt has shown how modernisation developed according to a multiplicity of pathways, hence his notion of 'multiple modernities'. The pioneer work of Eisenstadt has since been enriched by strands of research in 'entangled', 'fragmented' or 'other' modernities (see an overview in Costa et al. 2006) as well as 'multiple secularities' (Burchardt, Wohlrab-Sahr, and Middell 2015). Yet a constant in all of these works is the diagnosis of the worldwide exportation of the nation-state through European colonialism and imperialism. While the idea and ideals of 'modernity' was disseminated worldwide and acted to shake the institutional and symbolic foundations of the societies in which it was introduced, its cultural programme was variously appropriated and reinterpreted, opposed and contested. The products of these processes have been heterogeneous, and the Western models were nowhere reproduced as such and *in totto* (Eisenstadt 1999, 196–203). Yet Eisenstadt also insisted that while the outcomes of modernisation are certainly multiple, they are not infinite. Rather, they occur within the framework of the modern bureaucratic State[1] as the central societal regulator and the Nation as preferred and naturalised collective identity.

Peter van der Veer's *Imperial Encounters* (2001) illustrates how the construction of the modern nation-state in a country like Britain did not occur in isolation, but rather as part of a wider imperial project that bound coloniser and colonised. In his book, he analyses how the institutionalisation of the secularist principle of separation of Church and State was shaped by the colonial experience in India. The example of Britain and India serves to show how nation-state construction in Europe was actually a co-construction that had an equal impact on the colonies in six interwoven ways: first, how colonial administration contributed to disseminate modern ideals and the cultural programme of modernity in the colonies, and how these were then assimilated, reinterpreted, contested, and enacted; second, how colonial administration effectively contributed to the institutionalisation of a form of modern bureaucratic state in the colonies; third, how these processes

---

[1] I use capitals for State, Nation, Market, and Global when I am referring to more than the empirical, societal institutions they designate, for instance the idea and ideal of the State as a certain set of values, hopes, worldview, and meanings. Transferred to the discussion on the embedment of the social, I similarly capitalize the names of the National-Statist and Global-Market regimes to mark the difference with the actual nation-state and market.

were constitutively tied to the construction of a sense of nationalism in the colonies; fourth, how the imperial encounter contributed to the construction of the categories, among others, of the 'religious' and the 'secular'; fifth, that the category of religion was 'crucial in the emergence of nationalism' (Veer 2001, 53) in the colonies; and finally, that these processes ran two ways so that the formation of the nation and the construction of the category of religion, among others, occurred in both Britain and India as a result of the colonial relation. It seems sound to expand on this case and consider that other colonial cases would only show variations and modulations of this basic scenario, as do other countries that were not directly colonised but were nevertheless highly impacted by Western ideals and imperialism (e.g., China, Japan).

In sum, as Eisenstadt has noted, the nation-state had become the 'universal' and 'natural' modern political form by World War I. At the same time, religion was transformed within this frame in variegated although determinate trajectories across the globe, resulting in a new National-Statist religious regime installed against former 'traditional' regimes.

The transformation of religion in the national-statist regime

How did the institutionalisation of the national-statist regime affect religion? The reshaping occurred on two fronts: the actual empirical reshaping of religion, and the way religion emerged as a category. First and foremost, as has now been argued by a number of scholars, the 19th to 20th century consecrated the (re)invention of 'religion' (as a concept) as well as of 'religions' (as putative coherent entities), on the model of elitist post-Reformation Western Christianity and thus composed of the following: a scripturalist inclination supported by a rational and systematic theology delimited within a set of canonical sacred texts; differentiated, institutionalised, hierarchical, and bureaucratic organisations; a body of recognised clerics and religious 'virtuosi' (Weber); an emphasis on faith and belief; exclusive belonging on the model of Christian parishes; sober, weekly rituals; a clearly differentiated social space and time; the devaluation, even the repression of the particularistic, magic and superstitious elements of traditional and popular religion; the devaluation of emotional and experiential expressions in favour of rationalised, belief-centred forms; a distinction between private and public; a limitation and rationalisation of transcendent references, etc.

One cannot overstress the extent to which the changes brought forth by modernisation and colonisation in both Western and non-Western countries were radical. Nineteenth century Western colonialism and imperialism created Hinduism, Islam, Buddhism, Sikhism, Jainism, 'tribal religions' (Veer 2001, 26–27), Taoism, Confucianism (Goossaert and Palmer 2011), and Judaism (Heschell 2016), and one could add Christianity itself (Veer 2001, 27). All of these 'religions' were formerly vast landscapes of heterogeneous practices, beliefs and metaphysical currents. The (re)formation of the idea of religion went hand in hand with the practical – and often quite radical – transformation of the actual, empirical reality of religion as enacted from 'above', through the processes of nation-state building. The processes and outcomes of the modernisation of religion in non-Western countries, as in Western countries, were once again multiple, non-linear and context-dependent. Yet in all cases, these processes consisted in a major reformation of pre-modern, traditional religion and heralded the beginning of a distinct socio-historical era. There certainly would be a need here for an extensive global analysis in order to

National-statist Islam

Muslim majority countries did not escape this reformation of religion within a National-Statist frame. The case of Indonesia provides a paradigmatic example. Indonesia is the world's largest Muslim majority country with 88% of its population belonging to one of a myriad of Islamic currents, alongside significant minorities of Christians, Hindus, Confucians, Buddhists, and folk religions (Madsen 2011). In a remarkable synthetic and historically sweeping account, Howell (2007) describes how Islam was streamlined and invested in the anti-colonial struggle that led to Independence in 1945, and thereafter in the nation-state building pursued under Sukarno's authoritarian rule. As suggested above, the religion/superstition distinction is characteristic of the nation-state regime, and Indonesia provides a striking example of how these categories were used to regulate religion. In Indonesia, the opposition between rational, belief-based religion, and superstition was used as a criterion to distinguish between desirable and undesirable religion, for instance by undermining the practices of popular religion. As a consequence, non-Muslim, non-Christian, and Sufi-inspired mystical and devotional currents were targeted by the state, repressed and forced to conform or to disappear. Those movements which were successful in surviving were reformatted along the lines of scripturalism (the idea that the core of religion lies in canonical religious texts), worship of a unique transcendent deity, doctrinal rationalisation (along with the rejection of emotion as authentic religiosity), bureaucratic structuration and institutionalisation, and sober ritualisation within an exclusive, congregational frame. Islam was made to conform to the features of Christian churches within a nationalist framework and a modernist ideology whose core was the promotion of the modern state as the actor of progress. Hinduism, Buddhism, Confucianism (that of the Chinese ethnic minority) as well as Balinese traditional polytheism were similarly obliged to comply to this model and had to reinterpret their traditions (sometimes with a fair amount of creativity) in order to satisfy the state's definition of religion as 'belief in a supreme transcendent deity' inscribed in the constitution. Popular rituals were theologically reconstructed in order to become disengaged from the world of spirits. Meditation was downplayed, as were emotional devotional practices and other practices oriented towards the experience of immanent deities. Worship was re-oriented towards a transcendent being, and the divine approached via sober weekly collective liturgy, codified doctrines and official, 'canonical' texts. A restricted set of differentiated 'religions' were recognised by the state, while belonging to an exclusive religious community was made obligatory and appeared on national identity cards. All of this was directly and actively managed by the state, through the enforcement of the constitution, the surveillance of the Department of Justice, as well as through the funding of religious activities and publications by the Department of Religion (see also Beyer 2006).

The example of the Muhammadiyah Islamist movement, also described by Howell (2007), is useful to our discussion. The Muhammadiyah is the Indonesian version of the better-known Egyptian-borne Muslim Brotherhood, and also shares certain similarities with Pakistan's Jamaat-e-Islami (see Iqtidar 2011a, 2011b). Founded in 1912, the Muhammadiyah was institutionalised as a hierarchical and bureaucratic organisation that developed an Islamisation project seeking to conciliate modernity and Islam within a political imaginary and a nationalist framework. Its Islamist project was oriented towards the state and involved seizing political power: society was to be Islamised from the top down through the action of the state (this was largely the model of the other movements mentioned above, as well as of the Iranian Revolution of 1979). The movement sought to recruit mainly among urban and educated elites which were believed to be at the forefront of progress. These elites, it was believed, would 'naturally' pull the masses forward into their version of a modern, rationalised, and Islamised society. Hence even 'radical' Islamist movements contributed to the reshaping of religion within the national-statist framework through the construction of 'modern Islam', and not only the Westernised secular elites.

The global-market regime

According to Koenig (2005), the last decades of globalisation, conjunctly with the developments of communication technologies and Non-European immigration to Western countries, have challenged the political regulation of religion instituted in the nation-state's mission. For him, recent developments evidence the erosion of the 'charisma' (or sacredness) of the nation-state and its partial replacement by that of Human Rights, thereby allowing for new particularistic identities, including religious identities, to emerge as legitimate expressions of the universal which concurrence the nation (see also Beauchemin 2004). There is certainly much to keep from this analysis, yet it remains an essentially political analysis of the erosion of the container functionality of the nation-state. It is, in other words, an analysis of the dis-embedding of society from the nation-state as seen from within a political epistemology. This is why it fails to shed light on the structuring dynamics of the new configuration. The argument that our societies have shifted from an embedment within the nation-state to an embedment in Human Rights is not convincing, as Human Rights are not of the same nature as the nation-state and cannot pretend to regulate the entirety of our societies. Furthermore, the transformation of religion is a global affair, while the sacredness of Human Rights can only truly apply to the West, even though the UN has inscribed these rights in a charter. It is in any case hard to see what Human Rights have to do with the emergence of a global halal market and Islamic finance, the global efflorescence of Pentecostalism, the dissemination of Faith-based initiatives to replace the state in the provision of Welfare, or the rise of a transnational neo-shamanic movement and 'spiritual tourism', just to name a few relevant phenomena.

Countless analyses have insisted on the deregulation of religion. What is meant is that the modern types of institutional regulation by the state and religious institutions (the Churches) within the container of the territorial nation-state have been challenged and significantly hampered. Contrary to fragmentation diagnoses that insist on a prolonged state of deregulation and transition, the hypothesis here is that the organising principles of a new type of regulation are discernible, and that defining these sheds light on the global religious landscape. Yet this new regime is difficult to apprehend from within the political frame of the national-statist regime – which is also the conception that underpins the secularisation paradigm –, since it develops in a fairly different way. Political science and political sociology have proposed to understand this shift, brought on by the combined effects of the critique of the Keynesian Welfare state and the return of radical economic liberalism (i.e., neoliberal ideologies and associated management practices), as the move from 'governmentality' to 'governance'. Governmentality describes a vertical type of regulation by which the exercise of power imposes norms that diffuse from the centre towards the periphery, within a national territory (Portier 2008). As for governance, a term first defined in the field of economics, it describes a mode of regulation in which international and transnational fluxes (mainly economic, but also cultural) have challenged the former territorialised, state-led regulation, and have progressively replaced it by a decentralised, feebly institutionalised and horizontal mode of regulation in which a multiplicity of interested actors participate in the processes of decision-making. The change from governmentality to governance mirrors the shift from a national-statist, institutionalised type of regulation to a market type. It is a change in the very grammar or regime of regulation: it champions so-called transparent, objective, technical, professionalised, judicial and democratic processes over supposedly value-ridden, arbitrary, un-democratic vertical political regulation (Duchastel 2004; Gauthier, Martikainen, and Woodhead 2013a).

The shift from governmentality to governance shows how changes on the macro level of our societies need to be understood against the backdrop of the rise to societal dominance of economics from the late 1970s on. While the cusp of this shift is recent, it is a process that has been long in the making. From the 16th Century on, starting with the French Physiocrats and the moral philosophy of Bernard of Mandeville, up to Adam Smith's *Enquiry into the Nature and Causes of the Riches of Nations* published in 1776, the sphere of economics progressively autonomised from its embedment in traditional religious morality and its submission to the imperatives of the state, and thus the political sphere (as Smith's opus title illustrates). As Pierre Rosanvallon has argued in his history of economic liberalism (1989; see also Appleby 1978; Caillé 2005; Dumont 1977; Laval 2007; Slater and Tonkiss 2001), the market emerged in modern thought as an answer *to the political question of modernity*: by which mechanisms is a truly modern society to ensure optimal social regulation outside of a theological framework. The 'market' was therefore an idea before it ever was a massive social reality, and it was typically championed by liberals as an alternative to the state for social regulation. As capitalism rose, fuelled by belief in the supposedly automatic and value-free mechanisms of production and redistribution of wealth through free markets, the market concurred with the state – and almost won over in the late 19th Century (Polanyi 1957) – yet remained embedded within the objectives of the nation-state in the ideals of socialist, Welfare and (post-)colonial states alike.

The centrality of the state and the belief in its omnipotence and salvific power started to erode in the West in the course of the 1970s, at the tail end of the decades of the post-World War II's 'economic miracle'. Until this time, the radical free-market theories of the Neoliberal schools (Audier 2012) had been held in a marginal position by the Keynesian consensus and the combined arrangements of Fordism and Taylorism. Yet by the end of the 1970s, these old ideas in new clothes made a stark comeback in the combined policies of Reagan and Thatcher in the West, and the beginning of the liberalisation of the economy in China by Deng Xiaoping (Harvey 2005). By this time, Western capitalist societies were almost all rejoicing in the plentiful virtues of consumerism, which had by then become the dominant social and cultural ethos. Consumerism contributed to naturalise an economic rapport to the world – the idea that the world is made of things, material or not, that can be bought and sold (Slater 1997). Neoliberal ideas rapidly gained momentum in the 1980s, imposing themselves to the whole of the political spectrum. At this time, institutions such as the IMF, the World Bank and the WTO steered the new financialised economy created by American-led deregulation policies and imposed their programme aiming to transform the mission of the state in line with essentially economic objectives in all parts of the world. Contrary to common belief, neoliberalism has not lead to a reduction of the 'size' of the state: imposed by international economic institutions when it was not championed from within by national political actors, it has rather significantly redefined the state's mission (Saad-Filho and Johnston 2005). Deregulation, privatisation, free-trade international treaties, the exigencies of the afore-mentioned extra-national economic institutions, associations (G8, G20, ASEA, etc.), and notation agencies, as well as an enhanced concern for security have turned the mission of the state away from Welfare provision to the benefit of market actors (through the privatisation of state-owned companies and outsourcing), have undermined its sovereignty and power (Sassen 1996), and have submitted political action to economic factors such as profitability, cost-effectiveness, debt reduction, and growth (e.g., rather than reducing unemployment and building a social net). All in all, the neoliberal state is one whose essential function is to ensure the smooth and free exercise of trade through the insurance of propriety rights, the enforcing of security and the absorption of the costs of economic crises and market failures (Duchastel 2004; Saad-Filho and Johnston 2005).

Neoliberalism has had a significant impact on the mission of the state and the methods of management of public affairs, thereby aligning the state (and public and para-public administration more widely) on the principles and techniques of business and of the entre-preneurial world. As concerns religion, state regulation of religion has tended to shift from a vertical, governmentality type of regulation to a more horizontal, multi-actor governance model that has changed the rapports between the state and religious institutions and organisations (Martikainen 2013). Neoliberalism has therefore contributed to transform 'religion' from 'above' so to speak, by affecting the administrative, legal, political, and societal environment in which religious institutions evolve. It has also affected religion by contributing to the reformation of religious institutions' structure and functioning on the standards of business management, marketing, and accounting. In the same way that religions and religious movements institutionalised on the model of the modern bureaucratic state in the National-Statist regime, the current trend worldwide is the refor-mation of existing institutions and the emergence of new spiritual/religious movements on this entrepreneurial model (e.g., 'holistic spiritualities', Pentecostal churches, and radical Islamist movements such as ISIS and Boko Haram).

At the same time (in the West it was in fact prior), the spread of consumerism world-wide as a result of economic globalisation has affected the social and cultural environment from 'below'. Consumption became an important phenomenon in the 17th century in Europe through the practices of the emergent middle classes (Campbell 1987). Yet it is perhaps only in the 20th century, especially in the decades following World War II, that consumerism truly became the dominant cultural ethos, giving way to a profoundly morphed household, social and cultural reality, one in which the abundance and the circulation of objects and the continuous appeal to desire is central (Gauthier 2014a; Gauthier, Martikainen, and Woodhead 2013a, 2013b). The rise of consumerism as an ethos and matrix of lifestyle is inextricably tied to the development and democratisation of communication technologies, starting with television. As Charles Taylor has argued, consumerism developed in the West because it provided a formidable vehicle for the extension and radicalisation of the modern individualistic 'culture of authenticity and expressivity' (Taylor 1991, 2002). Consumption and commoditisation are far more than the mere circulation of objects, as marketers have understood far too well: it is based on the production, offer, appropriation, and expression of symbols (i.e., emotions, values, ideals, authenticity, experiences) that are crucial in the contemporary dynamics of identity, recognition, and belonging (Gauthier 2012, 2015). Consumption and its counterparts, advertisement and marketing, have penetrated the fabric of social life to the extent that we now live in *consumer societies* and *consumer cultures*. This means that consumerism shapes to a large extent the very dynamics of social life. A consumer culture is that in which the dominant values of society are not only 'organized through consumption practices but are also in some sense derived from them' (Slater 1997, 24–25), e.g., well-being, hedonism, happiness, personal satisfaction, choice, sovereignty, autonomy, individuality, reflexivity, self-realisation, and self-promotion. It is the culture of a market society, one in which increasing areas of social life are mediated by market relations in the form of the consumption of commodities. It is 'constituted as a culture both *for* consumers and *of* consumers: both a set of commodities for people to consume, and a set of representations of people as consumers' (Sassatelli 2007, 195; emphasis in original). Consumerism has shifted the modern project of the autonomous self away from the rationalist version promoted by Enlightenment philosophers such as Kant and later Nietzsche by providing 'a very particular set of material circumstances in which individuals come to acquire a reflexive relation to identity' (Lury 2011, 29).

The globalisation of the global-market regime

While consumerism, as the nation-state, is a Western invention, it has become a truly global phenomenon with the last phase of globalisation and the explosion of digital communication technologies. The emergence of a new urban, de-traditionalised middle class in the wake of economic development has transformed the landscape of almost every country on the globe, on all continents. It is this middle class which has acted as the main 'cultural carrier' (Campbell 1987) for the dissemination and appropriation of consumerism and the transformations of the last decades, as it had done earlier in Europe. Consumerism promotes choice as a fundamental process in the formation of the self and the expression of identity and belonging. These dynamics can also be found in non-Western countries, yet with local appropriations that differ from Taylor's European-born culture of authenticity and expressivity. A fundamental question for further research is precisely how consumerism is transformed and reshaped in non-Western societies. Yet the available research does attest to a common movement towards personalisation, a heightened valuation of the self, the importance of consumption in the dynamics of identity and belonging, as well as an increase in the importance of inner-worldly values such as well-being, success, affluence, and social mobility across those social classes affected by socio-economic changes.

A special note must be made on the individualism promoted by consumerism. While the consumerist 'revolution' (Taylor 2002) acts as a radicalisation of prior individualistic trends promoted by modernisation, this individualism is inassimilable to theories of narcissism and atomism. Consumer culture is individualistic, but it is an expressive type of individualism. This means that individuals need to express their identities through visible, public signs. Hence the movement towards lifestyle identities which also profoundly affects non-Western countries and the new middle classes especially. The expression of identities through visible, material and non-material signs requires that these signs be recognised. Contemporary individualism is paradoxically intensely social, as there is a constant need for forms of community, actual, or virtual, to recognise and validate these ever-constructing identities (Gauthier 2012, 2014b; Meintel 2014). This is why the use of Facebook, Twitter, Instagram, and other 'social media' is so widespread all over the world, since they cater to the dynamics of expression and recognition. The development of digital communications and the Internet significantly enhances the dynamics of neoliberalism and consumerism, yet do not constitute a logic of its own, contrary to the tenants of the mediatisation thesis, as I have argued elsewhere (Gauthier 2015). Following Taylor (2002), the consumerist brand of expressive individualism also reconfigures the public, which becomes an arena of mutual exposition rather than a 'common' (common oriented action, typical of the political project).

One of the most important effects of the embedment of global societies in the Market has been the de-differentiation of social spheres and the blurring of the boundaries that were instituted in the former National-Statist regime. While Casanova (1994) argued that the 'defendable core' of the secularisation thesis was the differentiation of social spheres, one can question whether this process was ever as accomplished as we commonly imagine, even in the case of Western countries. The differentiation of social spheres into well defined, institutionalised societal domains has been held as an unexamined truth by the bulk of social sciences. The differentiation process has been thought to be irreversible, as if each sphere had been liberated from external determinations and left to evolve into its 'natural' form. This is the case for religion, when one considers the classics, as well as the more recent writings of scholars like José Casanova and Marcel Gauchet (1985). Yet however accomplished may have been this process, scholars from all disciplines have pointed to a recent blurring of the boundaries between the differentiated spheres, including the blurring of the public/private division. These de-differentiation processes underlie Zygmunt Bauman's diagnosis of a 'liquid modernity' (2000). From our perspective, both of these processes, differentiation then de-differentiation, make sense: while the *State* requires well-defined societal domains and institutions to perform its social regulation function, the *Market*, on the other hand, demands deregulated, fluid, feebly institutionalised social spheres in order to perform its own specific type of immanent, horizontal type of social regulation (the 'free market' utopia). Hence the Market's challenge of the former, state-regimented societal order. The de-differentiation process has been widely ignored by the study of religion in comparison with other disciplines, and one can understand why: the object of social scientific study of religion, which remains tied to mostly substantive conceptions of religion, could dissolve in the process. José Casanova's de-privatisation/re-publicisation of religion thesis does not designate a cause. This, I would argue, has to with Casanova's inscription within the secularisation paradigm and, as a consequence, in an essentially statist and institutional, political perspective that is unable to seize the importance of economics in the underlying logics of change. The marketisation perspective, on the other hand, can offer such an explanation. The re-publicisation of religion, which exceeds the sole institutional level considered by Casanova, can be understood as a consequence of the rise of the neoliberal world order and the spread of consumerism.

While the neoliberal redefinition of the state decomposes the institutional social spheres to open them to market logics, consumerism furthers this process while also splitting open the divide between the private and the public with its expressive type of individualism. The trend in both cases supports a culture and a politics of publicity.

Following the de-differentiation of religion brought forth by its reformation within the Global-Market regime, religion has re-emerged in public life across the globe in old and new ways, including in the field of welfare provision, education, social integration (e.g., of immigrant populations), dispute settlement, healthcare, healing, entertainment, etc. For example, 'faith-based initiative' (Ashley and Sandefer 2013; Hackworth 2013) types of intervention have spread in a form or another worldwide. Parallel to this, expressive forms of religious practice have emerged (the case of the Muslim veil is paradigmatic, see Gauthier and Guidi 2016). As consumerism promotes individual choice as the main expression and accomplishment of one's subjectivity, the religious forms that are founded on the imperatives of choice are faring well, such as born-again movements and the nebula of personalised 'spiritualities' and rituals that cater to the contemporary quest culture of consumerism. On a general level, religion has been reformatted to address issues of ethics (how does one live? How to conduct a good life here and now?), identity, and belonging. The institutionalised, parochial, rationalised, modern forms of religious belief, belonging, and practice on the other hand are in decline. They are also forced to adjust to the new regime, often with important changes in their very substance (see, e.g., the contributions in Gauthier and Martikainen 2013; Martikainen and Gauthier 2013). On the other hand, the last few decades have seen the extraordinary rise of novel religious movements of an entirely new sort, non- or little-institutionalised, entrepreneurial, media-savvy, franchised, and transnational. These movements offer an experience-based, emotional, healing-oriented, and often charismatic brand of religion focused on meeting individual needs. Globally, the forms most corresponding to the National-Statist model are those the most affected by decline and the pressure for reform, while those espousing the Global-Market model are experiencing growth. All over the world, new religious manifestations are emerging, offering much more than compartmentalised religion and weekly rituals.

The erosion of the National-Statist regime signifies that the national frame is challenged and can no longer be considered the natural container for understanding contemporary religious dynamics. The nation is no longer the obliged community of reference, and the last decades have seen the emergence of de-territorialised global religious communities, such as the global Muslim *Ummah* (Roy 2004), but also the global Pentecostal family, the global community of Catholics (e.g., the experience of youth at the World Youth Day manifestation), the global community of First Nations, the international Hindutva, etc. Even national communities now tend to include their diasporas, with important consequences for religion in countries like China for instance (Goossaert and Palmer 2011). Similarly, and as a mass of scholarship has shown in the last years, the current trends affecting religion cannot be understood without paying significant attention to the transnational fluxes made possible by communication technologies, increased mobility, and the networks of a globalised economy. Meanwhile, methodological nationalism continues to be the norm in the social scientific study of religion, namely in 'post-secular' and 'multiple secularities' circles. From a secularisation perspective and a National-Statist political analysis, the phenomena described here appear marginal, dismissible, and incomprehensible, when they are not simply invisible. From the perspective defended here, they appear to be at the very heart of contemporary dynamics. The erosion of the sovereignty of the state, as well as that of the nation as the natural and most secure support for identity also explains the rise of conservative and fundamentalist movements which, faced with the blurring of the formerly recognisable landscape and the loss of certainty brought forth by economic and cultural globalisation, fuelled by the disenchantment regarding the utopian promises of politics, precisely aim to go back to a golden era, be it the times of the Prophet Mohammed (Salafism, ISIS), the pre-soviet imperial times (Hungary etc.) or Post-War America (Trump). Neo-fundamentalist movements (including religious radicalism) and populist-nationalist movements are two faces of the same coin, and build on each other's momentum. Religion often plays an important role in neo-nationalist movements (e.g., India, ex-Soviet block). These movements also tend towards authoritarian forms of government, which can readily be interpreted as the desire to re-instate both the Nation as the community of reference and the State as the undisputed societal regulator and purveyor of security, yet do so in a way that remains bound to the Market regime.

The transformation of religion in the global-market regime

Pursuing with the characteristics of religion as reshaped by the Global-Market regime, the portrait appears inherently variable, yet within a set of definable, common vectors. The religious landscape has been profoundly transformed following the arrival of new actors (women, immigrants, new religious authorities) and new religious movements (Global Pentecostalism, neo-Shamanism, neo-Pagan, neo-fundamentalism, etc.) A thorough analysis of these new successful movements would show how they are feebly institutionalised, networked, horizontal, entrepreneurial, and providers and promoters of an experience-based brand of religion in opposition to the rationalised and faith-based type of the National-Statist regime. At the same time, religious traditions have undergone important changes, both on the institutional level and that of practitioners, again moving towards an expressive, experience-based, charismatic, personalised, ethics and identity-oriented, immanent brands of religiosity, and cater to the needs for self-realisation, success, health, and happiness. Healing has become an important trope across the board, including in mainstream Christianity (e.g., laying of hands) and Islam (Touag 2014).

As a whole, religion has come out of its box, so to speak. It is no longer confined to a well-guarded, differentiated social sphere, and it has been re-publicised as a result of the expressive thread of consumer culture. Religion appears in many new guises, and mixes with other social spheres such as healthcare, education, law, politics, but also entertainment, cultural and subcultural movements, sports, arts, etc. On the institutional level, religious institutions and organisations are increasingly adopting neoliberal values, discourses, and practices (see, e.g., Moberg 2016; Schlamelcher 2013) as well as branding and marketing strategies (e.g., Einstein 2008, 2011). Use of digital media is now an obligation which affects religion by reformatting it according to the principle of visibility and recognisability (hence a branding effect) (Gauthier, Martikainen, and Woodhead 2013b; Gauthier and Uhl 2012). Religious organisations rally to answer the needs no longer catered for, following the dismantling of the Welfare or social state in areas relating to health, integration, education, legal counsel (e.g., dispute, marriage, and divorce settlement), social services, and social security more widely (see, e.g., Gray 2013 for Ireland).

Religion is no longer centred on belief, faith and creed as it reconfigures to answer practical as well as ethical and identity issues: how to live one's life, including social and intimate relationships. Emotional and mystical trends, which had been side-lined and sometimes even dismissed and repressed, have found new legitimacy and are thriving, as they offer formidable vehicles for the experiential culture of consumerism. Experience tends to become the defining criteria for authenticity (Gauthier 2012). The question of authenticity more broadly becomes central in this moving landscape, and modes of authority have shifted accordingly from traditional or bureaucratic modes to charismatic ones (Weber) (Gauthier and Mcintel, forthcoming). A striking example is the emergence of many new religious authority figures from the worlds of entertainment and business, with little or no frequentation of the instituted circuits of religious authority. Religion in the market regime is constitutively transnational, and affiliations tend to be cast against a global backdrop. Religion and identity are no longer contained by the Nation, which becomes available for reactionary and populist movements. Religious practice is no longer contained by the sober and weekly rituals and tends to revolve around extraordinary and ephemeral events such as festivals, seminars, and other mass or intimate forms of gathering (Gauthier 2014b). Similarly, communities are increasingly voluntary, and de-traditionalisation continues through urbanisation and the renewed critique of cultural particularisms. Self-realisation, self-discipline, self-discovery, individual responsibility, adaptability to change, mobility, empowerment, and personal progress are all neoliberal linked values promoted by religion in the market era.

The rise of market Islam

The case of Islam provides striking examples of some of the changes that can be linked to the rise of consumerism and neoliberalism. There is no place here to conduct a true case study, but the following simply aims at pointing to some transformations that authors specialised in Islam. This focus also aims to support the argument that these changes are global in nature and not confined to the West; neither are they simply a process of unilateral westernisation of the world. Social sciences continue to be highly interested in the links between Islam and Human rights, the state and democracy (e.g., Schulze 2008, 2012). Yet as a number of scholars have argued, recent reconfigurations are better understood when linked to consumer capitalism. Focusing on the Middle East, Haenni (2005) has argued that the religious revival in Muslim countries, accompanied by the increasing visibility of Islam corresponds neither to an atavistic return of mediaeval or traditional forms, nor to the victory of the political Islam incarnated by the Iranian revolution, but rather that it champions a new synthesis of Islam and modernity. According to Haenni, the matrix for this new configuration is the Market rather than the Nation-State, hence the appellation 'Market Islam' (*islam de marché*).[2] The Muslim revival that has been attested in all Muslim majority countries is correlated to the rise of as set of new values centred around self-realisation, health and economic as well as relational success (Haenni 2005: 7). These values turn the preoccupations of Muslims away from collective, social and

---

[2]Rudnyckyj (2009) has also coined the term 'Market Islam' in reference to the rise of Islamic management seminars in Indonesia and Malaysia. Rudnyckyj's notion embraces explicit phenomena which blend neoliberal ethics and Islamic religious practice and is thus narrower than Haenni's, which aims at qualifying the coherence of a broader spectrum of trends within Islam.

political projects towards more personal quests for salvation which coalesce in the emergence of a new entrepreneurial 'Muslim pride' (Haenni 2005: 11) born in the midst of widespread disappointment regarding the utopian promises of politics and state action. While the Iranian revolution played a role in the renewal of Islam and its re-publicisation throughout the world, Haenni argues that the characteristics of the recent transformations resonate with post-Cold War consumer capitalism more than political Islam. Market Islam has been promoted by new religious authorities such as business-trained-media-guru-turned-spiritual-reformer Amr Khaled (Haenni and Holtrop 2002; Haenni 2005; Gauthier and Uhl 2012) who insists on the 'reconciliation of religion and everyday life' and favours themes such as emotion, introspection, and the quest for happiness and success. More of a 'coach' or a 'big brother' than a charismatic leader in the classical sense, sporting a business suit without a tie nor a beard, the Egyptian-born Khaled insists that the Prophet Muhammad was a rich and successful merchant in preaches that are relayed worldwide via a media empire that includes satellite television and Internet. Assimilating notions, beliefs and techniques from New Age spirituality, popular psychology, self-help publications, and American-style management, Khaled aims for social efficacy rather than theological rationality in preaches that are easily assimilated, practical, and slogan-filled. Market Islam shifts the focus away from collective, politically oriented projects towards individualistic, practical concerns that find their full resonance in themes linked to economic performance (see also Krämer 2013 for Turkey). It introduces a prosperity theology in which material affluence and personal success are interpreted as signs of *baraka* (grace) and transform Islam in a direction that is reminiscent of the Puritan ethics that Weber (1971) famously argued were at the origin of the capitalist ethos (Haenni 2005: 85).

While these transformations first affected middle classes, the saturation of popular media with such themes has contributed to a much more profound penetration within the social fabric. To illustrate the importance of the impact of such new authorities, a research conducted in Ben Ali's Tunisia on fifty women who wore the Muslim veil (i.e., before the 2012 revolution, when veil wearing was forbidden in the public space) revealed that *all* of the interviewees, both those from lower and middle classes, and both 'liberal' and 'conservative' types, cited Amr Khaled as an important theological source for the legitimisation of their (then) rebel practice (Ben Salem and Gauthier 2011). From the perspective of Haenni, veil wearing (be it in its fashionable or integral varieties) is linked to this shift towards a Market Islam since it becomes important for Muslim women to *express* their religious identities publicly and that this expression operates through clothing, i.e., through consumption. The same logic applies to the exponential growth of *halal* consumption, which has not only become an extremely important market globally, but also extremely important for Muslims in diasporas and Muslim majority countries alike as a means of behaving as a 'good Muslim' and publicly expressing their religiosity (Bergeaud-Blackler 2012, 2015, 2017a, 2017b; Fischer 2008; Gauthier, forthcoming).

Similar transformations have been reported in the case of Indonesia,[3] the world's largest Muslim majority country in the world with 260 million inhabitants (see Howell

---

[3]My intention here is not to bring any novel data that would impress specialists of Indonesia. My sources are purely secondary. Yet being the largest majority Muslim country in the world, I am struck by how the sources I mention, especially

2005, 2009, 2012, 2015). There, dictator Suharto's New Order programme accelerated economic development (1968–1998), steered by Chicago University-trained economists, opened the country to foreign investments and trade. This process nevertheless remained under state control until the 1990s (e.g., state-owned companies in key development sectors), after which neoliberalism acted to privatise and further deregulate the economy. This first stimulated rapid growth and accelerated urbanisation, the de-territorialisation of social bonds, break with tradition, experience of ethnic diversity, and exposure to globalised communication networks. In addition, education rates climbed while 'more and more people experienced employment in places structured by instrumental rationality and rational-economic-thinking' (Howell 2007, 229). From the late 1970s on and increasingly thereafter, the attitude towards Sufism and mysticism began to change. Books on Sufism became best-sellers, and personalities began to encourage a positive attitude towards the mystical currents of *tasawwuf* and traditional, highly syncretic Indonesian Islam. This struck a chord with the new middle class, who felt attracted to these new, more personalised, emotional, experiential, self-realisation-oriented 'spiritual-but-not-religious' offers as has been the case in the West (Howell 2007, 244; see also Howell 2014a, 2014b; Njoto-Feillard 2012). The middle class consequently expanded in the 1980s–1990s, adopting a consumerist lifestyle, particularly in urban areas and among the youth (Hariyadi 2010). At the same time, Indonesia saw an explosion of books, magazines, television shows (talk shows, soap operas), newspapers, women's magazines, and later websites devoted entirely or partly to Islam. On the whole, religion exponentially increased in public visibility. The ever-expanding, globalising media-scape allowed for new religious authorities (Aa Gym, Arifin Ilham, Jefry Al Bukhori, Yusuf Mansur) to emerge from without the traditional *Ulama* amidst media empires and following the televangelist model, much like Amr Khaled (Haenni 2005; Howell 2008, 2013, 2014a, 2014b; Njoto-Feillard 2012; Watson 2005). For C.W. Watson, the rise in fame of such figures as Aa Gym and his 'approach to the implementation of Muslim precepts is more representative of the nature in Islam in Indonesia today than the activities of terrorists' (Watson 2005, 773) and, as Njoto-Feillard (2012) adds, the scriptural type of Islam promoted by the formerly dominant Modernist movements. This 'telecoranist' (Njoto-Feillard 2012, 211) model has penetrated the Indonesian economy by blending management techniques with Islamic content. Damir Rudnyckyj's study of the Iron industry has shown how figures such as Ary Ginanjar have built their lucrative businesses by developing highly successful 'spiritual training programmes' that blend management techniques, psychology (David Goleman's 'emotional intelligence'), and New Age-infused Islamic content in multimedia presentations. These programmes have been widely disseminated in key sectors of the Indonesian economy and beyond, successfully transmitting a new kind of neoliberal-friendly success-oriented brand of Islam (Rudnyckyj 2009, 2010).

As Julia Howell writes, in Indonesia, techniques for spiritual and personal development were readily interpreted as Sufi, 'as they enhance self-reflection and purification or deepen meditative awareness'. (Howell 2007, 240) The revival of Sufism in Indonesia in new urban

---

anthropologists, give a portrait of Indonesian religion that corresponds to the model I have been working on. What is also interesting is that these transformations have been ignored by other scholars, namely from Religious Studies and those with a mainly political outlook, who remain entrenched within the secularization paradigm and an essentially political conception of religion and related themes (secularization of Indonesia, the state and religion, compatibility of religion and democracy, etc.).

THE MARKETIZATION OF RELIGION

middle classes especially has to do with the ways in which it provided a legitimate vessel in which to coalesce, synthetise and Islamise new 'spiritual' influences, beliefs and techniques. If Sufism was inassimilable in the National-Statist era, it has appeared perfectly adapted in the emerging Global-Market era. According to Howell:

> A distinctive and remarkable feature of Indonesia's recent Islamic revival has been the upsurge of popular interest in Islam's mystical and devotional tradition, tasawwuf (Sufism). The resurgence of Sufism, especially among urbanistes [...] runs counter to the powerful current of scripturalist Islamic modernism that has been hostile to Sufism for most of the past century. (Howell 2008, 35).

New Age and personal development techniques, values, and themes permeated Indonesian cosmopolitan culture, yet were 'religiously decontextualized and psychologized or medicalized, in order to be assimilated to Islam' (Howell 2007, 242). Traditional practices such as meditation and *dzikir*, collective devotional recitations and chanting, which 'were seen as embarrassingly superstitious' now appear to Indonesian Muslim cosmopolitans as attractive, even scientifically validated ways to enhance modern lifestyles' (Howell 2007, 221). This new experiential rapport to religion, and to Islam in particular, has affected a wide spectrum of Indonesian society. In the former period, ruler Sukarno (1945–1967) had shunned from any public display of religiosity, and had insisted that religion must be rational (Howell 2007, 224). Suharto (1967–1998) followed in the steps of his forebear by pursuing the National-Statist formatting of religion, yet was obliged to espouse the new trends that were emerging in Indonesian society. Suharto therefore started to publicise his participation in hajj rituals and started insisting on his family's Quranic education during the course of the early 1990s. Lower social classes did not escape this reformation of religion, and were equally affected by television shows and other mass media. Lower classes have been key actors in the emergence of their own brand of phenomena, such as weekly mass street rallies in which devotional chants are sung in a highly effervescent atmosphere (Howell 2014a). In other words: exit sober and belief-centred rituality, enter event-based, temporary ritual communities.

The market formatting of Islam goes deeper than the aforementioned strands of popular religion. Modern Islamist movements such as the Muhammadiyah in Indonesia, the Muslim Brotherhood in Egypt and the in Pakistan, which were institutionalised within the former Nation-State regime, have also suffered changes. On the basis of ethnographic research on the Jamaat-e-Islami in Lahore, Iqtidar (2011b) accounted for the new difficulties the movement is experiencing in recruiting militants, a phenomenon which local organisers attribute in good part to the incompatibility of the new consumerist lifestyle with political involvement. Beneath a relative stability in the leaders' official rhetoric, which continues to emphasise the importance of the state as the main social regulator and preferred agent for social change, Humeira diagnoses a shift from a 'political imaginary' centred on the *State* to one centred on the idea of the *Market*, thereby corroborating Bayat's (2007) analysis of the situation in Egypt and Iran. Muslim modernist movements such as the Muslim Brotherhood and the Jamaat-e-Islami were and are militant and political, and strive to Islamise their respective societies from above through the action of the totalising state. The Indonesian Muhammadiyah, the country's largest, scripturalist Islamic organisation, provides another example as it shuns political activism in principle. In a lengthy study, Gwenaël Njoto-Feillard (2012) has described how the consumerist and neoliberal turn of the 1990s and 2000s has plunged the Muhammadiyah, which is highly bureaucratised yet not entirely vertically integrated as other modernist organisations in the world, in a serious crisis and an erosion of its influence, forcing it to negotiate with the new capitalist environment and the coextensive rise of an Indonesian brand of 'Market Islam'. In Indonesia as elsewhere, Islamist movements have an ambivalent attitude towards 'the market': it is seen as promoting reprehensible egotistical desires on the one hand, yet on the other it appears as a new space of autonomy and expression that can be a powerful mechanism for the transformation of societies, no longer from the top down, as in classical modern Islamism, via the action of the state, but rather 'from the bottom up', through the adoption of 'authentic' Muslim lifestyles, ethics and identities (Iqtidar 2011b; Njoto-Feillard 2012). The loss of state sovereignty to the hands of essentially economical supranational regulating bodies (IMF, World Bank, WTO, etc.) has multiplied the effects of disillusionment with regards to the state, and has acted to catalyse the shift from a Nation-State to a Market imaginary.

Radical Islam also provides a fertile ground for the interpretation and analysis within the framework of the Global-Market regime. The Jihadism of ISIS, for example, can be understood as a striking example of an entrepreneurial, radically transnational, highly mediatised, network type of Islamic radicalism that shuns the basic precepts of prior political Islamism, including a complete disregard for the nation-state. A caricature published in *The International New York Times* suggestively depicted a bearded ISIS jihadist standing in front of the ruins of the Libyan state, with the caption reading: 'You see a failed state, I see a brand opportunity'. This captures the dynamics of a movement oriented towards a politics of visibility that makes abundant use of the possibilities of Internet and social media to ignite franchising and vocations. Its highly branded communication aims at fascinating and recruiting amongst Western and non-Western youths in need of status, recognition, and participation in something bigger than themselves through born-again identities (Khosrokavar 2014, 2017; Roy 2016).

The above discussion is intended to show how similar trends have been unravelling in Muslim majority countries. Although national and regional colourations exist of course, the overall direction of the changes have been consistent.[4] As illustrated, the changes in Islam appear constitutively transnational, catalysed by heightened mobility and communication technologies. Furthermore, these trends have taken shape through intense, two-way relations between the Muslim diasporas in Western countries and Muslim majority countries. Trends like veil wearing ('fashion' or conservative) (Amiraux 2004; Göle 2003; Kiliçbay and Binark 2002), the exponential rise of halal or 'sharia compatible' consumption (Bergeaud-Blackler 2012, 2015, 2017a, 2017b; Rodier 2014), the emergence of Islamic media (Haenni and Holtrop 2002), Muslim fashion (Lewis 2015, 2016; Tarlo 2010), Muslim swim and sportswear (e.g., the *burkini*) (Gauthier and Guidi 2016), the revival of Islamic healing techniques (Touag 2014), Islamic tourism (e.g., sharia compatible 'all-inclusive' travel packages), and pilgrimage (e.g., the renewed importance of the hajj[5]), as well as the emergence of Islamic branding (Jafari and Sandicki 2016; Shirazi 2016), insurance and finance (Madi 2014) represent some of the major innovations of

---

[4]The case of the Gulf countries would require a specific treatment, but there is evidence that the marketization framework would also yield interesting results.
[5]Saudi authorities have invested in tourist accommodations and infrastructures, while the demand for the hajj pilgrimage has increased dramatically. Saudi authorities are sometimes at a loss as how to manage some of the new types of

the last few years. These are either old practices that have been invested with new meanings or entirely new practices which have, in a very short period of time, imposed themselves as the preferred means through which one expresses a Muslim lifestyle and belonging to the 'global *Ummah*' (Haenni 2005; Roy 2004). These phenomena are born outside of the instituted organisations that regulated Islam in the Nation-State regime. All are market born or find their full expressions through the possibilities of consumption and the Internet. As Haenni writes: 'The field of economics provides new Muslim religiosities not only their concrete supports (the market), but also their categories' (2005, 11), reframed according to the themes of self-realisation, personal responsibility, performance and competitiveness. The rise of a Market Islam is corollary to a neoliberal politicisation of Islam, as it accompanies state privatisation and the dismantling of the social net rather than the instauration of a sharia-based Islamic state (Rudnyckyj 2009; Haenni 2005). The global markets for halal products and Islamic finance, for instance, which represent tens of billions of dollars, are amongst the world's most important business sectors in terms of growth today (Bergeaud-Blackler 2017a, 2017b; Nasr 2009). The importance of these phenomena can therefore not be overrated, yet they are developing outside of the National-Statist framework, and remain practically invisible from within the secularisation paradigm's essentially political and institutional lens. In other words, this set of phenomena, which appear at best as marginal and irrelevant from the classic sociology of religion and religious studies perspective, are in my opinion anything but: they are at the core of a major transformation of the very substance of religion in the global era, and will only grow in importance in the near future. They illustrate a shift from a politically embedded type of religion to one in which consumerism and 'the market' are the structuring forces.

Conclusion

The secularisation paradigm is unfit to understand the trends highlighted above. The 'post-secular' hypothesis, centred on a few Western countries, is similarly impotent in seizing these global dynamics. Even the 'multiple secularities' current, which produces valuable research, evades the issues of the neoliberal and consumerist shaping of societies and cultures, as its analyses remain essentially bound to political issues. It is as if this strand of scholarship had inverted the former focus on the measure of Church decline into the measure of the 'degrees of secularity' of given nation-states. An empirically grounded alternative to the secularisation paradigm is urgently needed in order to better seize the ongoing mutations affecting religion, not only in the West but also worldwide. As I have attempted to show here, the world is an interconnected place – it already was before the latest wave of globalisation –, and therefore understanding the current transformations affecting religion must take this interconnectedness into account and counterbalance methodological nationalism with a transnational and global outlook. A refreshed perspective must accept to shift the framework of interpretation away from a state and institution-based one in order to acknowledge the importance of the socio-economic changes that have been brewing since the 1960s and have been manifesting

---

practices that have emerged in the last decade, such as self-portraits ('selfies') taken with cell phones inside the sacred space of the Kaaba shrine.

themselves increasingly since the 1980s and 1990s, enhanced by the latest wave of globalisation and the end of the Cold War. It is because scholars have not been looking in the right places that diagnoses of 'fragmentation' and 'open-ended transition' have been the object of a soft consensus. Suggesting there has been a shift from a National-Statist regime of religion to a Global-Market one signifies that global societies are interconnected in structural ways and that they form coherent – albeit complex, heterogeneous, singular and differentiated – wholes that coalesce around a defined set of organising principles. By evoking 'regimes', I have argued that this regulation has occurred within an embedding social sphere through its embodiment in a central actor and a corresponding level of community: first the Nation-State, as embodiment of High Modern Ideals and social utopianism, and more recently the Market, as the enforcer of an economistic ideal of horizontal and 'more efficient' social regulation, against a 'global' backdrop.

The marketisation thesis by no means signifies that the features of the National-Statist regime have disappeared. Changes of this magnitude and importance obviously do not happen overnight, and it is useless to attempt to date with any kind of precision 'when' the shift in balance might have occurred. If there was any sense to such an endeavour, the answer could only be differentiated, depending on the country and whether one considers urban or rural areas, social classes, and so on. The National-Statist and the Market regime are in many ways overlapping, and will continue to do so for some time, with movements of acceleration, slowing down, and a spectrum of variegated pathways (which are yet to be defined). Hence specific religious groups or movements do not need correspond to the characteristics portrayed. These are trends, and both the National-Statist and Market regimes are ideal-types in the strict Weberian sense, meaning that they are simplified portraits that are composed by highlighting and exaggerating certain characteristics in order that they may be manipulated scientifically and compared (Weber 1971). Yet a shift has occurred and is occurring, which has significantly modified the religious landscape, and it is important that social sciences step away from the secularisation framework in order to tune its analyses with the ongoing social change.

The claim here is wider in its implications than Beyer's (2013) stimulating hypothesis that we have left a 'Westphalian' world and have entered a 'post-Westphalian' one, although our analyses are partly similar. The Nation-State is a stronger and more general reference than Westphalia as it is truly global. It is grounded in a European Westphalian legacy, yet it far exceeds its limits (even the US can arguably be considered non-Westphalian in the strict sense). Hence attempting to define to which extent non-Western countries are Westphalian, as Beyer attempts in the case of India and Turkey, can only produce mitigated answers. Also, Beyer names the present 'post-Westphalian', for he is avowedly missing an organising principle on its own terms. While Beyer does recognise the new importance of the market and economics, he fails to side-step an essentially political analysis that would allow him to isolate the market as an overarching regulating principle and not dilute it amongst a series of other 'factors', such as media. Beyer is therefore unable to name the current situation and concludes that we are in an open-ended process whose outcomes are yet indiscernible. From the perspective developed here, *it is possible* to name the current global religious landscape and show how it has been evolving within a specific regime of religion, one I have called the Global-Market regime. While there is no telling where things may go in the future, there is less doubt about where we are.

Finally, the marketisation thesis must not be understood as meaning we should analyse religion by using the concepts of neoclassical economic theory (e.g., Rational Choice), on the contrary. The first and most superficial reason is that economic theory is fundamentally flawed in its assumptions (about the nature of Man as basically self-interested and maximising, and about the claim that its laws, as those of the market, are natural), even with respect to economic transactions, let alone non-economic ones, as a whole landmass of scholarship has shown, from Durkheim (see, e.g., Steiner 2005) to economist Keen (2011). 'Economics of religion' scholars translate religious phenomena (essentially church-type religion) into economic language, with the pretention that Rational Choice theory is universally valid and that it says something about *religion as such*. English language sociologists of religion have been insufficiently critical about an approach which, to paraphrase Mary Douglas, a couple of days of ethnographic research would suffice to prove utterly unfounded. The most profound reason is the following: Rational Choice adepts say nothing about the impacts of neoliberalism and consumerism on religion and societies more broadly. Rather they participate in the very phenomenon that needs to be analysed, e.g., the spread of the ideology according to which all social facts can be thought of in the terms of neoclassical (i.e., neoliberal) economics. The marketisation thesis defended here implies on the contrary that we understand that the rise to dominance of economics has non-economic effects and dimensions. At the core of this process, the market plays out a political function, that of a horizontal, supposedly 'optimal' and 'value-neutral' social regulator significantly different from the top-down, centralised, highly institutionalised social regulation typical of the Nation-State – one in which undetermined individuals freely exercise choice amidst a set of equal options. Rather than saying that the landscape of religion today is best thought of as a religious 'free market', the term 'marketization' as I am using it here points towards a reshaping of religion along a consumerist and neoliberal framework that has nothing natural about it. As the discussion on consumerism has shown, the 'Market' is a worldview, a set of values and meanings, a type of rapport to the self, to others and the world; it is an ethos that has corresponding consequences on identity and modes of belonging. Carried by the middle classes, marketisation does not so much stress the liberties of choice as the fact that seeing choice itself as something important that realises the modern project of the self is determined by macro-level social and historical global processes. As the case of Islam illustrates, the marketisation thesis thereby implies a move away from both the secularisation and Rational Choice paradigms in order to grasp an ongoing – but discernible – shift in the very meaning, location and substance of religion.

Disclosure statement

No potential conflict of interest was reported by the authors.

References

Amiraux, Valérie. 2004. "Être musulman : le dire, le montrer, le cacherDu difficile rapport entre privé et public." In *Etre musulmane, être musulman au Caire, à Dakar, Téhéran, Istanbul et Paris*, edited by Valérie Amiraux and Olivier Roy O., 19–24. Marseille: Indigène.

Appleby, Joyce O. 1978. *Economic thought and Ideology in Seventeenth Century England*. Princeton: Princeton University Press.

Arvidsson, Adam. 2006. *Brands: Meaning and Value in Media Culture*. Abingdon: Routledge.

Asad, Talal. 1993. *Genealogies of Religion. Discipline and Reasons of Power in Christianity and Islam*. Baltimore: The John Hopkins University Press.

Asad, Talal. 2003. *Formations of the Secular. Christianity, Islam, Modernity*. Stanford: Stanford University Press.

Ashley, David, and Ryan Sandefer. 2013. "Neoliberalism and the Privatization of Welfare and Religious Organizations in the United States of America." In *Religion in the Neoliberal Age. Political Economy and Modes of Governance*, edited by Tuomas Martikainen and François Gauthier, 109–128. Farnham: Ashgate.

Audier, Serge. 2012. *Néo-libéralisme(s). Une archéologie intellectuelle*. Paris: Grasset.

Baumann, Zygmunt. 2000. *Liquid Modernity*. Cambridge: Polity.

Bayat, Asef. 2007. *Making Islam Democratic: Social Movements and the Post-Islamist Turn*. Stanford: Stanford University Press.

Beauchemin, Jacques. 2004. *La société des identités. Éthique et politique dans le monde contemporain*. Montreal: Athéna.

Ben Salem, Maryam, and François Gauthier. 2011. "Téléprédication et port du voile en Tunisie." *Social Compass* 58 (3): 323–330. doi:10.1177/0037768611412136

Bergeaud-Blackler, Florence. 2012. ""Islamiser l'alimentation." Marchés halal et dynamiques normatives." *Genèses* 89: 61–87. doi:10.3917/gen.089.0061

Bergeaud-Blackler, Florence, ed. 2015. *Les sens du Halal. Une Norme dans un Marché Mondial*. Paris: CNRS.

Bergeaud-Blackler, Florence. 2017a. *Le Marché Halal ou l'Invention d'une Tradition*. Paris: Seuil.

Bergeaud-Blackler, Florence. 2017b. "Le marché halal mondial. Entretien avec Florence Bergeaud-Blackler, par François Gauthier." *Revue du MAUSS semestrielle* 49: 48–61. doi:N\A.

Berger, Peter L. 1990. *The Sacred Canopy. Elements of a Sociological Theory of Religion*. New York: Anchor Books.

Beyer, Peter. 2006. *Religion in Global Society*. London: Routledge.

Beyer, Peter. 2013. "Questioning the Secular/Religious Divide in a Post-Westphalian World." *International Sociology* 28 (6): 663–679.

Boltanski, Luc, and Eve Chiappelo. 1999. *Le nouvel esprit du capitalisme*. Paris: Galliimard.

Burchardt, Marian, Monika Wohlrab-Sahr, and Matthias Middell, eds. 2015. *Multiple Secularities Beyond the West. Religion and Modernity in the Global Age*. Leyden: De Gruyter.

Caillé, Alain. 2000. *Anthropologie du don. Le tiers paradigme*. Paris: Desclée de Brouwer.

Caillé, Alain. 2005. *Dé-Penser l'Économique. Contre le Fatalisme*. Paris: La Découverte/MAUSS.

Campbell, Colin. 1987. *The Romantic Ethic and the Spirit of Consumerism*. London: Blackwell.

Carrette, Jeremy, and Richard King. 2005. *Selling Spirituality: The Silent Takeover of Religion*. London: Routledge.

Casanova, José. 1994. *Public Religion in the Modern World*. Chicago: Chicago University Press.

Costa, Sergio, J. Mauricio Domingues, Wolfgang Knöbl, and Josué P. da Silva, eds. 2006. *The Plurality of Modernity: Decentring Sociology*. München: Rainer Hampp Verlag.

Douglas, Mary, and Baron Isherwood. 1978. *The World of Goods. Towards an Anthropology of Consumption*. New York: Basic Books.

Duchastel, Jules. 2004. "Du gouvernement à la gouvernance : crise ou ajustement de la regulation." In *La régulation néolibérale. Crise ou ajustement?*, edited by Raphaël Canet and Jules Duchastel, 17–47. Montreal: Athéna.

Dumont, Louis. 1977. *From Mandeville to Marx. The Genesis and Triumph of Economic Ideology*. Chicago: Chicago University Press.

Einstein, Mara. 2008. *Brands of Faith. Marketing Religion in a Commercial Age*. New York: Routledge.

Einstein, Mara. 2011. "The Evolution of Religious Branding." *Social Compass* 58 (3): 331–338.

Eisenstadt, Schmuel N. 1999. *Fundamentalism, Sectarianism, and Revolution. The Jacobin Dimension of Modernity*. Cambridge: Cambridge University Press.

Eisenstadt, Schmuel N. 2000. "Multiple Modernities." *Daedalus* 129: 1–29.

Fischer, Johan. 2008. *Proper Islamic Consumption: Shopping, Among the Malays in Modern Malaysia*. Copenhagen: Nias Press.

Gauchet, Marcel. 1985. *Le Désenchantement du Monde. Une Histoire Politique de la Religion*. Paris: Gallimard.

Gaulejac, Vincent de. 2005. *La société malade de la gestion. Idéologie gestionnaire, pouvoir managérial et harcèlement social*. Paris: Seuil.

Gauthier, François. 2009. "La religion de la " société de marché." *Revue du MAUSS permanente*. Accessed April 24, 2009. http://www.journaldumauss.net/spip.php?article494.

Gauthier, François. 2012. "Primat de l'authenticité et besoin de reconnaissance. La société de consommation et la nouvelle régulation du religieux." *SR* 41 (1): 93–111. doi:10.1177/0008429811429912.

Gauthier, François. 2014a. "Les ressorts symboliques du consumérisme. Au-delà de la marchandise, le symbole et le don." *Revue du MAUSS semestrielle* 44: 137–157.

Gauthier, François. 2014b. "Intimate Circles and Mass Meetings. The Social forms of Event-Structured Religion in the Era of Globalized Markets and Hyper-mediatization." *Social Compass* 61 (2): 261–271. doi:10.1177/0037768614524326.

Gauthier, François. 2015. "Consumerism, Media and Religious Change." In *Religion, Media and Social Change*, edited by Kenneth Granholm, Marcus Moberg, and Sofia Sjö, 71–87. London: Routledge.

Gauthier, François. 2017. *Robert H. Nelson, Economics as Religion, Review of Robert Nelson, Economics as Religion*. University Park, PA: Penn State Press 2014. p. 409. In *Revue du MAUSS semestrielle*, Accessed March 5, 2017. http://www.journaldumauss.net/./?Robert-H-Nelson-Economics-as.

Gauthier, François. 2018. "From Nation-State to Market. The Transformations of Religion in the Global Era, as Illustrated by Islam." *Religion* 48 (3): 382–417. doi:10.1080/0048721X.2018.1482615.

Gauthier, François. Forthcoming. "Extension du domaine du halal." *L'Homme*.

Gauthier, François, and Diletta Guidi. 2016. "Voile, halal et burkini. Le tournant expressif identitaire du religieux dans le régime du marché." In *Réguler le religieux dans les sociétés libérales*, edited by Amélie Barras, François Dermange, and Sarah Nicolet, 145–168. Geneva: Labor et Fides.

Gauthier, François, and Tuomas Martikainen, eds. 2013. *Religion in Consumer Society. Brands, Consumers and Markets*. Farnham: Ashgate.

Gauthier, François, Tuomas Martikainen, and Linda Woodhead. 2013a. "Introduction: Religion in Market Society." In *Religion in the Neoliberal Age. Political Economy and Modes of Governance*, edited by Tuomas Martikainen and François Gauthier, 1–20. Farnham: Ashgate.

Gauthier, François, Tuomas Martikainen, and Linda Woodhead. 2013b. "Introduction: Consumerism as the Ethos of Consumer Society." In *Religion in Consumer Society. Brands, Consumers and Markets*, edited by François Gauthier and Tuomas Martikainen, 1–24. Farnham: Ashgate.

Gauthier, François, Tuomas Martikainen, and Linda Woodhead. 2013c. "Acknowledging a Global Shift: A Primer for Thinking about Religion in Consumer Societies." *Implicit Religion* 16 (3): 261–276.

Gauthier, François, and Deirdre Meintel, eds. Forthcoming. "Questions of Authenticity. Special Issue." *Archives des Sciences Sociales des Religions*.

Gauthier, François, and Magali Uhl. 2012. "The Vatican On-line and Amr Khaled's Islamic TV-Preaching: Some Impacts of Internet on Religion in a Globalized World." *Australian Journal of Communication* 39 (1): 53–70.

Göle, Nilufer. 2003. *Musulmanes et Modernes. Voile et Civilisation en Turquie*. Paris: La Découverte.

Goossaert, Vincent, and David Palmer. 2011. *The Religious Question in Modern China*. Chicago: Chicago University Press.

Graeber, David. 2011. *Debt. The First 5'000 Years*. New York: Melville House Publishing.

Gray, Breda. 2013. "Catholic Church Civil Society Activism and the Neoliberal Government Project of Migrant Integration in Ireland." In *Religion in the Neoliberal Age. Political Economy and Modes of Governance*, edited by Tuomas Martikainen and François Gauthier, 69–90. Farnham: Ashgate.

Hackworth, Jason. 2013. "Faith, Welfare and the Formation of the Modern American Right." In *Religion in the Neoliberal Age. Political Economy and Modes of Governance*, edited by Tuomas Martikainen and François Gauthier, 91–106. Farnham: Ashgate.

Haenni, Patrick. 2005. *L'islam de Marché. L'Autre Révolution Conservatrice*. Paris: Seuil.

Haenni, Patrick, and Tjitske Holtrop. 2002. "Mondaines Spiritualités … 'Amr Khâlid, 'Shaykh' Branché de la Jeunesse Dorée du Caire." *Politique Africaine* 87: 45–68. doi:10.3917/polaf.087.0045

Hariyadi, Saja. 2010. Islamic Popular Culture and the New Identity of Indonesian Muslim Youths. Paper presented at the "18th Biennial Conference of the Asian Studies Association of Australia." Adelaide, Australia. 5–8th July, p. 13. Accessed January 20, 2017. http://www.academia.edu/5321255/Islamic_Popular_Culture_and_the_New_Identity_of_Indonesian_Muslim_Youths.

Harvey, David. 2005. *A Brief History of Neoliberalism*. Oxford: Oxford University Press.

Heilbrunn, Benoît. 2014. "Le monde des biens ou la naissance de l'anthropologie de la consumma-tion." *Revue du MAUSS semestrielle* 44: 108–124. doi:N/A.

Heschell, Susannah. 2016. "The Philological Uncanny: Jewish Constructions of Islam as a Deviant Genre of European Orientalism." Paper presented at the '2nd International Conference on Islamophobia: From Orientalism to Islamophobia?' Université de Fribourg, Switzerland, October 20–21.

Howell, Julia D. 2005. "Muslims, the New Age and Marginal Religions in Indonesia: Changing Meanings of Religious Pluralism." *Social Compass* 52 (4): 473–493. doi:10.1177/0037768614524322.

Howell, Julia D. 2007. "Modernity and Islamic Spirituality in Indonesia's New Sufi Networks." In *Sufism and the 'Modern' in Islam*, edited by Martin van Bruinessen and Julia D. Howell, 217–244. London: IB Tauris.

Howell, Julia D. 2008. "Modulations of Active Piety: Professors and Televangelists as Promoters of Indonesian 'Sufisme'." In *Expressing Islam: Religious Life and Politics in Indonesia*, edited by Fealy Greg and White Sally, 35–57. Singapore: Institute of Southeast Asian Studies.

Howell, Julia D. 2009. "The New Spiritualities, East and West: Colonial Legacies and the Global Spiritual Marketplace in Southeast Asia." In *Islam in Southeast Asia. Critical Concepts in Islamic Studies*, edited by Josepth Chinyong Liow and Nadirsyah Hosen, 277–289. London: Routledge.

Howell, Julia D. 2012. "Introduction: Sufism and Neo-Sufism in Indonesia Today." *Review of Indonesian and Malaysian Affairs* 46 (2): 1–16.

Howell, Julia D. 2013. "Pluralist Currents and Counter-Currents in the Indonesian Mass Media: The Case of Anand Krishna." In *Religious Pluralism, State and Society in Asia*, edited by Formichi Chiara, 216–235. London: Routledge.

Howell, Julia D. 2014a. "'Calling' and 'Training': Role Innovation and Religious De-Differentiation in Commercialised Indonesian Islam." *Journal of Contemporary Religion* 28 (3): 401–419. doi:10.1080/13537903.2013.831650

Howell, Julia D. 2014b. "Christendom, the Ummah and Community in the Age of Televangelism." *Social Compass* 61 (2): 234–249. doi:10.1177/0037768614524322

Howell, Julia D. 2015. "Revitalised Sufism and the new Piety Movements in Islamic Southeast Asia." In *Routledge Handbook of Religions in Asia*, edited by Bryan S. Turner and Oscar Salemink, 276–292. Routledge: Abingdon.

Iqtidar, Humeira. 2011a. *Secularizing Islamists? Jama'at-e-Islami and Jama'at-ud-Da'wa in Urban Pakistan*. Chicago: Chicago University Press.

Iqtidar, Humeira. 2011b. "Secularism beyond the State: 'State' and 'Market' in Islamist Imagination." *Middle Asian Studies* 45 (3): 535–564. doi:10.1017/S0026749X11000217

Jafari, Aliakbar, and Özlem Sandicki, eds. 2016. *Islam, Marketing and Consumption. Critical Perspectives on the Intersections*. London: Routledge.

Jorion, Paul. 2008. *La crise: Des subprimes au séisme financier planétaire*. Paris: Fayard.

Keen, Steve. 2011. *Debunking Economics. The Naked Emperor Dethroned?* London: Zed Books.

Kepel, Gilles. 2012. *Quatre-vingt-treize*. Paris: Gallimard.

Khosrokavar, Farhad. 2014. *Radicalisation*. Paris: Éditions de la Maison des sciences de l'homme.

Khosrokavar, Farhad. 2017. "Le nouveau djihadisme européen." *Revue du MAUSS semestrielle* 49: 31–47.

Kiliçbay, Baris, and Mutlu Binark. 2002. "Consumer Culture, Islam and the Politics of Lifestyle. Fashion for Veiling in Contemporary Turkey." *European Journal of Communication* 17 (4): 495–511. doi:10.1177/02673231020170040601

Koch, Anne. 2014. *Religions-ökonomie. Eine Einfuhrung*. Stuttgart: Kohlhammer.

Koenig, Matthias. 2005. "Politics and Religion in European Nation-States. Institutional Varieties and Contemporary Transformations." In *Religion and Politics. Cultural Perspectives*, edited by Berhard Giesen and Daniel Suber, 291–315. Leyden: Brill.

Krämer, Gudrun. 2013. "Modern but not Secular: Religion, Identity and the Ordre Public in the Arab Middle East." *International Sociology* 28 (6): 629–644. doi:10.1177/0268580913503875

Kuhn, Thomas S. 1962. *The Structure of Scientific Revolutions*. Chicago: University of Chicago Press.

Laval, Christian. 2007. *L'Homme Économique. Essai sur les Racines du Néolibéralisme*. Paris: Gallimard.

Lewis, Reina. 2015. *Muslim Fashion. Contemporary Styles Culture*. Durham: Duke University Press.

Lewis, Reina. 2016. "The Commercial Limits of the *Ummah*? National and Regional Taste Distinctions in the Modest Fashion Market." In *Islam, Marketing and Consumption. Critical Perspectives on the Intersections*, edited by Aliakbar Jafari and Özlem Sandikci, 83–101. Abingdon: Routledge.

Lury, Celia. 2011. *Consumer Culture*. 2nd ed. New Brunswick, NJ: Rutgers University Press.

Madi, Özlem. 2014. "From Islamic Radicalism to Islamic Capitalism: The Promises and Predicaments of Turkish-Islamic Entrepreneurship in a Capitalist System (The Case of IGIAD)." *Middle Eastern Studies* 50 (1): 144–161. doi:10.1080/00263206.2013.864280

Madsen, Richard. 2011. "Secularism, Religious Change, and Social Conflict in Asia." In *Rethinking Secularism*, edited by Craig Calhoun, Mark Juergensmeyer, and Jonathan Antwerpen, 248–269. Oxford: Oxford University Press.

Martikainen, Tuomas. 2013. "Multilevel and Pluricentric Network Governance of Religion." In *Religion in the Neoliberal Age. Political Economy and Modes of Governance*, edited by Tuomas Martikainen and François Gauthier, 129–160. Farnham: Ashgate.

Martikainen, Tuomas, and François Gauthier, eds. 2013. *Religion in the Neoliberal Age. Political Economy and Modes of Governance*. Farnham: Ashgate.

Mauss, Marcel. (1920) 1969. "La nation." In *Oeuvres 3. Cohésion sociale et division de la sociologie*, edited by Marcel Mauss, 573–625. Paris: Minuit.

McGuire, Meredith. 2008. *Lived Religion. Faith and Practice in Everyday Life*. Oxford: Oxford University Press.

Meintel, Deirdre. 2014. "Religious Collectivities in the Era of Individualization." *Social Compass* 61 (2): 196–206. doi:10.1177/0037768614524321.

Moberg, Marcus. 2016. "Exploring the Spread of Marketization Discourse in the Nordic Folk Church Context." In *Making Religion. Theory and Practice in the Discursive Study of Religion*, edited by Frans Wijsen and Kocku von Stuckrad, 239–259. Leiden: Brill.

Moberg, Marcus, and Tuomas Martikainen. 2018. "Religious Change in Market and Consumer Society: The Current State of the Field and New Ways Forward." *Religion* 48 (3): 418–435. doi:10.1080/0048721X.2018.1482616.

Nasr, Vali. 2009. *The Rise of Islamic Capitalism*. New York: Free Press.

Nelson, Robert H. (2001) 2014. *Economics as Religion. From Samuelson to Chicago and Beyond*. University Park, PA: University of Pennsylvania Press.

Njoto-Feillard, Gwenaël. 2012. *L'islam et la réinvention du capitalisme en Indonésie*. Paris: Karhala.

Orléan, André. 2011. *L'Empire de la valeur*. Paris: Seuil.

Polanyi, Karl. (1944) 1957. *The Great Transformation. The Political and Economic Origins of Our Time*. Boston: Beacon Press.

Polanyi, Karl. 2001. *The Great Transformation. The Political and Economic Origins of Our Time*. Boston: Beacon Press.

Portier, Philippe. 2008. "Les mutations de la gouvernementalité sous la Ve République." In *Droit, Politique et Littérature*, edited by Pascal Morvan, 255–268. Bruxelles: Bruylant.

Portier, Philippe. 2010. "Conclusion. 'Modernités plurielles'? Une approche longitudinale des modèles nationaux de régulation du croire dans les démocraties occidentales." In *Pluralisme religieux et citoyenneté*, edited by Micheline Milot, Philippe Portier, and Jean-Paul Willaime, 241–271. Rennes: Presses Universitaires de Rennes.

Rodier, Christine. 2014. *La Question Halal. Sociologie d'une Consommation Controversée*. Paris: Presses universitaires de France.

Roof, Wade Clark. 1999. *Spiritual Marketplace. Baby Boomers and the Remaking of American Religion*. Princeton: Princeton University Press.

Rosanvallon, Pierre. 1989. *Le Libéralisme Économique. Histoire de l'Idée de Marché*. Paris: Seuil.

Rosanvallon, Pierre. 1990. *L'État en France de 1789 à nos Jours*. Paris: Seuil.

Roy, Olivier. 2004. *L'Islam Mondialisé*. Paris: Seuil.

Roy, Olivier. 2016. *Le djihad et la mort*. Paris: Seuil.

Rudnyckyj, Daromir. 2009. "Market Islam in Indonesia." *Journal of the Royal Anthropological Institute (N.S.)* 15: S183–S201.

Rudnyckyj, Daromir. 2010. *Spiritual Economies. Islam, Globalization, and the Afterlife of Development*. Ithaca: Cornell University Press.

Saad-Filho, Afredo, and Deborah Johnston. 2005. *Neoliberalism: A Critical Reader*. London: Pluto Press.

Sandıkcı, Özlem. 2018. "Religion and the Marketplace: Constructing the 'New' Muslim Consumer." *Religion* 48 (3): 453–473. doi:10.1080/0048721X.2018.1482612.

Sassatelli, Roberta. 2007. *Consumer Culture. History, Theory and Politics*. London: SAGE.

Sassen, Saskia. 1996. *Losing Control? Sovereignty in an Age of Globalization*. New York: Columbia University Press.

Schlamelcher, Jens. 2013. "The Decline of the Parishes and the Rise of City Churches: The German Evangelical Church in the Age of Neoliberalism." In *Religion in the Neoliberal Age. Political Economy and Modes of Governance*, edited by Tuomas Martikainen and François Gauthier, 53–67. Farnham: Ashgate.

Schulze, Fritz. 2008. "Die Konzeption von Pluralismus im neo-modernistischen Islam Indonesiens." In *Religion und Identität – Muslime und Nicht-Muslime in Südostasien*, edited by Fritz Schulze and Holger Warnk, 65–76. Wiesbaden: Harrassowitz.

Schulze, Fritz. 2012. "Der islamische Staat als Demokratie - Indonesien." In *Staatsdenken in der islamischen Welt: Zwischen Fundamentalismus und politischer Emanzipation*, edited by Lino Klevesath and Holger Zapf, 225–252. Baden-Baden: Nomos.

Seele, Peter, and Lucas Zapf. 2017. "Economics." In *Oxford Handbook for the Study of Religion*, edited by Michael Stausberg and Steven Engler, 112–123. Oxford: Oxford University Press.

Shirazi, Faegheh. 2016. *Brand Islam. The Marketing and Commodification of Piety*. Austin: University of Texas Press.

Slater, Don. 1997. *Consumer Culture and Modernity*. London: Polity.

Slater, Don, and Fran Tonkiss. 2001. *Market Society*. London: Polity.

Spickard, James V. 2007. "'Religion' in Global Culture: New Directions in an Increasingly Self-Conscious World." In *Religion, Globalization, and Culture*, edited by Peter Beyer and Lori Beaman, 233–252. Leyden: Brill.

Steiner, Philippe. 2005. *L'École Durkheimienne et l'Économie*. Geneva: Droz.

Stolz, Jörg, and Jean-Claude Usunier. 2014. "Religion as Brands. New Perspectives on the Marketization of Religion and Spirituality." In *Religion as Brands. New Perspectives on the Marketization of Religion and Spirituality*, edited by Jean-Claude Usunier and Jörg Stolz, 3–25. Farnham: Ashgate.

Tarlo, Emma. 2010. *Visibly Muslim. Fashion, Politics, Faith*. Oxford: Berg.

Taylor, Charles. 1991. *The Malaise of Modernity*. Toronto: Anansi.

Taylor, Charles. 2002. *Varieties of Religion Today. William James Revisited*. Cambridge, MA: Harvard University Press.

Tönnies, Ferdinand. 1970. *Gemeinschaft and GEsellschaft. Grundbegriffe der reinen Soziologie*. Darmstadt: Wissenschaftliche Buchgesellschaft.

Touag, Hanifa. 2014. "Healing by Islam: Adoption of a Prophetic Rite—roqya—by Salafists in France and Belgium." In *Religion as Brands. New Perspectives on the Marketization of Religion and Spirituality*, edited by Jean-Claude Usunier and Jörg Stolz, 109–121. Farnham: Ashgate.

Usunier, Jean-Claude. 2014. "9591″: The Global Commoditization of Religions through GATS, WTO, and Marketing Practices." In *Religion as Brands. New Perspectives on the Marketization of Religion and Spirituality*, edited by Jean-Claude Usunier and Jörg Stolz, 27–43. Farnham: Ashgate.

Veer, Peter van der. 2001. *Imperial Encounters. Religion and Modernity in India and Britain*. Princeton: Princeton University Press.

Watson, Bill. (C. W.) 2005. "A Popular Indonesian Preacher: The Significance of Aa Gymnastiar." *Journal of the Royal Anthropological Institute* 11: 773–792. doi:10.1111/j.1467-9655.2005.00261.x

Weber, Max. 1971. *Économie et Société*. 2 vols. Paris: Plon.

Weintraub, Jeff. 1997. "The Theory and Politics of the Public / Private Distinction." In *Public and Private in Thought and Practice. Perspectives on a Grand Dichotomy*, edited by Weintraub Jeff and Kumar Krishan, 1–42. Chicago: University of Chicago Press.

Wimmer, Andreas, and Nina Glick Schiller. 2002. "Methodological Nationalism and Beyond: Nation-State Building, Migration and the Social Sciences." *Global Networks* 2 (4): 301–334. doi:N/A.

Religious change in market and consumer society: the current state of the field and new ways forward

Marcus Moberg and Tuomas Martikainen

ABSTRACT

This article provides a critical appraisal of how the concept of the 'market' has been understood and employed in previous scholarship on religion and religious change in market society. The discussion focuses on the respective virtues and weaknesses of approaches that view 'religious markets' in terms of a de facto empirical entity on the one hand, and approaches that instead employ the 'market' as a metaphor for how the religious field is structured and organized on the other hand. The article then proceeds to outline and argue for the adoption of a broader marketization-focused perspective that views ongoing changes in the religious field against the backdrop of wider neoliberal socio-economic restructurings of the global political economy and social institutional fields.

Introduction: from markets to market and consumer society

The study of religion and religious change in market and consumer society has evolved into a diverse and constantly expanding field of study (e.g., Gauthier and Martikainen 2013; Martikainen and Gauthier 2013). Primarily situated within the sociological study of religion, this scholarship has mainly been focused on the various ways in which the social and cultural conditions of neoliberal market society and consumer culture has worked to affect changes and transformations in the religious field. Notwithstanding some significant areas of overlap, the main focus of this scholarship thus differs substantially from much previous work in the broader 'economics of religion' (e.g., McCleary 2011) tradition that has primarily utilized market and economic theory for the purposes of providing explanations for the assumed 'fundamental' logics and dynamics of collective and/or individual religious behavior. The key terminology and conceptual apparatus commonly employed in the scholarship on religious change in market and consumer society is, however, still in need of further refinement (cf. Stolz and Usunier 2018, 2). This applies in particular to the multitude of diverging and often unspecified understandings of the very concept of the 'market' that continues to characterize much of the work in the area. Maintaining that a reasonable degree of conceptual clarity constitutes a key prerequisite for the proper consolidation and further development of any field of research, this article provides a critical appraisal of how the concept of the 'market' (along with closely related terms and concepts such as 'product' and 'consumer') has been understood and employed in previous scholarship on religion and religious change in market and consumer society. In light of our critical assessment of the current state of the field, we proceed to outline and argue for the benefits of adopting a broader approach that views ongoing changes in the religious field against the backdrop of wider global socio-economic changes that have followed in the wake of the proliferation and implementation of neoliberal ideology and an accelerating general marketization of ever more social and cultural domains.

Throughout history, the various meanings attached to the concept of the 'market' have undergone a range of notable shifts and transformations. In pre-modern times, the 'market' denoted a more specific mode, physical space, and event for the actual exchange of goods. Since the advent of the modern era, however, the concept of the market gradually took on much broader meanings as a primary organizing principle for economic, and to varying extents, social life on the whole. As Slater and Tonkiss point out, although this understanding of the market has gained increasing prominence through the global spread of neoliberal ideology since the early 1980s, its origins can nevertheless be traced back to the early liberalism and classical economics of thinkers such as Smith, Mill, and Ricardo in the 18th and 19th centuries. Indeed, early modern social thought gave rise to several different understandings of the market, all of which were intimately 'bound up with competing modern projects – both intellectual and political – aiming to explain and govern the social' (Slater and Tonkiss 2001, 2). Early modern social thought thus lay the foundations for the subsequently much further developed notion of a 'market society' and its eventual full actual realization in the post-World War II era.

The first decades of the post-war era were largely governed by the corporatist ideology and 'managed capitalism' of Keynesian political economy. This period also witnessed a gradual transition from an industrialized and standardized mass-production focused 'Fordist' economy towards a more flexible, specialized, and services-oriented 'post-Fordist' economy – a development that also played a central role in propelling the rise of consumerism and the establishment of consumer culture throughout the Western world, and beyond (e.g., Lury 2011, 1–3). By the early 1970s, however, corporatist structures were facing new and mounting challenges, most notably due to the accelerating general financialization of the global economic system and the re-configuring of previous structures of competition and global trade following the rise of new economic powers, particularly in South East Asia (e.g., Slater and Tonkiss 2001, 135). These developments helped spur a new renaissance for liberal and freer market ideologies along with their visions for the proper organization of society. Indeed, as already hinted at, market ideologies are not adequately understood as pertaining merely to the economic sphere proper; typically, they also comprise broader visions about the 'good' society, its organization, the proper role of its citizens, and so on. Following Slater and Tonkiss (2001, 3) it is therefore crucial to note that there are always important distinctions to be made 'between the complex range of transactions that take place in actual market settings and the market ideal'. As they highlight in connection to Carrier's (1997) notion of 'the Market Idea', a set of more particular conceptualizations of the market and its meaning have played 'a central role in organizing the modern West's conceptual and normative universe' through the erection of 'modern social myths', the persuasive power of which have been particularly 'evident in the neoliberal restructuring of advanced capitalist and transitional economies since the 1980s' (Slater and Tonkiss 2001, 9).

The currently globally dominant political economic ideology of neoliberalism is based on a very particular type of 'Market Idea': an unwavering belief in the power, efficiency, and rationality of the free, non-regulated market. In the neoliberal vision, individual freedom and flourishing is best supported and realized when as many social functions and spheres as possible are subsumed under an all-encompassing market logic. In this vision, the primary task of the state therefore becomes to actively facilitate the creation of markets where these do not already exist. In order for this to be achieved, state-controlled social functions and sectors are to be deregulated, subjected to conditions of enterprising and competition, and, wherever possible, be either outsourced or privatized. In theory, neoliberal ideology thus promotes a minimalist 'night watchman' model of the state according to which the state is supposed to maintain control only over those social functions and institutions that are required for the maintenance and facilitation of *laissez-faire* capitalism. Following the enthusiastic adoption of neoliberal ideology by the Thatcher and Reagan administrations in the United Kingdom and the United States as well as transnational financial institutions such as the World Bank and the International Monetary Fund (IMF) in the early 1980s, neoliberal ideology and policy has since spread and become widely adopted in a variety of state and other institutional settings on a worldwide scale (e.g., Harvey 2007, 1–2).

Beginning in the early 1980s and continuing to this day, the study of religion in market and consumer society has thus largely emerged and evolved during a time period that has been particularly characterized by an accelerating spread and increasing perpetuation and normalization of neoliberal ideology, along with its language and terminology, across ever more social and cultural domains, including academia. This time period has also witnessed a range of highly significant actual global socio-economic structural changes following the emergence of the so-called 'new economy' in the late 1990s (i.e., marking a general transition from a manufacturing-based to a service-based economy) followed by the so-called 'knowledge economy' and the exponential growth of the financial sector in the first years of 21st century. As expressed by (the expressly critical and arguably more contentious) Sennett, these developments 'left an enduring trace on non-business institutions, particularly institutions of the welfare state' as 'the values of the new economy have become a reference point for how government thinks' (Sennett 2006, 7–8).

As such, these developments have greatly affected the basic structure and organization of contemporary societies across the globe. As Gauthier points out, mirroring similar developments in the sphere of industry, business, and commerce proper, the post-war, post-industrial period has witnessed a gradual transformation of previous hierarchical, bureaucratic, and centralized national-statist models of social organization and regulation towards a market model that foregrounds horizontal and decentralized network-types of organization (Gauthier 2015, 72). These thoughts are echoed by Sennett (2006, 45–46) who makes the observation that 'Big government and civic institutions have tried to dismantle their institutional past following this model.' The above developments have thus come to propel a set of 'complex and multifarious set of processes through which economics has dislodged politics as a structuring and embedding force' (Gauthier 2015, 71–72). As part of these developments, consumerism has also emerged as the principal, both social and cultural, ethos of contemporary societies (e.g., Slater 1997, 24–25), along with the consumer as 'master category of collective and individual identity'

(Trentmann 2006, 2). No longer considered a 'passive dupe' the consumer has 'reappeared as a "co-actor" or "citizen consumer" in a variety of settings in state, civil society and market' (Trentmann 2006, 3). As is discussed in more detail in the Introduction to this special issue, the consequences of these developments for contemporary religion, religious life, and organization have been manifold. To name just a few of the most notable ones, the rise of market and consumer society has coincided with a set of major transformations in the global religious field, including a sharp decline in institutional forms of religion, an increasing elevation of the subjective over the collective, and a growing emphasis on the experiential over reason across different types of religions and religious traditions (Gauthier, Woodhead, and Martikainen 2013, 4).

In light of these observations, we take as our point of departure that the 'market', in the sense described above, already clearly has come to constitute a defining feature of many current religious developments. The changes that are occurring within the religious field today both challenge previous religious understandings, forms of organization, preferred ways of action, etc., as well as create novel forms of social thought, identities, and activities that cannot be path-dependently understood as mere modifications of the 'historical', but rather in the context of market and consumer society. Even challenges to the broader contemporary social and economic order can be expected to be deeply related to the operational logic of the 'market'.

The study of religion and religious change in market and consumer society: a brief general overview

Scholarly inquiry into the relationship between religion and markets, capitalism, and consumer culture come in many different shapes and forms. As religions and religious communities have historically often formed integral components of the very fabric of societies and cultures on the whole, they have obviously also always been deeply implicated in various types of economic affairs and practices. In this sense, as Passas (1994, 225) observes, 'It appears that there is no clear-cut distinction separating religious organizations from commercial ones and the two are best conceived as the ideal-type ends of a continuum' (cf. Martikainen 2012, 178). Although historical and contemporary relationships between religion and wider socio-economical arrangements long remained a somewhat under-researched area within the study of religion in general, a substantial and constantly growing scholarly literature is now coalescing around the subject. Based on a general, although by no means comprehensive, review of this literature it is possible to identify at least five main strands or categories of studies. We want to point out, though, that what follows is a general categorization of work that primarily focuses on the various ways in which the social conditions of market and consumer society works to affect changes and transformations in the religious field. We have therefore deliberately excluded the (by now quite extensive) body of work in the Rational Choice approach (e.g., Stark and Finke 2000) which would, in the broadest of categorizations, certainly qualify as a category in its own right.

A first main category would include studies that focus on various types of historical relationships between religion, markets, and economic arrangements, usually those of Christian churches in Europe and the United States (e.g., Moore 2001; Noll 2001; Giggie and Winston 2002).

A second and fast-growing diverse main category includes studies primarily focused on various types of cases of the general 'commodification' of religion (or certain forms of religion) in contemporary (mostly Western) consumer-capitalist societies (e.g., Passas 1994; Martikainen 2001; Kale 2004; Twitchell 2004, 2007; Clark 2007; Mottner 2008; Luhr 2009; Kitiarsa 2010). This category also contains studies with a more specific focus on religion, marketing, branding, and advertising (e.g., McDaniel 1986; Frankl 1987: Percy 2000; Keenan and Yeni 2003; Martikainen 2006; Einstein 2008; Sengers 2010; Muskett 2015), including studies of the 'textual poaching' (Johnstone 2009) of religion/spirituality *in* advertising (e.g., Rice and Al-Mossawi 2002; Marmor-Lavie, Stout, and Lee 2009). Interestingly, as many of these latter contributions stem from fields such as consumer, advertising, and marketing research, they are frequently aimed at offering suggestions for advertisers and marketers interested in catering to various 'religious' or 'spiritual' markets and niche publics. For example, as Marmor-Lavie, Stout, and Lee (2009, 2) state: 'As a core value in society, spirituality becomes a central concern for marketers and consumer researchers attempting to determine how the "needs" ... and characteristics of spiritually inclined customers should be addressed through advertising messages.' These studied thus highlight an increasing, albeit mostly instrumental, interest in religiously or spiritually 'inclined' customers or consumers on the part of advertisers and marketers themselves.

Explorations of the impact of consumer culture on contemporary Christian life and practice from a theological perspective could be viewed in terms of a separate third category of studies. While the majority of these explorations principally have been aimed at presenting normative theological critiques of the (usually detrimentally seen) impact of consumer culture on religious life and tradition (e.g., Budde and Brimlow 2002; Stevenson 2007), others have instead been more interested in offering critical reflections on consumer culture deemed relevant for modern theology (e.g., Beaudoin 2004; Miller 2008).

A fourth and significant main category is composed of studies dealing with various instances of the commodification of various forms of alternative spirituality in general (e.g., Heelas 2008) or in relation to more specific phenomena such as so-called Complementary and Alternative Medicine (e.g., Partridge 2005, 40–41) or alternative spiritual practices in the workplace (e.g., Williams 2003; Nandram and Borden 2010). Many studies in this category have been strongly critical in tone, often portraying alternative spirituality or 'New Age' related products as heavily commodified consumer-capitalist 'colonizations' or 'co-optations' of various 'Eastern' beliefs (e.g., Lau 2000; York 2001, 367; Carrette and King 2005). Indeed, as Heelas (2008, 6) reflects: 'Of all the controversies surrounding contemporary inner-life spiritualties, by far and away the most significant within the academy and beyond revolves around the criticism that the great majority (or virtually all) of provisions and activities serve as consumer products.' However, as Taira (2008, 231) has rightly observed, as studies focusing on the commodification of alternative spirituality seldom theorize capitalism as such, the arguments they present rarely amount to much more than ideological critiques in which 'the problem of capitalism itself remains in the background'.

A final fifth main category consists of studies focusing on the impact of market imperatives and consumer culture ideologies and practices in various Islamic contexts and the global proliferation of halal and 'sharia-friendly' products and provisions worldwide (e.g., Sandikci 2011; Shirazi 2016). The establishment of scholarly journals such as the

Journal of Islamic Marketing and the publication of reference works such as the *Handbook of Islamic Marketing* (Sandikci and Rice 2011) attests to the growing scholarly interest in this area.

This general review of the field of religions, markets, and consumer culture research clearly reveals notable differences in how central notions, terms, and concepts such as the 'market', 'economy', 'product', and 'consumer' are approached and understood (cf. Gauthier, Martikainen, and Woodhead 2013, 5–6; the Introduction to this special issue). Among these, the perhaps most significant respects in which studies in the area differ from one another is in their various approaches and understandings of the meaning of the 'market'. Partly, this discrepancy results from differences in disciplinary anchoring and the empirical case study focused nature of much of this work. But it is likely also partly a consequence of the ways in which previous studies have differed considerably when it comes to their respective theorizations of the 'market', or lack thereof, and it is to this issue that we now turn.

'Religious markets' and 'markets for religion' – factual or metaphorical?

As noted, the scholarship on religion and religious change in market and consumer society generally remains marked by a high degree of ambiguity when it comes to how the concept of the 'market' is approached and understood. Looking at the field as a whole, it is possible to identify a general dividing line between studies that argue for or assume the existence of a 'religious market' or 'market for religion' as an *actual empirical entity* on the one hand, and studies that instead primarily employ the concept of the market as a heuristic device, analogy, or *metaphor* for how the religious field appears to be organized on the other hand. In the following, we move to discuss the respective virtues and weaknesses of these two approaches in relation to a few concrete examples.

The market as an organizing principle of the social: the 'religious market'/ 'market of religion' as a de facto empirical entity

In line with the general understanding of the market initially introduced through early modern social thought, many studies of religion in market and consumer society have been based on an understanding of the market as a general, and indeed principal, organizing principle for social life on the whole. Especially following Warner's (1993) widely debated assertion that a 'new paradigm' was emerging in the United States in the early 1990s, spearheaded by early studies that viewed changes and developments in the religious field within a framework for an 'open market system' for religion (e.g., Bilhartz 1986; Hatch 1989), this approach has become firmly established in the sociological study of religion in the United States.

Since new paradigm research tends to be based on an understanding of the market as an organizing principle of the social as a whole, it follows that the religious field often is viewed as forming a de facto market that comprises actual religious 'products', '-goods', '-services', and other provisions and is essentially governed by market logics and imperatives such as competition, supply, and demand. Consequently, changes and developments in the field of religion are viewed as being best studied using theoretical perspectives derived from economic and market theory (e.g., McCleary 2011, 7–8). Inspired in particular by theoretical perspectives on so-called 'Supply-Side' economics, the new paradigm approach seeks to disprove the secularization thesis through demonstrating that free 'market competition' in the religious field (as is argued to largely be the case in the United States) is conducive of religious vitality, whereas the enduring presence of national religious 'monopolies' (as is argued to largely be the case throughout much of Europe) instead works to constrain religious innovation and vitality, thus serving to further religious stagnation and decline (for a critical discussion of the Supply-Side approach see for example Bruce 2014).

Studies in this tradition nevertheless tend to vary when it comes to the extent to which they *expressly* employ and theorize the concept of the market as an actual empirical entity. While some studies are indeed expressly based on the premise that the religious field constitutes and operates as a de facto market in the same sense as, for example, the market for leisure activities, others are much more ambiguous in their understandings and articulations and instead tend to balance between viewing the market as a de facto empirical entity on the one hand and as an analogy for the ways in which the religious field operates and develops on the other hand.

An earlier and widely read example of a study that assumes the existence of a 'religious market' as an actual empirical entity would be Roof's *Spiritual Marketplace* (1999), which is based on the general premise that 'An open, competitive religious economy makes possible an expanded spiritual marketplace which, like any marketplace, must be understood in terms both of "demand" and "supply"' (Roof 1999, 78). Aiming to understand notable transformations in the religious landscape of the United States since the beginning of the post-war era Roof contended that

> Religion in any age exists in a dynamic and interactive relationship with its cultural environment; and, in our time [the mid- and latter part of 1990s] we witness an expansion and elaboration of spiritual themes that amounts to a major restructuring of religious market dynamics. (Roof 1999, 78)

Spiritual Marketplace thus provides an early example of a study that takes inspiration from economic and market theory for the purposes of constructing a general analytic and interpretive framework for making sense of broader developments in the religious field of the United States in the post-war era. But since the study does not contain any theorization of the concept of the market, nor any type of deeper substantial theoretical discussion of other closely related concepts such as 'economy', 'product', or 'consumer', its engagement with economics and market theory really amounts to little more than a selective and rather shallow employment of its language and terminology.

An example of a frequently referenced study that balances between a de facto market- and market analogy approach can be found in Einstein's *Brands of Faith* (2008), which provides a detailed analysis of how market imperatives and consumer culture has affected the general character of the religious landscape in the United States and served to propel a rapid increase in marketing and branding practices among religious communities themselves. Expressly situating her study in the new paradigm and Supply-Side tradition, Einstein (2008, 19) maintains that 'Viewing religion as a product, rather than as a social mandate' provides many clues as to why religion has remained vital in the United States while it has declined throughout much of Europe. She ultimately comes to conclude that 'faith brands' exist for three principal reasons: first, in contemporary society, religion is compelled to 'compete against other discretionary activities'. Second, religious communities and groups increasingly find themselves in a situation in which they also have to 'compete against the constant barrage of images and information in today's culture'. And, third, generational and cultural shifts have brought about a situation in which younger generations are less attracted to religion than previous generations (Einstein 2008, 193). Similar to Roof's *Spiritual Marketplace*, the focus of *Brands of Faith* can likewise be characterized as broad as it aims to highlight how the proliferation of marketing and banding practices has brought about notable changes in the religious field and served to facilitate the emergence of new religious 'products' and 'faith brands'. But with the exception of the concept of 'brands' (and to some extent the concept of 'marketing') *Brands of Faith* does not contain any theorization of the concept of the market or other concepts central to the study such as 'product' and 'consumer'. While there is certainly merit to many of the observations presented in the book, it still remains unclear whether the 'market' in Einstein's account is to be understood as a de facto empirical entity or more as an analogy for the ways in which the religious field appears to be organized in the context of the United States. Although the study does indeed primarily focus on religious 'products' and 'brands', both of these concepts nevertheless ultimately derive their analytic and heuristic value (or lack thereof) from the particular ways in which they are situated and positioned within particular theorizations and understandings of the market.

In sum, Roof's and Einstein's accounts thus both provide examples of studies that employ terms and concepts such as 'religious market', 'markets for religion', religious 'market share', '-monopoly', '-competition', '-product', '-suppliers', '-customers', '-consumers' '-demand', etc. as central parts of their analytic apparatus without adequately specifying the precise meaning of most of these terms and concepts.

When it comes to how the term 'market' is employed, studies that argue for, or just simply assume, the actual existence of 'religious markets' as actual de facto empirical entities need to be able to convincingly demonstrate the factuality of at least two closely related things. First, they need to show that (at least some, if not all) religious communities actually, at least to some extent, *view themselves* as being situated within a 'market' and that they therefore have become more open to adopt marketing practices; become more prepared to understand their services or provisions in terms of 'products' that can be marketed and branded; and become more prone to view their members and potential members in terms of 'customers' or 'religious consumers'. Indeed, the mere existence of publications such as *Church Executive* and the more recent rise of the 'church consultant' (Einstein 2008, 60–62) provide good grounds for arguing that this is at least the case with respect to certain types of Christian churches in the United States. Nearly two decades ago already, Roof (1999, 78) also touched upon this question, although more vaguely, when he wrote that:

> in recent times especially, religious messages and practices have come to be frequently restylized, made to fit a targeted social clientele, often on the basis of market analysis, and carefully monitored to determine if programmatic emphases should be adjusted to meet particular needs.

Second, studies arguing for the actual existence of 'religious markets' as actual de facto empirical entities also need to be able to move beyond merely highlighting 'similarities between religion and marketing' (Einstein 2008, 74) and demonstrate that (at least some, if not all) religious communities *purposefully* create religious 'products' and 'services' and that they *purposefully* engage in practices that would generally be considered marketing from the perspective of the fields of economics and marketing themselves (as opposed to, for example, merely spreading information about their activities). While it is certainly possible to approach religious communities through theoretical lenses that view all forms of social life and action in economic terms, it is still well worth considering the expressed intentions and motivations of religious actors themselves (many of who might outright reject any association with 'market' associated practices). This is not least because religion has, at least traditionally, been understood to promote moral altruism and to be characterized by an 'other-regarding orientation' rather than the type of 'self-interest and egoistic motivation' that is characteristic of consumerist values (Usunier 2014, 42). Further, as Usunier points out, as 'religion often implies non-choice (i.e., converting is considered evil and becoming an infidel), it violates the fundamental belief of commoditization in free choice and rationality' (Usunier 2014, 42; cf. Bruce 2014, 197).

These observations highlight the need for future studies to take more seriously the 'symbolic rivalry' that exists between economic and market meanings and (traditionally considered non-economic) religious meanings (Usunier 2014, 43). Future studies in the area could therefore usefully align more closely with cultural approaches to markets that emphasize 'market enculturation' and the ways in which 'the economy seems increasingly made up of informational and symbolic work on goods that are themselves increasingly "non-material"' (Slater and Tonkiss 2001, 176). The two books discussed above both constitute examples of previous studies that have indeed gone some way in bringing our attention to these types of questions. While their agenda-setting efforts and contributions should be commended, their shortcomings with regard to conceptual clarity nevertheless point to a need for future work in the area to be more specific in its usage of key terms and concepts such as 'market', 'product', and 'consumer'. This should by no means be taken to suggest that future work should be grounded in any one type, or any particular set of, theorizations of the concept of the market. Future work should be especially wary of adopting rigid and essentialist theoretical models that purport to explain what a market or product 'really is'. This is not least since such approaches will likely only serve to theoretically predetermine that which should be explained. We are therefore simply highlighting the need for future work to provide clearer articulations and explanations of their respective approaches and understandings of the concept of the market, as well as the precise meaning of associated concepts such as product, consumer, etc. (whatever they may be).

The 'market' as a metaphor for the religious field

Apart from new paradigm research, market *metaphors* have more recently also started to be employed in a broader sense to capture the changing and diversifying character of the religious landscape in the West as a whole. The decidedly more diverse and entrepreneurial character of the religious landscape of the United States when compared to that of Europe is routinely noted in work of this type. For example, as Davie has more recently (2015, 135) observed, whereas the religious landscape of the United States 'is made up of tens of thousands of free-standing congregations that aggregate themselves into denominations, none of which has, or has had, a legally privileged position in the federal state', the 'increasing range of choices' currently available on the religious field in Europe is largely emerging 'over the top of a historically dominant church with (more or less) a comprehensive network of parishes across the country' (Davie 2015, 135). While the market-approach constitutes but one aspect of the much broader debate on European/American exceptionalism (e.g., Berger, Davie, and Fokas 2008), as Davie notes, it has nevertheless become 'increasingly present in analyses of religion in Europe' (Davie 2015, 135).

Similar to the arguments of many new paradigm theorists, in Davie's recent account, the different trajectories along which the religious field has developed in the United States and Europe may thus be explained by notable differences in the 'religious economies' or 'religious markets' of these respective two regions. When applied to the specific case of Britain, Davie (2015, 135) contends that the contemporary British religious field can be thought of as being organized along the lines of 'two religious economies that run side by side'. While one can be considered a 'market of active churchgoers who choose their preferred form of religious activity and join the religious organization which expresses this most effectively', the other largely 'retains the features of a public utility and exists, for the most part, for those who prefer not to choose, but who are nonetheless grateful for a form of religion which they can access as the need arises' (Davie 2015, 135). As Davie goes on to argue, while the British religious market remains divided along these two main lines, there has more recently occurred a 'degree of rebalancing as the concept of choice begins to outweigh a sense of obligation in the religious lives of most British people' (Davie 2015, 135).

In this account, however, the type of 'choice' intended is significantly different from that of many 'economics of religion' (and especially Rational Choice) approaches in that it is juxtaposed with a 'sense of obligation' rather than being viewed as a central component of human behavior as such. Nor does the 'market' automatically emerge as a general organizing principle in the field of religion in this account. Rather, in what might perhaps be seen as an illustration of the general permeation of market-related language and terminology across social fields as a whole, including the work of academics, the concepts of the 'economy' and 'market' are instead primarily used in a metaphorical sense as heuristic devices.

This, however, does not detract from the fact that the precise meaning of these concepts, as well as their relation to one another, remains highly elusive and ambiguous in this account. Given this lack of explanation and specification, we might certainly ask what their heuristic value actually amounts to. For example, to assume that the religious field (or some part of it) is organized on the basis of market logic just because some religious communities can be shown to engage in market and consumer society associated practices such as marketing or branding, or because people increasingly can be shown to exercise individual choice in matters of religious engagement and affiliation, amounts to a 'conceptual leap' that is possible only if one also assumes that the categories of the 'economy' and the 'market' are one and the same (Usunier 2014, 33). It seems clear, therefore, that future studies that wish to employ the concepts of the 'market' or 'economy' in a metaphorical sense would need to more clearly spell out their reasons for doing so and provide more detailed explanations of what added analytic value the employment of such concepts actually brings.

Religious marketing, products, and consumers

As we hope to have been able to illustrate through our discussion so far, to speak of various types of *relationships* or *associations* (e.g., in terms of 'similarities', 'shared elements', etc.) between religion, markets, and consumer culture practices is one thing. But to speak of, and thereby at least implicitly assume, the *factuality* of 'religious markets' or 'markets for religion' (e.g., in terms of 'religious market dynamics', 'religious supply and demand', etc.) in and of themselves is an entirely different thing. We believe it is important to recognize, at the very least, that the two should not be confused, and certainly not be equated nor conflated, with one another. The key point to note is that each and every particular theorization of the 'market' will always serve to determine how other related key terms and concepts such as 'religious marketing', 'religious products', and 'religious consumers' are approached and understood. In a way that reflects the sometimes highly ambiguous ways in which the concept of the 'market' has been employed and understood, these latter terms and notions have also typically been employed in unspecified and sometimes highly ambiguous ways in previous scholarship on religious change in market society.

These issues have recently been explored by Usunier (2014), who offers a critical assessment of the degrees to which it makes sense to talk about similarities between religion and religious communities vis-à-vis religious products, services, and the marketing of religion. He starts out by highlighting that the mere establishment of product category 9591 on 'religious services' in the Central Product Classification (CPC) scheme of the General Agreement on Trade Services (GATS) of the World Trade Organisation (WTO) in 1995 might certainly be taken as a good a sign as any of the actual contemporary 'commoditization' of religious products and services. Usunier views commoditization as being 'based on an object-centered view of economic exchange whereby subjects exchange a wide range of tangible and intangible commodities (latissimo sensu, i.e., products, services, rights, institutions, and social behaviors), on markets' (Usunier 2014, 29–30). As such,

> Commoditization occurs when a previously non-market object (e.g., religion, blood, adoption, etc.) enters the market. The commodity itself is at the very center of the market process in which price, volume, and competition between suppliers to capture consumers are viewed as the central elements of market dynamics guided by unlimited free and rational choice. (Usunier 2014, 30)

The crux is that, in a traditional marketing perspective, commodities need to be as standardized as possible so as to be able to, as far as possible, remove any obstacles that would make it more difficult for potential consumers to make comparisons between similar products and to be able to exercise free choice (Usunier 2014, 30). Similar to our discussion of the ideational dimensions of market society, consumerism, and the category of the consumer above, Usunier (2014, 33) highlights commoditization as involving a complex 'communication task' characterized by 'the systematic use of vocabulary and discourse to acquaint people with a newly commoditized (or a to-be-commoditized-in-the-near-future) object'. However, the mere fact that religious services have gained legal inscription through inclusion in the WTO-GATS framework does not automatically produce religious markets but 'needs the additional legitimizing power of practices and words' as provided by politics, media, business, and academia (Usunier 2014, 33). Similarly, Muniesa, Millo, and Callon (2007, 3) underline how any conception of the market, older or more recent, is always and 'precisely the outcome of a [social] process of "economization"', the aim of which is to render 'things more "economic" or, more precisely, at enacting particular versions of what it is to be economic' (cf. Usunier 2014, 33). In other words, before any notion of a religious economy or market can take on currency as a specific economy or market in and of itself, and before products and services can take on meaning as specifically *religious* products or services, they first need to be rendered and 'made' so through active and conscious efforts of construction by 'religious entrepreneurs', academics, or both. Put another way, like any type of market, product, or service, 'religious markets', 'products', or 'services' do not simply come into being by and of themselves; they too have to be actively constructed as such.

Concerning religious communities and marketing, Usunier (2014, 40) examines how well the classic four 'Ps' of marketing (i.e., Product, Price, Place, and Promotion) apply to the supposed similarities between marketing practices and religion. He arrives at the conclusion that, while '2 Ps (place and promotion) readily apply to the marketing of religions (as quasi-firms) and religious products and services', this is less the case with both product and price policy. As Usunier points out, while

> there is certainly utility in several religious services ... marketing makes a difference between religion and religious services. While the latter may, to a certain extent be commoditized, this does not imply that religion itself should be considered a commodity. (Usunier 2014, 31)

To the above, we could also add several additional and closely related questions having to do with the supposed subjects of religious marketing and the supposed 'consumers' of religious products and/or services. For example, we might want to ask who exactly should be viewed as a consumer of a 'religious product' and under what circumstances. As Trentmann (2006, 6) reminds us, when considering such questions, 'the starting point is not how people have certain bits of information about goods, prices, etc. but when information is processed and systematized in such a way that it creates a sense of being a consumer'. So, similar to the ways in which economies, markets, and products have to be constructed *as* such, so, too, do 'consumers of religion' have to be 'made' so through different types of legitimizing language. This is not least since people who some academics would consider 'consumers of religion' are unlikely to consider themselves in that way. Problematic issues of the kind discussed above become even more accentuated in Rational Choice and Supply-Side approaches to religion, as is discussed in more detail in the Introduction to this special issue.

Religion in an era of marketization

In light of the critical discussion above, we now turn to the concept of marketization, which occupies an increasingly central position in various types of scholarship on political economy, politics, consumer-capitalism, and consumer culture. The concept has, however, been utilized in a range of different, and sometimes contrasting, both evocative and heuristic capacities (e.g., as a general umbrella term for coupling together the values promoted by neoliberal ideology). Although the concept of marketization retains many connections to other related concepts such as 'commodification', 'commoditization', or 'commercialization', it is most usefully taken to denote the more general and extended historical process whereby a market logic has come to provide a means of *thinking about* social institutions and individuals more generally, such that notions of competition, enterprise, utility and choice can be applied to various aspects of people's working lives, access to public services and even private pursuits. (Slater and Tonkiss 2001, 1, emphasis added)

In this approach, marketization is thus conceived of as a primarily *ideational* process that chiefly involves the 'the permeation of market exchange as a social principle' (Slater and Tonkiss 2001, 25) across different social and cultural domains and sub-systems, which are gradually but increasingly visibly 'subjected to a deliberate policy of economizing' (Schimank and Volkmann 2012, 37).

Although not always conceptualized in terms of marketization, some very similar observations on the ideational dimensions of these developments have also been presented by commentators such as Thrift (2005) who has highlighted the ways in which capitalism and its associated values and imperatives has become a 'theoretical enterprise in which various essentially virtual notions (network, the knowledge economy, the new economy, community of practice) are able to take on flesh as, increasingly, the world is made in these notions' likeness' (Thrift 2005, 6; cf. Mautner 2010, 4). The concept of marketization is thus most usefully taken to denote the historical, both ideational and actual, process whereby economistic thinking gradually comes to permeate society and culture on the whole, including in particular spheres traditionally considered non-economic such as the educational, healthcare, and religious spheres (e.g., Moberg 2017). In this understanding, marketization is consequently primarily intended to capture the process whereby economistic thinking impinges on social and cultural spheres from the 'outside' in ways that have tangible both ideational and actual empirical effects and consequences (cf. Moberg 2017). As Gauthier points out, viewing ongoing developments in the present-day religious field within such a broader interpretative framework does not amount to an argument for the reduction of social realities to economic determinants but should rather be understood as an attempt at drawing our attention to 'the *noneconomic* [i.e., the ideological, ideational, and discursive] dimensions and effects of market economics and their correlates in globalizing societies' (Gauthier 2015, 72, emphasis added).

In this understanding, marketization is therefore not adequately understood as a phenomenon that affects social spheres or sub-systems in isolation from one another. So, rather than talking about the marketization *of* religion specifically as if 'religion' constituted a sphere that could be approached and analyzed separately from other social spheres, it is much more fruitful to view ongoing changes and transformations in the religious field within a broader context of an increasingly marketized social and cultural environment on the whole. Such an approach would strive to avoid reducing changes in the religious field 'to historical, path-dependent explanations as in the modernisation paradigm' in favor of a more sustained focus on the 'new opportunity structure in which religions now operate' (Martikainen 2012, 180). This, then, provides an alternative framework for approaching the changing modes of religious organization and agency in market and consumer society. For the fact remains that even though most religious communities and organizations do not identify as businesses or firms, they have clearly become ever more willing to discursively present their activities and services through a market-idiom in terms of 'products' and to engage with their members or adherents in terms of 'customers' and/or 'consumers' (c.f. Moberg 2017). Part of the explanation for this undoubtedly relates to how market and economics-related terminology has developed into a central trait of the language of modern social institutions and organizations more generally, especially following the proliferation of new public management in the 1990s. The fact that traditional institutional Christian churches with long-standing historical and structural relationships to nation states and core social establishments have been particularly prone to adopt such languages lends further support to this view (Moberg 2017).

This (emergent) approach to the character and fate of religion in market and consumer society is thus one that strives to highlight the role of 'market Ideas' (Carrier 1997) – in the sense of market economics-inspired ideologies and discourses – as prime vectors of contemporary social and cultural change on the whole, including religious change. In its broader emphasis on religion *in* market and consumer society, this approach to the concept of marketization thus closely relates to, but also extends significantly beyond, the understanding presented in the Introduction to this special issue.

Concluding remarks

This article has provided an overview and critical appraisal of the current state of the scholarship on religion and religious change in market and consumer society. Our discussion aimed to highlight in particular how the field would benefit from a firmer consolidation of its conceptual language, and especially when it comes to how central, both heuristic and analytic, terms and notions such as 'market', 'product', 'service', 'consumer', etc. are approached and understood. In our discussion we made a general distinction between work that approaches 'religious markets'/'markets for religion' in terms of a de facto empirical entity on the one hand, and work that employs the notion of the 'market' as an analogy or metaphor for how the religious field appears to be structured and organized on the other hand. We argued that work with the former approach would need to be more specific in their theorizations of the concept of the 'market' and closely associated concepts such as 'product' and 'consumer'. Work with the latter approach would also need to be more specific about what new insights can actually be gleaned by viewing the religious field through a market analogy or metaphor. Again, if the precise meaning of the concept of the 'market' itself remains elusive in such work, then what does it's heuristic value actually amount to?

Lastly, we outlined and argued for the benefits of adopting a broader marketization-focused perspective that views currently ongoing changes in the religious field against the wider backdrop of neoliberal restructurings of the global political economy. This broader approach does not by and of itself solve the problem of conceptual ambiguity that currently still haunts the field. But it does point to the need for future studies of religion in market and consumer society to align more closely with the perspectives and theories of the fields of economics, marketing, political economy, and economic sociology.

Viewing marketization as an outcome of global processes of neoliberal change, though embedded in numerous local variants, makes it possible to see processes of religious marketization around the world as a direct result of politico-economic changes that have taken place since the 1980s. This has been a challenge for Western-centric sociology of religion, which is why we have seen an increasing amount of new studies springing from anthropology, marketing, consumer research, etc. focusing on non-Western societies and religions in unexpected places, and often with limited engagement with the main body of Western sociology of religion, as referred to earlier in this article. Ultimately, in order to test the suggestions of this article and special issue, we need to turn our gaze beyond Western contexts in order to be able to appreciate the full magnitude of the religious changes that are now taking place as a consequence of broader socio-economic and cultural developments.

Disclosure statement

No potential conflict of interest was reported by the authors.

References

Beaudoin, Tom. 2004. *Consuming Faith: Integrating Who We Are With What We Buy*. Chicago: Sheed and Ward.

Berger, Peter L., Grace Davie, and Effie Fokas. 2008. *Religious America, Secular Europe? A Theme and Variations*. Aldershot: Ashgate.

Bilhartz, Terry D. 1986. *Urban Religion and the Second Great Awakening: Church and Society in Early National Baltimore*. Cranbury, NJ: Associated University Presses, 1986.

Bruce, Steve. 2014. "Authority and Freedom: Economics and Secularization." In *Religions as Brands: New Perspectives on the Marketization of Religion and Spirituality*, edited by Jörg Stolz and Jean-Claude Usunier, 189–204. Farnham: Ashgate.

Budde, Michael, and Robert Brimlow. 2002. *Christianity Incorporated: How Big Business is Buying the Church*. Grand Rapids: Brazos Press, 2002.

Carrette, Jeremy, and Richard King. 2005. *Selling Spirituality: The Silent Takeover of Religion*. London: Routledge.

Carrier, James G. 1997. "Preface." In *Meanings of the Market: The Free Market in Western Culture*, edited by James G. Carrier, vii–xvi. Oxford: Berg.

Clark, Lynn Schofield, ed. 2007. *Religion, Media and the Marketplace*. Toronto: Rutgers University Press.

Davie, Grace. 2015. *Religion in Britain: A Persistent Paradox*. Oxford: Wiley-Blackwell.

Einstein, Mara. 2008. *Brands of Faith: Marketing Religion in a Commercial Age*. New York: Routledge.

Frankl, Razelle. 1987. *Televangelism: The Marketing of Popular Religion*. Carbondale: Southern Illinois University Press.

Gauthier, François. 2015. "Religion, Media and the Dynamics of Consumerism in Globalising Societies." In *Religion, Media, and Social Change*, edited by Kennet Granholm, Marcus Moberg, and Sofia Sjö, 71–88. London: Routledge, 2015.

Gauthier, François, and Tuomas Martikainen, eds. 2013. *Religion in Consumer Society: Brands, Consumers and Markets*. Farnham: Ashgate.

Gauthier, François, Tuomas Martikainen, and Linda Woodhead. 2013. "Introduction: Religion in Market Society." In *Religion in the Neoliberal Age: Political Economy and Modes of Governance*, edited by Tuomas Martikainen and François Gauthier, 1–18. Farnham: Ashgate.

Gauthier, François, Linda Woodhead, and Tuomas Martikainen. 2013. "Introduction: Consumerism as the Ethos of Consumer Society." In *Religion in Consumer Society: Brands, Consumers, Markets*, edited by François Gauthier and Tuomas Martikainen, 1–26. Farnham: Ashgate.

Giggie, John Michael, and Diane H. Winston, eds. 2002. *Faith in the Market: Religion and the Rise of Urban Commercial Culture*. Piscataway, NJ: Rutgers University Press.

Harvey, David. 2007. *A Brief History of Neoliberalism*. Oxford: Oxford University Press.

Hatch, Nathan O. 1989. *The Democratization of American Christianity*. New Haven, CT: Yale University Press.

Heelas, Paul. 2008. *Spiritualities of Life: New Age Romanticism and Consumptive Capitalism*. Oxford: Blackwell.

Johnstone, Carlton. 2009. "Marketing God and Hell: Strategies, Tactics and Textual Poaching." In *Exploring Religion and the Sacred in a Media Age*, edited by Christopher Deacy and Elisabeth Arweck, 105–121. Hampshire: Ashgate.

Kale, Sudhir H. 2004. "Spirituality, Religion, and Globalization." *Journal of Macromarketing* 24 (2): 92–107. doi:10.1177/0276146704269296.

Keenan, Kevin L., and Sultana Yeni. 2003. "Ramadan Advertising in Egypt: A Content Analysis with Elaboration on Select Items." *Journal of Media and Religion* 2 (2): 109–117. doi:10.1207/S15328415JMR0202_04.

Kitiarsa, Pattana. 2010. "Towards a Sociology of Religious Commodification." In *The New Blackwell Companion to the Sociology of Religion*, edited by Bryan S. Turner, 563–583. Chichester: Blackwell.

Lau, Kimberly. 2000. *New Age Capitalism: Making Money East of Eden*. Philadelphia: University of Pennsylvania Press.

Luhr, Eileen. 2009. *Witnessing Suburbia: Conservatives and Christian Youth Culture*. Berkeley: University of California Press.

Lury, Celia. 2011. *Consumer Culture*. Oxford: Polity Press.

Marmor-Lavie, Galit, Patricia A. Stout, and Wei-Na Lee. 2009. "Spirituality in Advertising: A New Theoretical Approach." *Journal of Religion and Media* 8 (1): 1–23. doi:10.1080/15348420802670868.

Martikainen, Tuomas. 2001. "Religion and Consumer Culture." *Tidskrift for kirke, religion og samfunn* 14 (2): 111–125.

Martikainen, Tuomas. 2006. "Consuming a Cathedral: Commodification of Religious Places in Late Modernity." *Fieldwork in Religion* 2 (2): 127–145. doi:10.1558/fiel2008v2i2.127.

Martikainen, Tuomas. 2012. "Towards a New Political Economy of Religion: Reflections on Marion Maddox and Nicolas de Bremond d'Ars." *Social Compass* 59 (2): 173–182. doi:10.1177/0037768612440956.

Martikainen, Tuomas, and François Gauthier, eds. 2013. *Religion in the Neoliberal Age: Political Economy and Modes of Governance*. Farnham: Ashgate.

Mautner, Gerlinde. 2010. *Language and the Market Society: Critical Reflections on Discourse and Dominance*. New York: Routledge.

McCleary, Rachel M, ed. 2011. *The Oxford Handbook of the Economics of Religion*. Oxford: Oxford University Press.

McDaniel, Stephen W. 1986. "Church Advertising: Views of the Clergy and General Public." *Journal of Advertising* 15 (1): 24–29. doi:10.1080/00913367.1986.10672985.

Miller, Vincent J. 2008. *Consuming Religion: Christian Faith and Practice in a Consumer Culture*. New York: Continuum.

Moberg, Marcus. 2017. *Church, Market, and Media: A Discursive Approach to Institutional Religious Change*. London: Bloomsbury Academic.

Moore, Laurence R. 2001. *Selling God: American Religion in the Marketplace of Culture*. Bridgewater, NJ: Replica Books.

Mottner, Sandra. 2008. "Marketing and Religion." In *The Routledge Companion to Nonprofit Marketing*, edited by Adrian Sargeant and Walter W. Wymer, 97–113. Abingdon: Routledge.

Muniesa, Fabian, Yuval Millo, and Michel Callon. 2007. "An Introduction to Marker Devices." In *Market Devices*, edited by Michel Callon, Yuval Millon, and Fabian Muniesa, 1–12. Oxford: Blackwell.

Muskett, Judith A. 2015. "Reflections on the Shop Windows of the Church of England: Anglican Cathedrals and Vicarious Religion." *Journal of Contemporary Religion* 30 (2): 273–289. doi:10.1080/13537903.2015.1025557.

Nandram, Sharda S, and Margot Esther Borden, eds. 2010. *Spirituality and Business: Exploring Possibilities for a New Management Paradigm*. Heidelberg: Springer Verlag.

Noll, Mark A., ed. 2001. *God and Mammon: Protestants, Money, and the Market, 1790–1860*. Oxford: Oxford University Press.

Partridge, Christopher. 2005. *The Re-enchantment of the West, Vol. 2: Alternative Spiritualities, Sacralization, Popular Culture and Occulture*. London: Continuum.

Passas, Nikos. 1994. "The Market for Goods and Services: Religion, Commerce, and Deviance." In *Between Sacred and Secular: Research and Theory on Quasi-Religion*. Religion and the Social Order, vol. 4, edited by Arthur L. Greil and Thomas Robbins, 217–240. London: Jai Press.

Percy, Martyn. 2000. "The Church in the Market Place: Advertising and Religion in a Secular Age." *Journal of Contemporary Religion* 15 (1): 97–119. doi:10.1080/135379000112161.

Rice, Gillian, and Mohammed Al-Mossawi. 2002. "The Implications of Islam for Advertising Messages: The Middle Eastern Context." *Journal of Euromarketing* 11 (3): 71–95. doi:10.1300/J037v11n03_05.

Roof, Wade Clarke. 1999. *Spiritual Marketplace: Baby Boomers and the Remaking of American Religion*. New Jersey: Princeton University Press.

Sandikci, Özlem. 2011. Researching Islamic Marketing: Past and Future Perspectives." *Journal of Islamic Marketing* 2 (3): 246–258.

Sandikci, Özlem, and Gillar Rice, eds. 2011. *Handbook of Islamic Marketing*. Northampton, MA: Edward Elgar.

Schimank, Uwe, and Ute Volkmann. 2012. "Economizing and Marketization in a Functionally Differentiated Capitalist Society – a Theoretical Conceptualization." In *The Marketization of Society: Economizing the Non- economic*, edited by Uwe Schimank and Ute Volkmann, 37–63. Research Network 'Welfare Societies' conference papers. University of Bremen. Accessed October 9, 2016. http://welfare-societies.com/uploads/fi le/WelfareSocietiesConferencePaper-No1_Schimank_Volkmann.pdf.

Sengers, Erik. 2010. "Marketing in Dutch Mainline Congregations: What Religious Organizations Offer and How They Do It." *Journal of Contemporary Religion* 25 (1): 21–35. doi:10.1080/13537900903416796.

Sennett, Richard. 2006. *The Culture of the New Capitalism*. New Haven: Yale University Press.

Shirazi, Faegheh. 2016. *Brand Islam: The Marketing and Commodification of Piety*. Austin: University of Texas Press.

Slater, Don. 1997. *Consumer Culture and Modernity*. Cambridge: Polity Press.

Slater, Don, and Fran Tonkiss. 2001. *Market Society: Markets and Modern Social Theory*. Cambridge: Polity Press.

Stark, Rodney, and Richard Finke. 2000. *Acts of Faith: Exploring the Human Side of Religion*. Berkeley: University of California Press.

Stevenson, Tyler Wigg. 2007. *Brand Jesus: Christianity in a Consumerist Age*. New York: Church Publishing.

Stolz, Jörg, and Jean-Claude Usunier. 2018. "Religions as Brands? Religion and Spirituality in Consumer Society." *Journal of Management, Spirituality & Religion*. doi:10.1080/14766086. 2018.1445008.

Taira, Teemu. 2008. "The Problem of Capitalism in the Scholarship on Contemporary Spirituality." In *Postmodern Spirituality*, edited by Tore Ahlbäck, 230–244. Åbo: The Donner Institute for Religious and Cultural History.

Thrift, Nigel. 2005. *Knowing Capitalism*. London: Sage.

Trentmann, Frank. 2006. "Knowing Consumers: Consumers in Economics, Law and Civil Society." In *The Making of the Consumer: Knowledge, Power and Identity in the Modern World*, edited by Frank Trentmann, 1–27. Oxford: Berg.

Twitchell, James B. 2004. *Branded Nation: The Marketing of Megachurch, College Inc., and Museumworld*. New York: Simon & Schuster.

Twitchell, James B. 2007. *Shopping for God. How Christianity Went from in Your Heart to in Your Face*. New York: Simon & Schuster.

Usunier, Jean-Claude. 2014. "'9591': The Global Commoditization of Religions through GATS, WTO, and Marketing Practices." In *Religions as Brands: New Perspectives on the Marketization of Religion and Spirituality*, edited by Jörg Stolz and Jean-Claude Usunier, 27–43. Farnham: Ashgate.

Warner, Stephen R. 1993. "Work in Progress Toward a New Paradigm for the Sociological Study of Religion in the United States." *American Journal of Sociology* 98 (5): 1044–1093. doi:10.1086/230139.

Williams, Oliver F., ed. 2003. *Business, Religion, & Spirituality: A New Synthesis*. Notre Dame, IN: University of Notre Dame Press.

York, Michael. 2001. "New Age Commodification and Appropriation of Spirituality." *Journal of Contemporary Religion* 16 (3): 361–372. doi:0.1080/13537900120077177.

Governing religious identities: law and legibility in neoliberalism

Marian Burchardt

ABSTRACT
This article explores from a Foucauldian perspective how, in the neoliberal age, religious diversity has become a new form of governmentality that is based on practices of classifying and categorizing people according to religious criteria. Contributing to studies on religion and marketization, the article explores how religious diversity is promoted as a category of social order and coexistence and develops two ideas: first, religious diversity is a legal-political form of governmentality geared towards rendering complex populations legible for administrative purposes. Second, religious diversity reflects an economic form of governmentality, in that its legal doctrinal cognates (subjective definitions of religion, sincerity of belief, etc.) call forth liberal notions of consumer choice. While both are premised on the idea that people have identities, there are potential tensions between both forms, as the first tends to favor collectives and the second favors individuals. The article is based on research in Spain and Canada.

Introduction

In this article, I suggest that there is considerable merit in going beyond the currently dominant use of religious diversity as a *descriptive* category that depicts the existence of several different religious traditions in a given territory and that becomes subject to regulatory intervention by state actors such as legislatures, courts and administrative bodies (Beckford 2003). Rather, I argue that we should explore how religious diversity is itself turned into an epistemic and administrative category through which states observe societies, render populations legible and contribute to configuring their cultural identities. Pursuing this idea, I employ Foucault's notion of governmentality, which means the ways that power operates through practices of classification, labeling and naming whereby people are registered through particular social categories. I suggest that 'religious diversity' does exact this, and that the rise of diversity as a new form of governmentality is borne from the characteristics of neoliberal market society.

During the last three decades, sociologists have stressed that, for many religious communities, the increasingly transnationally connected world and its populations are markets in which they compete for adherents (Roof 2001; Finke and Stark 2005; for a classical statement see Berger 1967). Efforts to win adherents thus turn people into possible consumers, their faith into a product and a commodity, and their ways of winning the hearts, minds and souls of people into marketization strategies. More recently, scholars have opened a novel perspective by showing how neoliberalism, financial capitalism, marketization and consumerism provide the model for how to manage religious groups or traditions, how these increasingly consider their organization in management terms, and how today's capitalism is directly concerned with religion (Gauthier and Martikainen 2013; Martikainen and Gauthier 2013; Schenk, Burchardt, and Wohlrab-Sahr 2015). I seek to add to this scholarship by showing how religion is an aspect of labor that needs to be accommodated in the workplaces and management processes of state bureaucracies and private companies under certain circumstances. Accounting for that fact, and in order to create social environments that are attractive for religiously diverse workforces, some Western nation-states such as Canada and Spain have developed policies and regulatory frameworks based on the notion of religious diversity.

Accommodating aspects of employees' personal lives that are seemingly external to production processes such as religion has acquired particular importance in advanced knowledge economies in which labor is not easily replaceable by industrial reserve armies but instead valued as an individualized asset and reconfigured as 'human capital' (Harvey 1989; Castells 1996). Thus, in globalized and increasingly deregulated labor markets in which human mobility and transnational migration provide national economies and companies with the opportunity to draw from global pools of human capital in order to optimize their demands for labor, the term diversity has turned into the new paradigm of living with heterogeneity and economic development (Reuschke, Salzbrunn, and Schönhärl 2013; Matejskova and Antonsich 2015; Vormann 2015).

This suggests that cultural difference is in fact no longer seen as something merely 'external' to economic processes, but as an asset and a potentially productive aspect of human capital.[1] Richard Florida expressed this idea most succinctly when he insisted that 'diversity and creativity work together to power innovation and economic growth' (Florida 2002, 262). Research in critical political economy, geography and urban studies has investigated how diversity has become a major paradigm for policy-makers, managers, heads of public administrations and planners under neoliberalism (Fainstein 2005; Vormann 2015). Scholars have shown how diversity discourses and policies are viewed to improve competitiveness and how their spread has been linked to the introduction of market logics into institutional fields of all kinds. However, these insights have not yet been taken up in research on religious diversity in the sociology of religion.

In order to fill this lacuna, I explore how relationships between states and religion in Western immigrant societies have been reconfigured so as to make them fit with the principles and functional requirements of transnational, deregulated labor markets. Such reconfiguration has chiefly been the work of governments, courts and state bureaucracies. My argument is that the notion of religious diversity is central to this process as an epistemic category, regulatory practice and cultural narrative.

---

[1]Significantly, the recognition of religious diversity also produces costs. In the US, such costs emerge for instance from 'floater holidays', in Europe's more expansive welfare state mainly because of the necessary institutional adaptations.

I explore this process by employing a transatlantic comparison focused on the cases of Canada and Spain, especially the province of Quebec and the region of Catalonia. Within the broader scenario of Western immigrant societies and the nation-states of which they are part, both regions have experienced particularly pronounced debates about religious diversity over the last two decades. Quebec has seen fiercer contestations about the place of religion in the public sphere than any other Canadian province. These contestations include: the so-called accommodation crisis in 2007; the subsequent public discussions and deliberations that took place in the context of the well-known 'Bouchard-Taylor Commission' in 2008; the Liberal Party's attempt to ban full-face veiling (Bill 94) in 2010; the Parti Quebecois' (PQ) project to make secularism part of Quebec's Charter of Rights and Freedoms and to impose the principle of state neutrality on state employees that formed part of its proposed 'Charter of Quebec Values'; and finally the Religious Neutrality Bill passed by the Liberal Party-led government in October 2017, suspended just two months later by a Quebec court following a legal appeal (Burchardt 2016, 2017). Similarly, political and cultural contestations related to migration-driven diversity reached more intense levels in Catalonia than in the rest of Spain. Catalan citizens became engaged in multiple anti-mosque campaigns (Astor 2012). No less than 12 Catalan municipalities have regulated the wearing of the Islamic full-face veil, but citizens have also manifested themselves in favor of the religious rights of migrants (Burchardt, Griera, and García-Romeral 2015). In addition, the Catalan government has passed in 2009 a new 'Law on Centers of Worship' [*ley sobre los centros de culto*] with the aim of providing equitable conditions for the establishment of religious places for all religious groups.

In response to migration-driven changes in the religious make-up of national populations, state bureaucracies in liberal democracies with market economies face two major pressures. On the one hand, they face political and cultural pressures to maintain some degree of normative integration and social cohesion. Frequently, their supposed failure to do so is blamed on decreasing cultural homogeneity and results in mediatized xenophobia, cultural anxieties and popular nationalist sentiment (Lentin and Titley 2011). On the other hand, they face what has broadly been termed 'pressures of globalization' or, in other words, the demand to transform national economies in line with the principles of neoliberalism as infamously summarized in the Washington consensus (liberalization, deregulation, privatization), and to transnationalize their capital and labor markets in order to increase their global competitiveness and avoid economic penalties. As I will demonstrate below, in this context the concepts of secularism and religious diversity have been central in capturing the imagination of politicians and law-makers, steering popular sentiments about conviviality, and shaping notions of legitimate cultural difference in public and private domains (Burchardt and Michalowski 2015). Importantly, while Quebec and Catalonia are part of the same economic sphere of transnational neoliberal capitalism, dominant ideas about the relationships between secularism and religious diversity in these nations turned out to be inversed. While in Quebec debates about secularism acquired a strongly identitarian dynamic and fed into reinvigorated nationalisms which favored a secular public sphere over and against religious diversity, in Catalonia secularism became simply a concept to legitimate the respect for, and political promotion of, religious diversity. The reason for these differences is the configuration of nexus between diversity and nation-building. Whereas Catalans feel that outperforming Spain by enhancing economic competitiveness through diversity policy enhances the popularity of their nation-building project, Quebeckers, on the contrary, mainly feel that the Canadian constitution, with its official multiculturalism, forces them into accepting certain forms of religious diversity that many consider excessive as a condition for economic success in a globalized world. In other words, if multiculturalism-type diversity is promoted by liberals as the price to be paid for economic success, it is felt by republican nationalists as ultimately undermining national cohesion.

Governing diversity: culture, economy, religion

Thus far, in scholarly debates, most sociologists of religion have focused on how state bureaucracies have responded to religious diversity as one (among several) outcomes of migration (Madeley 2003; Koenig 2005). While lauding this scholarship for its insights in the dynamics that drive institutional change in the field of law and policy around religion, my aim here is different. I seek to show how the concept of religious diversity itself has migrated into the political and social imaginaries of state actors as well as in civil society. In so doing, religious diversity has come to serve as a concept for states in order to steer the regulation of religion in new directions. As a consequence, state practices themselves have co-produced religious diversity by relying upon the idea that people have religious identities. In other words, I am interested in how the concept has itself reshaped the ways in which citizens are able to draw on religion as a marker of difference in ordinary practices of classification and categorization (Jenkins 2000).

While in the study of religion, the questioning of how diversity became a concept that has helped to reshape social hierarchies and justify particular policies is relatively novel, this question has already been addressed in urban studies (Fainstein 2005), political theory (Vormann 2015) and the study of nationalism (Yücel 2016). Scholars have noted how diversity became a policy buzzword, how it turned from a means to achieve goals such as justice into an end in itself, and how diversity changed perceptions of policy-makers. In Germany, for instance, Rodatz (2012, 70) observed that municipal authorities began to 'view migrant districts as productive sites of "diversity" featuring resources for the "local economy" and "civil society"'.

At the same time, scholars note the depoliticizing effects diversity discourse has on the field of discrimination, difference and equality. While discrimination laws and policies generally address practices of exclusion, diversity discourse often focuses on the positive effects of cultural differences and sometimes tends to aestheticize them. Lentin and Titley (2008, 9) therefore, see diversity as a 'cost-free form of politics attuned to the need of late capitalist consumer societies'. More generally, Yücel (2016, 1) has criticized that 'most of the authors who have dealt critically with the topic have stressed the plasticity and ubiquity of diversity, considered at times as discourse, at others as practice or policy, and sometimes as both'. In another recent intervention, Matejskova and Antonsich (2015) cogently described the political force of diversity discourse in Foucauldian terms. However, by arguing that the main problem of diversity is merely its tendency to individuate difference, they also misconstrue its deeper political effects. Diversity discourse problematizes the ways that membership in ethnic and religious groups is tied to class position and proposes as a remedy some measure of social mobility for those facing marginalization and exclusion due to group-related discrimination. However, its real political consequence is that it fundamentally accepts and fails to raise questions about the very nature of vertical social hierarchies in capitalist society.

The intricacies of diversity as a concept that draws together recognition and rule, emancipation and enforced alterity had already been noted in debates around multiculturalism, a term which diversity has partially displaced. Similar to diversity, regimes of multiculturalism entwine the emancipation of minority cultures from enforced national cultural homogeneity with the official sanctioning of cultural differences whereby particular, often ethno-religious 'cultural' definitions of people are privileged over other definitions – despite the fact that not everybody might share such cultural definitions. In a well-known critique, Žižek (1997, 44) argued that multiculturalism was the ideal form of ideology of global capitalism. He saw multiculturalism as the

> attitude which, from a kind of empty global position, treats each local culture the way the colonizer treats colonized people – as 'natives' whose mores are to be carefully studied and 'respected' [...] In the same way that global capitalism involves the paradox of colonization without the colonizing Nation-State metropole, multiculturalism involves patronizing Eurocentrist distance and/or respect for local cultures without roots in one's own culture.

In a related critique, Bauman (2011, 46) observed that multiculturalism, as a theory of cultural pluralism that postulates the support of liberal tolerance for identities, is a conservative force:

> Its achievement is the transformation of social inequality, a phenomenon highly unlikely to win general approval, into the guise of 'cultural diversity', that is to say, a phenomenon deserving of universal respect and careful cultivation. Through this linguistic measure, the moral ugliness of poverty turns, as if by the touch of a fairy's wand, into the aesthetic appeal of 'cultural diversity'. The fact that any struggle for recognition is doomed to failure so long as it is not supported by the practice of redistribution gets lost from view along the way.

As states and cities recognize cultural diversity, they increasingly address people on the basis of their membership in groups, organized as categories of identity. They thereby increasingly incite people to view themselves and their own form of being on these same terms. There has been a trenchant critique of the essentialisms that come with these ways of governing people. Other scholars have, in turn, defended multiculturalism against these critiques (Kymlicka 2013). Yet as a regime that handles the effects of transnational mobility, the governmentality of diversity is clearly linked to the operations of multinational capital, as Žižek showed.

Intervening in this debate and taking it to the sphere of religion, I draw on Foucault's notion of governmentality, which denotes the ways in which power operates through practices of classification, labeling and naming, that is, through tying people to particular social categories. Defined by Foucault (1988, 146) as the contact point between technologies of power and technologies of the self, governmentality refers to practices that govern human behavior through particular forms of address, which shape subjectivities and identities. While Foucault's main concern lay with the classification of people in administrative categories as inseparable from the constitution and policing of those categories of people, this also includes modern identity categories such as religion. I suggest that contemporary regimes of religious diversity increasingly work through practices of classification. As a consequence, states understand, recognize and govern citizens through their religious identities, offer services and impose sanctions linked to them. Religious diversity increasingly qualifies citizenship. Following Foucauldian intuitions, Ian Hacking (2006) argued that modern science has little in common with broader everyday life understandings of humans, and that science was, therefore, chiefly about 'making up people'. Similarly, I argue that the religious believers on which regimes of religious diversity are founded do not exist prior to these regimes and that religious diversity is indeed a form of 'making up people(s)'. While remaining agnostic about causal directions, I note here the parallelisms between the rise of neoliberalism, the rise of multiculturalism and subsequently of the diversity paradigm and the way it is premised on the idea that people have identities.

I begin by scrutinizing changes in the legal regulation of religion in Canada and Spain, and argue that legal regulations entail the basic categories that allow state bureaucracies to render populations legible and manageable in market terms. I then discuss the policies and projects of religious diversity that have been grafted onto these legal frameworks by concentrating on developments in Quebec and Catalonia.

Legal governmentality

Canada

Since the 1960s, Canada has been pursuing immigration policies based on a mix of instrumentalist concerns oriented towards the needs of labor markets, bio-political concerns about demographic reproduction, and humanitarian ethics. Similar to the American Hart-Cellar Act of 1965, this has meant a radical shift from previous policies, which explicitly excluded or discriminated against specific national and ethnic groups through quota regulations. Canada is known for being the first country in the world to adopt an official policy of multiculturalism. This policy was first launched in 1971 by liberal Prime Minister Pierre Trudeau, then taken up in Canada's first constitution in 1982, and officially affirmed in the *Multiculturalism Act* in 1988 under the conservative Prime Minister Brian Mulroney. Interestingly, multiculturalism was initially animated by the need to clarify the relationships between Catholic Francophones and the (mostly Protestant) Anglophones in the context of increasing demands for recognition by other groups, namely Ukrainians. The concept of diversity figures prominently in the 1988 act. It states that the Canadian government is committed to 'recognize and promote the understanding that multiculturalism reflects the cultural and racial diversity of Canadian society and acknowledges the freedom of all members of Canadian society to preserve, enhance and share their cultural heritage' and to 'foster the recognition and appreciation of the diverse cultures of Canadian society and promote the reflection and evolving expressions of those cultures'. Diversity is indeed a key term in Canadian discourses on identity and citizenship. Contrary to the case in Western Europe, however, the term has not replaced that of multiculturalism but has evolved in tandem with it (Vertovec and Wessendorf 2010). Importantly, while cultural and racial diversity are staked out as distinct grounds, religion is not mentioned in the Act. Yet, as in most other liberal constitutions in the world, the Canadian constitution bans discriminations based on religion and has improved the status of religion as one of the 'fundamental freedoms' (Joppke and Torpey 2013).[2]

---

[2]One important objection to this notion is that the legal definition of religion limits it to 'conscience' thereby demoting it (see for instance Ogilvie 1996).

Following the adoption of the constitution, a number of court cases and decisions have contributed to the development and eventual hegemony of a highly subjective definition of religion that appeared to have a particularly positive spin on the integration of religion and neoliberal capitalism. Widely known as the 'sincerity of belief' doctrine, the emergence of this subjective concept of religion had, as a precondition, the abandonment of certain privileges of Christianity that some scholars have viewed as a kind of 'shadow establishment' of Christianity in Canada (Beaman 2003; Chagnon and Gauthier 2013). In 1985, in the case R. vs. *Big M Drug Mart,* the Supreme Court ruled that the *Lord's Day Act* that prescribed the closing of shops on Sundays violated section 2 of the Charter, which guarantees fundamental freedoms such as the freedom of belief, speech and religion. If through this ruling the Court officially recognized Canada's increasing religious plurality, in 2004, in the case *Syndicate Northcrest* vs. *Amselem,* it went one step further. The case involved an apartment owner's claim to erect a temporary religious structure on his balcony as a way of celebrating a Jewish festival of *Sukkot.* Against the claims of Syndicate Northcrest, a partial owner of the building, that this constituted a violation of the ownership rules, the court ruled that he did indeed have the right to erect the structure. It also used this opportunity to develop a liberal definition of religious freedom built around the notion that, in order to be protected, religious practices should be based person's sincere conviction and religious beliefs, that the examinations of a person's beliefs must be minimally intrusive, and that the changing of religious beliefs over time did not compromise their sincerity.

Eventually, in 2006, the Supreme Court had to decide whether a Sikh student at a Montreal high school should be allowed to wear his ceremonial dagger (*kirpan*) while in the school. The Court ruled that by banning the *kirpan* from the school on grounds of safety, the school commission had violated the student's right to religious freedom and had failed to take Canadian values of multiculturalism into account.

Taken together, these judgments developed an expansive and individualistic concept of religious freedom, which – combined with the judicial and political emphasis on the value of multiculturalism – protects religion in a very wide sense in both public institutions and private markets. Importantly, instead of recognizing particular religious traditions or protecting particular sets of beliefs, practices and symbols, it protects all of them under the umbrella term 'diversity' to the extent that they are based on sincere convictions and do not conflict with other Constitutional values or the rights of others. 'Sincerity of belief' and 'diversity' are thus the basic categories through which Canadian law renders populations legible in religious terms, for both governmental purposes and the citizens themselves.

Spain

Unlike Canada, Spain has been a country of emigration for much of the 20th century. This trend only reversed around the end of the century when Spain's booming economy, relatively generous citizenship and naturalization laws as well as its increasingly cosmopolitan global image helped to attract millions of immigrants from across the globe. As a consequence, the regulation of migration-driven religious diversity became an important issue but unfolded in a legal context that was entirely different. Following the transition to democracy, the Spanish Constitution of 1978 recognized the freedom of religion and declared the Spanish state to be non-confessional and neutral towards religion, but it also encouraged the state to entertain cooperative relationships with religious communities. While the Constitution thus recognized religious pluralism and may be seen as endorsing a model of 'open secularism', the Concordat between the Vatican and Spain signed under Franco's rule in 1953 helped to maintain entrenched privileges of Catholicism, especially in the field of education (Guia 2015). In addition, Catholic privilege is maintained through Catholicisms's legal framing as national heritage (Astor, Burchardt, and Griera 2017).

In the midst of Franco's declining system of National Catholicism, a new Law on Religious Liberty had already been passed in 1967 that allowed non-Catholic associations to be founded. This law was again amended in 1980 so as to specifically stipulate cooperative relationships between the state and religious communities that had achieved 'deep rootedness' in Spanish society. The state's Advisory Commission on Religious Freedom is the public entity to grant this status according to the fulfillment of a number of criteria (sufficient number of members and places of worship, cultural and social activities, historical roots in the country). Following the Jews' and Protestants' request to be recognized in these terms, in 1984 the Spanish state declared that these communities had achieved this status, and in 1989 the *Muslim Association of Spain* petitioned it as well. These acts of recognition were, in turn, the basis for the signing of official agreements between the Spanish state and the religious communities that granted them a number of institutional privileges. As Astor argues:

> the generous set of rights and privileges established by the 1992 agreement between the state and the CIE [Islamic Commission of Spain] thus reflected the celebratory climate surrounding religious diversity characteristic of the period. Elites from across the political spectrum saw religious diversity, which was still relatively minimal in Spain at the time, as a tool that they could leverage to demonstrate their support for a modern and plural society. (Astor 2014, 1723)

The developments in Spain strikingly contrast with Canada. First, the historical timeline suggests that political activism around the legal regulation of religion was not primarily a response to immigration and transnationalizing labor markets, but was instead animated by the impulse to transform Spain into a modern, democratic and cosmopolitan society. Part of this impulse was to improve Spain's international image, which, together with the country's improved economic situation, in turn attracted millions of migrants from Africa, South Asia and Latin America who would then be able to enjoy a hugely improved situation with regard to practicing their religion upon arrival, compared to earlier historical periods. A similar mechanism drove the establishment of architecturally sophisticated 'cathedral mosques' in large Spanish cities during the 1990s. As Astor showed, municipal activism around these mosques was animated by urban governments' desire for 'enhancing the global and cosmopolitan image of their cities through promoting multicultural architecture and strengthening relations with foreign governments and investors' (2014, 1723). Spanish cities began to use religious diversity to market themselves to global audiences of investors, politicians, workers and tourists as a part of entrepreneurial strategies of urban regeneration.

Second, unlike Canadian law that recognizes religion as an individual right in the *abstract* (while adding a more collective spin through multiculturalism policies), Spanish law recognizes a *concrete* and specific set of religions and the state engages in concrete relationships with them. Tying institutional privileges to this type of classification provides incentives not only for citizens but also for religious organizations to fashion themselves in such terms. Among others, this was apparent in schisms in the Islamic field around questions of representation through umbrella bodies and in the eagerness of Jehova's Witnesses and Buddhists to be recognized as deeply rooted. The Mormons achieved this status in 2003, Jehova's Witnesses in 2006, Buddhists in 2007 and the Orthodox Churches in 2010.

Third, while in Canada the basic categories employed to render populations legible in religious terms are 'sincerity of belief' and diversity, in Spain the legal meaning of religious diversity is qualified through the concept of 'deep rootedness'. Importantly, the criteria used to assess deep rootedness have varied and included numerical size and territorial presence as well as historical significance. Interestingly, the concept of deep rootedness does not appear to favor flexible political and bureaucratic responses to migration-driven demographic shifts, as it puts the burden of proof on the shoulders of religious communities. In everyday bureaucratic practice, however, Spanish bureaucracies use wider catalogues of religious traditions with whom they collaborate. For instance, many cities maintain relationships with Sikhs and Hindus, although these groups do not enjoy the status of deep rootedness. This points to the fact that religious diversity is not only shaped by legal regulations but equally by policy programs and projects. As such programs and projects are often carried out at subnational levels, in the following section I zoom in on Quebec and Catalonia and describe the major differences between both cases.

Promoting and contesting religious diversity: policies, projects and neoliberal governmentality

By and large, the legal governmentality of religion applies to both national and provincial levels in a similar way. While Quebec has a fair degree of sovereignty in matters of migration and Catalonia has, over the last two decades, invested much political effort to acquire greater autonomy over religious issues, both regions are bound to overarching constitutional frameworks. In order to understand what kinds of political and bureaucratic practices both regions have utilized to develop their own forms of governmentality, and to contrast the ways these procedures are linked to their nationalist ambitions, I begin with two ethnographic observations.

In September 2013, the government of Quebec publicized its plans for a 'Charter of Quebec Values', formerly called the 'Charter of Secularism'. A central component of the Charter was to ban the wearing of ostentatious religious signs for all employees in the state sector. Shortly thereafter, a big Toronto hospital belonging to Lakeridge Health initiated an advertising campaign in the Montreal press calling for hospital staff whose jobs may be threatened by the Charter to move to Toronto and to come and work in an atmosphere of respect for diversity.[3] Under the slogan 'We don't care what's on your head. We care what's in it', they construed the Charter as a welcome opportunity to diversify their workforce. The idea of competition between Montreal and Toronto is nothing new and economic questions have always played a role in polemics over

---

[3]See http://globalnews.ca/news/835892/ontario-hospital-uses-draft-quebec-charter-to-recruit-nurses-and-doctors/. Accessed 30 June 2016.

Quebec nationalism and independence. The corporate sector and banks have always been major opponents of Quebec's independence and, more generally, private business and entrepreneurial middle classes are widely viewed as the carriers of anti-independence sentiments. As a result of these dynamics but also because of the historically greater representation of Anglophones in private business and commerce, anti-independence, pro-Canadian attitudes, pro-religious diversity and pro-neoliberal and business attitudes have been amalgamated to form a consistent whole in the eyes of many Quebeckers. Suddenly, however, the specters of capital flight turned into specters of labor flight and became clearly linked to religion.

Similarly, Catalonia witnessed diverse municipal attempts to ban Islamic full-face veiling between 2010 and 2014 (Burchardt, Griera, and García-Romeral 2015; Burchardt and Griera 2018). A group of city governments also brought the issue into the Catalan parliament obliging the legislature to discuss it, hoping that the members of parliament would pass a regional regulation against face veiling. However, in interviews, some of the conservative party activists that pushed the initiative told me that the ban was unlikely to be passed because of economic considerations. According to them, economic relationships with Saudi Arabia and the Emirates were too important to be put at risk because of a small number of niqab-wearing women. Moreover, people from the Emirates are also considered an important tourist clientele. Such discussions take place in a context in which Catalonia is increasingly engaging in building and fortifying its own international relations as this allows the Catalan government to behave like a state. At the same time, unlike Quebec, Catalonia has, at least since the late 19th century, been more economically developed than the rest of Spain and has tied its independence project to its self-image as a potent economic performer.

Though ultimately unsuccessful, the PQ plans for a Charter of Secularism in Quebec illustrate historically grown preferences amongst many Quebeckers for a more secular public sphere and their understanding of religious diversity as something to be contained or at least privatized (see also Joppke and Torpey 2013). As a part of a series of attempts to increase Quebec's secularity, the Charter debates reflected Quebec's particular history of secularization, its experience with modernity and the ways in which Quebec nationalism has taken a decidedly secularist turn since the 1990s. For many Quebeckers, the public recognition and governmentality of religious diversity runs up against notions of Republican citizenship and their desire for national unity.

These dynamics are clearly visible in the controversies around 'reasonable accommodation'. Reasonable accommodation involves the legal obligation of employers and organizations to accommodate people who are disadvantaged by providing exceptions to general rules if these general rules lead to unjust treatment (Beaman 2012). While most claims to reasonable accommodation are discussed and solved bilaterally between claimants and employers, critical or controversial cases are also assessed and adjudicated through a special advisory service on reasonable accommodations that the Commission of Human Rights and Youth has established. Interestingly, Quebec is the only Canadian province to have such a service. Yet despite the existence of such means of civil counseling and arbitration, reasonable accommodation became hotly contested in Quebec since the middle of the 2000s through the massive mediatization of a series of controversial cases. In one instance, non-Jewish construction workers at a Jewish hospital were asked to have their non-kosher lunch sandwiches outside the hospital premises; in another one, the leadership of a Jewish high school with mostly Hassidic Jewish boys asked the owner of a gym to blind their windows so that the students would not be exposed to the gym-wear clad bodies of female gym users during school breaks. A third instance involved a group of 260 Muslims in a traditional maple-sugar cabin in the Montérégie region. After dinner, the group asked the owner for a private space in which to pray. The owner offered them the dance hall, which was being used by another family, and interrupted the music for ten minutes. These instances, and certainly their mediatization, led to the perception among sections of Quebec's populace that they 'over-accommodated' minority claims, either because of lacking national self-esteem, or else because Canadian law forced them to do so.

The report following the hearings of the Bouchard-Taylor commission that discussed these cases with citizens explicitly promoted a mechanism they called 'concerted adjustment' over and against the 'legal route' of reasonable accommodation. Qualifying the latter as 'top-down' and leading to an antagonistic situation of winners and losers, they sought to promote a dialogical approach that was 'contextual, deliberative and reflexive' (Bouchard and Taylor 2008, 52).

While reasonable accommodation is indeed a legal obligation, the description as 'top-down' contradicts the perception of the members of the advisory service in the Human Rights Commission that I interviewed. As mentioned before, most cases are effectively managed between the concerned parties and, in their view, even the involvement of the Commission does not lead to a strong judicialization of the claims and the procedure. On the one hand, one can interpret these recommendations as an effort to enhance citizen involvement and bottom-up democracy in the regulation of religious diversity. On the other hand, they can also be seen as an effort to prevent state authorities from getting overly entangled in debates over religious diversity and to keep religious issues private.

While also claiming that in Quebec religion was (supposed to be) a private affair, the 2013 campaign for a Charter of Secularism sent an entirely different message. Part of the campaign included a number of visual depictions meant to explain to people which kinds of religious symbols were not ostentatious, and hence allowed, and which were to be banned for state employees, as wearing them on the job supposedly undermined the principle of state neutrality. One of the depictions showed drawings of persons wearing a large Christian cross, a Sikh turban, a Jewish kippah, as well two Muslim women, one with a hijab and the other with a niqab (see Figure 1). While, as mentioned before, Canadian law does not recognize religion by granting privileges to particular religious traditions, this depiction clearly identifies particular traditions and effectively classifies people as members of these communities (and not others), and creates distinctive subclasses according to the kind of self-identifying symbols people may display. Paradoxically, secularist campaigns to ban certain religious symbols in Quebec may, therefore, have the same effect for the governmentality of religious diversity as the explicit recognition of specific religious traditions in Spain's framework of 'deep rootedness'. They incite people to consider themselves in terms of the religious categories and symbols offered to them and to link these symbols to religion as a part of their 'identity'.

While Quebec has thus developed its own form of the governmentality of religious diversity, albeit in primarily negative terms since the 1990s, Catalonia has become a veritable champion of religious diversity. Despite several changes in government, Catalan state authorities developed a pioneering approach towards a proactive engagement with religious diversity that has been hailed as exemplary in the Spanish and also wider European

Figure 1. Promotional poster for the Charter of Quebec Values.

context (Griera 2016). In 2000, the regional government formed the Secretariat for Religious Affairs. Initially, a conservative nationalist regional government created this agency in order to develop direct relationships between Catalonia and the Vatican, among other things. Soon after, however, the agency was charged with promoting religious diversity and monitoring issues related to religion both at the regional level and in concert with municipal authorities. Moreover, the agency has the task to develop the autonomous regulatory capacities of the regional government in religious affairs and the 'Catalanization' of religious leaders. On the surface, 'Catalanization' refers to language acquisition and the use of Catalan in religious interactions but in practice it also means the fostering of the sense of belonging to the Catalan nation among the leaders and of their commitment to the project of independence.

This government agency, despite recent budget cuts due to Spain's ongoing economic crisis, is by now thoroughly established and unique in the Spanish context. Though it is comprised by only a few employees, it exerts influence throughout the province by offering regular educational activities for civil servants working on issues of civil participation, migration and integration in Catalan municipalities. With the aim to put the standing of religious minorities on par with that of the Catholic Church, one of the first steps on the diversity agenda was signing agreements with religious minorities in 2005 that officially recognized their presence and positive contribution to Catalan society and made them eligible for limited funding to promote religious activities, and regulated the accommodation of minority practices in the fields of pastoral care and places of worship in hospitals, prisons, schools and cemeteries. By signing these contracts, Catalan authorities clearly reproduced Spanish practices of governmentality, based as they are on discreet religious categories.

However, the incorporation of religious newcomers has not been without problems. During the 2000s, Catalonia has experienced a wave of protests against mosque constructions (Astor 2012) and, since 2010, municipalities have launched efforts to ban the Islamic full-face veil. Against this backdrop, it is particularly striking that urban and municipal officials working in departments that handle issues related to religion generally hold positive attitudes towards incorporating migrants' and other newcomers' religions and make strong efforts to organize local religious life in smooth ways. As a part of my ethnographic fieldwork in Catalonia, between 2013 and 2015 I visited 20 Catalan cities and interviewed members of urban administrations working for departments of civil participation, immigration and integration, among others. Generally, urban bureaucrats, many of which were trained in the social sciences and social work, described religious coexistence in their cities in relatively positive terms and marshaled numerous examples in order to showcase the unproblematic ways in which new religious communities were being integrated into the textures of urban institutions. However, they were less convinced that locals and newcomers were also able to integrate socially in everyday life. Importantly, they oftentimes criticized local native populations for spreading rumors about migrants and being ill-informed about migrants' cultures, religion and ways of life. They clearly felt that they had a pedagogical mandate to educate people towards more positive attitudes towards religious diversity.

This also resonates with the central place religious diversity occupied in recent governmental activities. In 2014, the Catalan government's *Advisory Council on Religious Diversity* published a report entitled 'Religious Diversity in Open Societies: Criteria for Decision-Making'. The Catalan vice-president opened the report with the following words:

> Catalonia will always be a country of welcome, integration and cohesion. For this reason, we understand religious diversity as an opportunity to augment the cultural wealth of our country that is increasingly cosmopolitan [...] We have to start from the assumption that religion is fundamental for human beings and therefore has a great significance for society.[4]

---

[4]http://governacio.gencat.cat/web/.content/afers_religiosos/consell_diversitat/doccadr1_es.pdf; p. 5, accessed 2 July 2016, translation mine.

While the most commonly used official wording speaks of the 'promotion of religious diversity', I suggest that urban bureaucrats also developed practices of 'marketing' religious diversity. This is illustrated by the founding of the *Office of Religious Affairs* by the City Council of the Catalan capital city of Barcelona in the late 1990s. Importantly, this office is an outcome of earlier interfaith and ecumenical initiatives that were formed in the context of the 1992 Olympic Games, in which they were part of a broader effort in city marketing that aimed to produce globally circulating images of Barcelona as a diverse city.[5] Today, the Office of Religious Affairs manages and markets religious diversity 'upstream' through facilitating relationships between city officials and religious leaders as well as 'downstream' by supporting and managing positive relationships between religious communities and local residents, for instance in the context of public religious festivals and places of worship.

To a large extent, efforts to promote religious diversity in Catalonia can be explained by the desire of the regional state to recruit migrants as members of religious communities into the Catalan nation-building project. However, for both elites and ordinary people, this project has an important economic dimension, as many Catalans pride themselves on economically outperforming the rest of Spain and being an economic force in Europe in its own right. Interestingly, within popular understandings, not only do Catalans see themselves as economically more developed, but also more modern and more cosmopolitan than Spaniards in other Spanish provinces. They also view themselves as more secular. Indeed, as historical and sociological studies show, Catalans have the lowest rates of religious participation on the Iberian Peninsula and the social role of Catholicism has been on the decline since the late 19th century (Dowling 2012). Against this backdrop, the Catalan vice-president's insistence that 'religion is fundamental for human beings' and his emphasis on religious diversity are rather astonishing. I argue that such religious interpellations must be understood as distinctive efforts to render complex population legible and to produce a matrix of conviviality that enshrines and consecrates cultural difference as religious diversity and that at once issues calls for liberal tolerance as a way of living with such difference.

Conclusions

The idea that nation-states and city administrations shape and produce diversity is certainly not a new development. In her comparative study on the ways in which the concept of diversity changes practices and policies of immigrant integration in Antwerp, Amsterdam and Leeds, Maria Schiller has shown that diversity has regrouped and reassembled categories of difference, tying ethnicity, sexual orientation and disability in often uneasy ways together. The concept of diversity has thus worked to move people under the radar of bureaucracies, planners, and policy-makers in formations that do not necessarily exist, or at least not in the same fashion, independently from bureaucratic classification.

In this article, I have explored how such practices of governmentality, premised as they are on the idea that people have identities and should be governed on the basis of these

---

[5]In the Italian city of Turin as well the Olympic Games provided the occasion for the establishment of more enduring and marketable interfaith relationships.

identities, play out in the field of religion. While running up against powerful processes of secularization, the promotion and marketing of religious diversity through urban and governmental programs and projects rests on the idea that religion does – almost by necessity – become more important in contexts of migration-driven diversity and that societies characterized by transnationalized labor markets must continually reckon with the need to 'integrate' religion into forms of sociality and civil participation that sustain them. Against this backdrop, the transatlantic comparison between Quebec and Catalonia yields several significant lessons. It shows that religious diversity becomes a premise of governmentality even in highly secularized societies but it does so in different ways. These differences can be explained by two major factors: the integration into global capitalism and transnational labor markets and nationalism. Catalonia is clearly more integrated into global capitalism than Quebec and economic success is a central element of its national self-image and of nationalist campaigns. Quebec, by contrast, remains an economic underdog in comparison to the rest of Canada by most measures and this notion too is a central part of Quebec's self-image. Parallel to this, there is a palpable public sense that embracing the agenda and politics of religious diversity and multiculturalism that is so characteristic of Canada would mean giving up on its national distinctiveness for the sake of enhancing economic competitiveness. Apart from the economically integrated business class, there is among many people resentment towards 'diversity' that stems from this scenario and which exists despite the relatively smooth functioning of accommodations through the work of an educated bureaucracy. It thus seems that the close interdependence between labor migration and economic success in today's capitalism favor normative claims towards the promotion of religious diversity, a fact which may actually also point up the limits of earlier assumptions about the interdependence between secularization and economic modernization. More research is needed in order to explore how ordinary citizens who are called to inhabit the symbolic universes of religious diversity in neoliberal capitalism and to recognize themselves in its regime of recognition actually fashion for themselves such identities and whether or not they act according to them.

Disclosure statement

No potential conflict of interest was reported by the author.

References

Astor, Avi. 2012. "Memory, Community, and Opposition to Mosques: The Case of Badalona." *Theory and Society* 41 (4): 325–349.

Astor, Avi. 2014. "Religious Governance and the Accommodation of Islam in Contemporary Spain." *Journal of Ethnic and Migration Studies* 40 (11): 1716–1735.

Astor, Avi, Marian Burchardt, and Mar Grier. 2017. "The Politics of Religious Heritage: Framing Claims to Religion as Culture in Spain." *Journal for the Scientific Study of Religion* 56 (1): 126–142.

Bauman, Zygmunt. 2011. *Culture in a Liquid Modern World*. Cambridge: Polity Press.

Beaman, Lori G. 2003. "The Myth of Pluralism, Diversity, and Vigor: The Constitutional Privilege of Protestantism in the United States and Canada." *Journal for the Scientific Study of Religion* 42 (3): 311–325.

Beaman, Lori G., ed. 2012. *Reasonable Accommodation: Managing Religious Diversity*. Toronto: UBC Press.

Beckford, James A. 2003. *Social Theory and Religion*. Cambridge: Cambridge University Press.

Berger, Peter L. 1967. *The Sacred Canopy: Elements of a Sociological Theory of Religion*. New York: Open Road Media.

Bouchard, Gerard, and Charles Taylor. 2008. *Fonder L'Avenir. Le temps de la Conciliacation*. Commission de consultation sur les pratiques d'accommodement reliées aux différences culturelles, Gouvernement du Québec.

Burchardt, Marian. 2016. "Does Religion Need Rehabilitation? Charles Taylor and the Critique of Secularism." In *Working with A Secular Age. Interdisciplinary Perspectives on Charles Taylor's Master Narrative*, edited by Florian Zemmin, Colin Jager, und Guy Vanheeswijck, 137–158. Boston: De Gruyter.

Burchardt, Marian. 2017. "Recalling Modernity: How Nationalist Memories Shape Religious Diversity in Quebec and Catalonia." *Nations and Nationalism* 23 (3): 599–619.

Burchardt, Marian, and Mar Griera. 2018. "To See or not to See: Explaining Intolerance Against the "Burqa" in European Public Space." *Ethnic and Racial Studies*. Advance online publication. doi:10.1080/01419870.2018.1448100.

Burchardt, Marian, and Ines Michalowski, eds. 2015. *After Integration: Islam, Conviviality and Contentious Politics in Europe*. Wiesbaden: Springer.

Burchardt, Marian, Mar Griera, and Gloria García-Romeral. 2015. "Narrating Liberal Rights and Culture: Muslim Face Veiling, Urban Coexistence and Contention in Spain." *Journal of Ethnic and Migration Studies* 41 (7): 1068–1087.

Castells, Manuel. 1996. *The Rise of the Network Society: The Information Age: Economy, Society, and Culture*. New York: John Wiley & Sons.

Chagnon, R., and Francois Gauthier. 2013. "From Implicitly Christian to Neoliberal: The Moral Foundations of Canadian Law Exposed by the Case of Prostitution." In *Religion in the Neoliberal Age. Political Economy and Modes of Governance*, edited by Tuomas Martikainen and Francois Gauthier, 176–191. Farnham: Ashgate.

Dowling, Andrew. 2012. "For Christ and Catalonia: Catholic Catalanism and Nationalist Revival in Late Francoism." *Journal of Contemporary History* 47 (3): 594–610.

Fainstein, Susan S. 2005. "Cities and Diversity Should we Want it? Can we Plan for it?" *Urban Affairs Review* 41 (1): 3–19.

Finke, Roger, and Rodney Stark. 2005. *The Churching of America, 1776–2005: Winners and Losers in our Religious Economy*. New Brunswick, NJ: Rutgers University Press.

Florida, Richard. 2002. *The Rise of the Creative Class*. New York: Basic Books.

Foucault, Michel. 1988. "The Political Technology of Individuals." In *Technologies of the Self: A Seminar with Michel Foucault*, edited by Michel Foucault, Luther H. Martin, Huck Gutman, and Patrick H. Hutton, 145–162, Amherst: University of Massachusetts Press.

Gauthier, Francois, and Tuomas Martikainen, eds. 2013. *Religion in Consumer Society. Brands, Consumers, Markets*. Farnham: Ashgate.

Griera, Mar. 2016. "The Governance of Religious Diversity in Stateless Nations: The Case of Catalonia." *Religion, State & Society* 44 (1): 13–31.

Guia, Aitana. 2015. "Completing the Religious Transition?: Muslims and Catholics Navigate Secularism in Democratic Spain." *New Diversities* 17 (1): 95–110.

Hacking, Ian. 2006. "Making Up People." *London Review of Books*, August 17: 23–26.

Harvey, David. 1989. *The Condition of Postmodernity*. Oxford: Blackwell.

Jenkins, Richard. 2000. "Categorization: Identity, Social Process and Epistemology." *Current Sociology* 48 (3): 7–25.

Joppke, Christian, and John Torpey. 2013. *Legal Integration of Islam: A Transatlantic Comparison*. Cambridge: Harvard University Press.

Koenig, Matthias. 2005. "Incorporating Muslim Migrants in Western Nation States – A Comparison of the United Kingdom, France, and Germany." *Journal of International Migration and Integration* 6 (2): 219–234.

Kymlicka, Will. 2013. "Neoliberal Multiculturalism?" In *Social Resilience in the Neoliberal Era*, edited by Peter A. Hall and Michele Lamont, 99–124. Cambridge: Cambridge University Press.

Lentin, Alana, and Gavan Titley. 2008. "More Benetton than Barricades? The Politics of Diversity in Europe." In *The Politics of Diversity in Europe*, edited by Gavan Titley and Alana Lentin, 9–30. Strasbourg: Council of Europe Publishing.

Lentin, Alana, and Gavan Titley. 2011. *The Crises of Multiculturalism: Racism in a Neoliberal Age*. London: Zed Books.

Madeley, John. 2003. "A Framework for the Comparative Analysis of Church–State Relations in Europe." *West European Politics* 26 (1): 23–50.

Martikainen, Tuomas, and Francois Gauthier, eds. 2013. *Religion in the Neoliberal Age: Political Economy and Modes of Governance*. Farnham: Ashgate.

Matejskova, Tatiana, and Marco Antonsich. 2015. "Introduction: Governing through Diversity." In *Governing through Diversity. Migration Societies in Post-Multiculturalist Times*, edited by Tatiana Matejskova and Marco Antonsich, 1–18. Basingstoke: Palgrave Macmillan.

Ogilvie, Margaret H. 1996. *Religious Institutions and the Law in Canada*. Scarborough, ON: Carswell.

Reuschke, Darja, Monika Salzbrunn, and Korinna Schönhärl, eds. 2013. *The Economies of Urban Diversity: Ruhr Area and Istanbul*. Basingstoke: Palgrave.

Rodatz, Mathias. 2012. "Produktive "Parallelgesellschaften" Migration und Ordnung in der (Neoliberalen) "Stadt der Vielfalt"." *Behemoth* 5 (1): 70–103.

Roof, Wade C. 2001. *Spiritual Marketplace: Baby Boomers and the Remaking of American Religion*. Princeton: Princeton University Press.

Schenk, Susanne, Marian Burchardt, and Monika Wohlrab-Sahr. 2015. " Religious Diversity in the Neoliberal Welfare State: Secularity and the Ethos of Egalitarianism in Sweden." *International Sociology* 30 (1): 3–20.

Vertovec, Steven, and Susanne Wessendorf, eds. 2010. *Multiculturalism Backlash: European Discourses, Policies and Practices*. New York: Routledge.

Vormann, Boris. 2015. "Urban Diversity: Disentangling the Cultural from the Economic Case." *New Diversities* 17 (2): 119–129.

Yücel, Clémence Scalbert. 2016. "Diversity Talk and Identity Politics: Between Consensus and Resistance." *Nationalism and Ethnic Politics* 22 (1): 1–8.

Žižek, Slavoj. 1997. "Multiculturalism, or, the Cultural Logic of Multinational Capitalism." *New Left Review* (September–October): 28–51.

Religion and the marketplace: constructing the 'new' Muslim consumer

Özlem Sandıkcı

ABSTRACT
Despite the prediction that modernization would lead to secularization, the past 30 years brought a global resurgence of religion. As many scholars note, religion has gained a new visibility in the contemporary political economy and become firmly embedded within the identity politics. The changing role of religion is linked to the growing influence of neoliberalism and the expansion of the market logic. In this study, I look at the intersections between Islam, consumption, and market and trace the shifts in the conceptualizations of Muslims in relation to the changing market dynamics and the broader socio-political and economic structures. I discuss three phases through which the view of Muslims as modern consumers in search of distinction and propriety comes to dominate the view of Muslims as non- or anti-consumers: exclusion, identification, and stylization. I conclude by discussing the implications of the study for the current understandings of the marketization of religion.

Introduction

'Modesty sells', declares the popular weekly Economist, pointing to the growing Muslim retail market in the United Kingdom which according to the analysts 'remains woefully underserved by mainstream shops' (Economist 2016). It is not only the Economist; business media and consultancy agencies advise managers not to ignore Muslim consumers and attend to the needs of this large yet untapped segment. H&M, Zara, Uniqlo, Tommy Hilfiger, and Dolce and Gabbana, among others, are discussed as global brands that successfully reach out to the 'new' Muslim consumer. This article explores the formation of Muslim consumer subjectivity and the emergence of the so-called Islamic market. By consumer subjectivity, I am referring to the forms of personhood that privilege making choices in the marketplace and consuming freely as anchors of selfhood (e.g., Dolan 2009; Miller and Rose 1997). I am particularly interested in tracing the shifts in the marketers' discourses and conceptualizations of Muslims in relation to the changing market dynamics and the broader socio-political and economic developments.

In recent years, the relationship between religion and economy has come under increasing scrutiny and scholars from a diverse set of disciplines, including anthropology, sociology, geography, cultural studies, and marketing, have sought to go beyond the parameters of the classical economic theory to account for the new forms of religiosity, religious practices, and organizational forms (e.g., Comaroff and Comaroff 2001; Engler 2016; Gauthier and Martikainen 2013; Gauthier, Martikainen, and Woodhead 2013a, 2013b; Jafari and Sandikci 2016; Lewis 2015; Osella and Osella 2009; Robbins 2004; Rudnyckyj 2009; Sandikci and Ger 2010). Covering a broad spectrum of contexts, ranging from Pentecostal movements to new age spirituality, mega churches, and Islamic fashion, these studies explore the co-constitutive relationship between religion and economics that locates the market at the very center of the analytical framework. Key to this emerging interest is, as Gauthier, Martikainen and Woodhead note, 'the observation that the new form of cultural political economy, which has emerged in the last half of the twentieth century and become dominant since the 1980s, has had profound consequences for religious belief, practice and expression worldwide' (2013b, 269). Marketization, the expansion of market logic into non-market domains (Fairclough 1992; Slater and Tonkiss 2001), has been a defining feature of the contemporary neoliberal political economy, reconfiguring all domains of life including religion.

Market logic prioritizes monetized and profit-driven production of goods and services and seeks to transform 'every human interaction into a transient market exchange' (Ciscel and Heath 2001, 401). As markets subsume greater portions of everyday life, being a consumer emerges as a dominant mode of identity. However, the development of consumer subjectivity is not a natural process but a socio-cultural construction in which marketing plays an important role (Beckett 2012; Miller and Rose 1997; Trentmann 2006). From a Foucauldian perspective, marketing can be understood as a set of techniques that aim to produce, mobilize, and govern consumer subjectivity. Foucault (1991) first used the term 'governmentality' to discuss the particular ways through which modern states govern populations to bring about a condition of individual self-awareness and agency. Foucault argued that liberal governance operates not by coercion but by granting liberties to people. That is, through the shaping of desires and aspirations which in turn shapes the 'conduct of conduct', people are positioned as simultaneous wardens and practitioners of their own freedom (Foucault 1982). Power operates implicitly as individuals learn how to make free choices within a limited range of possible actions and assert themselves as sovereign subjects.

The notion of governmentality has proven particularly useful in studying marketing practices and consumer subjectivity (e.g., Arvidsson 2001; Binkley 2006; Dolan 2009; Hackley 2002; Miller and Rose 1997; Trentmann 2006). This approach emphasizes deployment of discourses in the production of consumer subjectivity and shows how key authorities such as marketing research and advertising agencies along with media institutions discursively construct normative models of how to consume efficiently and authentically. For example, in a seminal study on the topic, Miller and Rose (1997) document the use of psychological sciences in the construction of advertisements in Britain and show how psychological knowledge has been connected with the technologies of advertising and marketing 'to make possible new kinds of relations that human beings can have with themselves and others through the medium of goods' (3). Following studies has further revealed that changes in consumer subjectivity cannot be separated from the complex intertwining of multiple social processes and, hence, the intentional practices of marketing professionals and media experts 'occur at particular points when the potential consumer already feels receptive to such discursive practices' (Dolan 2009). New visions of consumer subjectivity and discursive appeals to consume according to one's individuality and unique lifestyle develop simultaneously with new structures of everyday life.

Following these perspectives, I discuss the expansion of market logic into the Islamic social sphere and explore the emergence of the 'new Muslim consumer'. In particular, I examine the discourses of marketing experts and the media and trace the changes in the conceptualization and articulation of Muslim identity in relation to the changing social, political, and economic dynamics. I discuss three phases through which the view of Muslims as modern consumers in search of distinction and propriety comes to dominate the view of Muslims as non- or anti-consumers: exclusion, identification, and stylization. Rather than forming parts of a linear process, these phases should be perceived as analytical categories used to explain different forms of subjectivity valorized independently or collectively in particular socio-temporal contexts. I conclude by discussing the implications of the study for the analyses of the marketization of religion and the intersections between Islam, consumption, and market.

Religion and market

There is a complex and puzzling relationship between religion and market. One perspective considers the relation to be antagonistic; that is, religion and market stand in opposition to each other (e.g., Haddorff 2000; Loy 1997). This approach, drawing upon Marx and Weber, perceives the market as a destructive force that threatens to dissolve the very fabric of society. For Marx, capitalist economy turns everything to commodities and leads to alienation. Under the oppressive conditions of the market, religion's role is limited to providing comfort to the masses. For Weber, modernization fosters the process of secularization. While the authority of religion declines against the secular institutions, traditional ways of practicing religion diminishes. In short, in modern capitalist economies the market emerges as the dominant organizing form and religion loses its influence in shaping society and social interactions.

In the 1980s, following liberal economic theory's spilling outside of its original sphere, a second strand of research emerged in the US, which projected to understand the dynamics of religion with the tools of neoclassical economics. According to the proponents of the religious market theory, also known as the Rational Choice current, religious organizations act like firms competing for market share and people shop for the alternatives that best satisfy their religious needs (e.g., Iannaccone 1991; Stark and Finke 2000). This model adopts the neoclassical economic view of market as a spontaneous creation, driven by calculative, self-interested and profit-maximizing agents. Accordingly, religious marketplace is perceived as 'a space in which various religious ideas and communities can be freely selected by religious consumers and where religious competition produces an environment of creativity and adaptability' (Koenig 2016, 87). In contrast to the antagonistic approaches, adaptive perspective considers market values to be compatible with religion. Rather than exerting a negative effect, by expanding religious options and enabling competition, market contributes to religious vitality.

The third approach can be traced back to the classical works of the Durkheimian school, according to which the sacred and the profane exist symbiotically and 'redefine themselves according to the dominant ethos of society' (Haddorff 2000, 491). The implication of this is to consider that in modern, secularized societies where the market becomes dominant, religion can be understood as taking on market like character. According to this perspective, though, what is meant by 'the market' diverges from the abstract construction of neoclassical theory. Rather, the notion of the market is a moral ideal, one that is historically contingent. As sociological approaches have shown, markets are historically contingent constructions, situated within broader socio-political structures, and are subject to power dynamics that limit free choice (e.g., Callon 1998; Fligstein 2001; Granovetter 1985). Following this, a growing body of research seeks to capture the historical specificities of the market dynamics and examines 'the emergence of forms of religio-ethno-economic practice which are completely integral to consumer capitalism' (Comaroff and Comaroff 2001; Gauthier 2018; Gauthier, Martikainen, and Woodhead 2013b, 269; Hefner 2010).

Moving beyond the metaphor of market to explain religious growth or decline, this perspective aims to understand how market interacts with religion to organize, mobilize, and legitimize new, situated forms of belongings, experiences, and identities. For example, the literature on megachurches, New Age movements, and prosperity religion shows how marketization, globalization, and mediatization help mobilize people transnationally and allow for the configuration of new practices and expressions of faith that combines religious, economic and socio-cultural discourses (Redden 2016; Van Hove 1999). Similarly, several studies look into the relation between Islamism and neoliberal globalization and reveal how socioeconomic restructuring transforms everyday experiences of Islam and how new forms of piety inform marketplace dynamics (e.g., Fischer 2009; Izberk-Bilgin 2015; Osella and Osella 2009; Rudnyckyj 2009; Sandikci and Ger 2007). In line with this perspective, I explore the particularities of Islam-market interaction and discuss how the notion of the 'Muslim consumer' and the 'Islamic' consumption practices has evolved in the contemporary political economy.

Muslims in the marketplace

Until recently, marketing, consumption, and branding have been concepts that were seldom discussed in relation to Islam and Muslims. Today, however, there is a growing academic and managerial interest in understanding the dynamics of the so-called Islamic or halal economy and devising marketing strategies that will enable companies to effectively respond to the needs of what is claimed to be a highly attractive consumer segment. One can trace such interest in the growing number of research articles appearing in academic journals, the publication of books and handbooks, the establishment of specialist periodicals such as the *Journal of Islamic Marketing* and the *International Journal of Islamic Marketing and Branding*, the organization of academic conferences and executive workshops in various parts of the world, the production of high profile consultancy reports, and the circulation of news stories about Muslim consumers and entrepreneurs in the trade press and popular media. Next, I discuss the changes in the conceptualizations of Muslim consumer identity through three phases of exclusion, identification, and stylization.

Exclusion

For centuries, Muslims have engaged in consumption and trade; yet, Muslim consumers and businesses remained almost invisible in the mainstream Western marketing theory and practice. For example, a subject search in the flagship journals of the field, such as the *Journal of Marketing, Journal of Consumer Research*, and *Marketing Science*, returns no results for the period prior to the 2000s. It is important to note that, until recently, religion in general has remained as an understudied topic within marketing studies. One might speculate that marketing scholars have largely subscribed to the secularization theory and expected that with modernization religion would recede from the public sphere, including the market. Thus, given this general tendency, the lack of attention on the Islam, consumption, and marketing linkage might appear as not too surprising. However, a closer look suggests that there have been additional factors underlying this omission.

First has been the marginalization of Muslims as low income and uneducated people who do not qualify as consumers of branded products. While rich Muslims from the oil states of the Gulf were known to engage in extravagant consumption in New York, London, or Paris, much of the Muslim world was considered to be in the grip of poverty, consisting of people barely sustaining their lives. There was and still is truth to this observation. According to the latest statistics, around 40 percent of the Muslim population languishes in abject poverty, with nearly 350 million living on less than US$1.25 a day (COMCEC 2014). The United Nations Food and Agriculture Organization lists more than half of the world's 57 Muslim nations as low-income food deficit countries (FAO 2014). Such bleak numbers contribute to an image of Muslims as economically unworthy of attention. The historical legacy of widespread poverty and lack of purchasing power appears to have placed Muslims outside the scope of marketing and rendered their marketplace behaviors almost invisible.

However, beyond economic dynamics, the omission is also related to the stereotypical images of Muslims as traditional and uncivilized people. As Said (1978) lucidly demonstrated in his book *Orientalism*, the prevailing Western view of Islam and Muslims as the inferior Other of the West has been a historical construct, a trope that was based on false and romanticized images of the Middle East and Asia. Said argued that Western writings of the Orient depict it as an irrational, weak, feminized 'Other' in contrast to the rational, strong, masculine West. Underlying this contrast was, according to Said, the need to create 'difference' between West and East that can be attributed to immutable 'essences' in the Oriental make-up (1978, 65–67). In the business context, such Orientalist representations worked to produce and reinforce an essentialist view of Islam as incompatible with capitalist market ideology and Muslims as outside the values and practices of Western consumer culture. Several prominent sociological analyses carried out in the 1990s further propagated the discourse of incompatibility (e.g., Barber 1995; Huntington 1997; Turner 1994).

For instance, in his book *Orientalism, Postmodernism and Globalism*, Brian Turner argued that 'consumerism offers or promises a range of possible lifestyles which compete with, and in many cases, contradict the uniform lifestyle demanded by Islamic fundamentalism' (1994, 90). Turner interpreted the cultural, aesthetic, and stylistic pluralism fostered by postmodernism and the spread of global system of consumption as contradicting the fundamentalist commitment to a unified world organized around incontrovertibly true values and beliefs. Similarly, in his provocatively titled *Jihad vs. McWorld*, Barber (1995) described the rise of Islamic fundamentalism as a reactionary response to Westernization and the spread of a global system of market capitalism and consumption. While these studies privileged the West as the natural space of market, they framed the non-West both as outside the market and antagonistic to the ethos of consumerism.

In the 20th century, in much of the Muslim geography, Islam acted as an important force mobilizing people against Western colonialism and imperialism. The terms such as 'political' or 'revolutionary' Islam were used in conjunction with such liberatory and mobilizing potential of religion (Esposito 1998; Roy 2004). An important part of the anti-colonial and anti-imperialist uprisings was the boycott of Western products and services and the rejection of Western lifestyles that signified the colonial/imperialist West (Ezra 2000; Jafari 2007). However, failing to acknowledge the historical complexities underlying the relationships between the West and Muslims, many analysts have interpreted consumption resistance merely as an evidence of Islam's anti-capitalist and anti-market essence.

The view of Islam as an anti-Western force was also echoed in the writings of the scholars of Islamic economics. Islamic economics developed in the post-colonial era of 1970s as a response to the 'assertions of superiority of Western knowledge' (Zaman 2008, 17) and aimed to offer an Islamic alternative to the capitalist and communist economic systems (Chapra 2000; Khan 1995). In a broader perspective, Islamic economics can be considered part of an ongoing project of the 'Islamization of knowledge' (Al-Faruqi 1982). The founders of the field defined the purpose of Islamic economic system as to promote justice and equality (Al-Sadr 1961) and 'believed that applications of Islamic laws and guiding principles in the economic sphere would bring advances in human welfare and be superior to Western systems for handling economic affairs, which promote only material welfare' (Zaman 2008, 19). Proponents called for re-instigating Islamic traditions against the secular Western project of modernization and advocated the merits of Islamic principles in conceptualizing, guiding, and organizing economic affairs (e.g., Khan 1995; Siddiqi 1995).

Followers of the doctrine claim that the moral imperatives embedded in an Islamic economic system differentiate it from both capitalism and communism. First and foremost, the application of Quranic injunctions and Islamic norms were expected to prevent injustice in the distribution and acquisition of material things and motivate people to use wealth for performing obligations that would please Allah and the society rather than pursuing individualistic materialist pleasures (Zaman 2008). As devout Muslims know that 'spendthrifts are the brethren of Satan' (Qur'an 17:27), in an Islamic economy consumption would be lower and savings would be higher than a non-Islamic economy (Khan 1995). While religious norms would encourage Muslims to control their spending, *zakat* (obligatory almsgiving) would spur growth in the long run and improve societal welfare (Siddiqi 1995).

Given the emphasis on justice and equality, scholars of Islamic economics tend to exhibit a diffident attitude toward consumption. In general, excessive attention to materialistic desires is seen as futile, egotistic, and crass. In response to the perceived decadence of Western consumerism, an Islamic economic model calls for moderation and prohibition of envy. As proponents explain, while Islam does not encourage asceticism, it commands Muslims to be moderate in spending and refrain from extravagance and ostentatious and luxurious lifestyles (Khan 1992). Similarly, scholars identify envy as an important source of waste and unhappiness characterizing capitalist economies and emphasize that Islam prohibits Muslims from envying others and teaches believers to be content with whatever they own (Arif 1985). Thus, depicting consumerism as wasteful, harmful, immoral, and fostering individualism, hedonism, and materialism, the advocates of Islamic economics preach Muslims to live modest lives and refrain from conspicuous consumption. As Kuran (2004, ix) argues, by casting the Western consumer culture and capitalist market system as Mammon and presenting Islam as an antidote against its harms and evils, Islamic economics 'has promoted the spread of antimodern, and in some respects deliberately anti-Western, currents of thought all across the Islamic world'.

Overall, for a long period of time, various economic, political, and theological factors have contributed to a widely held belief in the incompatibility of Islam and capitalism, rendering Muslims rather invisible and irrelevant for the mainstream marketing theory and practice. Prevailing in this exclusionary perspective has been an image of Muslim as non- or anti-consumer, a subject position that situated the Muslim self-outside the boundaries of Western consumption culture. A Muslim, whether due to obligation (Islamic norms), choice (anti-colonial resistance) or inability (poor financial resources), seemed to lack the expected capacities, freedoms, and duties of the consumer proper.

Identification

While an image of Muslims as outside the capitalist market and consumption system dominated popular representations, lived experiences suggest the opposite. Indeed, in the 1990s, anthropologically oriented analysis began to report that new consumption objects and practices that explicitly draw from Islamic references have become increasingly visible (e.g., Armbrust 1996; Robinson 1997; Starrett 1995). Religious consumption is not a new phenomenon and people have always used religious commodities, such as prayer mats, rosaries or statues (McDannell 1995; Tarocco 2011). However, while these products typically have direct association to acts of worship, the emerging Islamic consumptionscape included objects that lacked such connection: pop music and romance novels, toys, coloring books, calendars, and greeting cards, and clothing. For many scholars, the increasing visibility and proliferation of objects defined and promoted as religiously appropriate signaled the changing nature of the relationship between Islam, market, and consumption (e.g., Fischer 2009; Hasan 2009; Izberk-Bilgin and Nakata 2016; Jafari and Süerdem 2012; Jones 2010; Maqsood 2014; Sandikci 2017; Sandikci and Ger 2010; Schulz 2006).

Underlying this change has been several interrelated macro-level developments. Since the 1980s, neoliberal restructuring has characterized the development path of much of the developing countries, including the Muslim-majority ones (Ong 2006; Rudnyckyj 2009). The severe economic crisis of the 1970s led to questioning of the state-led development models and created an environment that favored less protection and more liberalization. In the context of the general anti-Keynesian ideological wave that characterized the West at the time, the neoliberal model was promoted to the less-developed world as an innovative growth strategy. The ramifications of neoliberal globalization have extended well beyond the economic realm to the political, social, and cultural domains (Appadurai 1996; Harvey 2005). Liberalization of trade and capital movement encouraged Western businesses to outsource their production to developing countries to take advantage of the cheap supply of labor and resources. The changing manufacturing landscape along with the growth of financial markets in developing countries created opportunities for local entrepreneurs and helped boost the emergence of a new industrial and professional class in these countries.

On the consumption side, an unprecedented inflow of foreign consumer goods dramatically changed the marketplaces of developing countries. As global brands became available and abundant in economies once characterized by scarcity, new patterns of consumption emerged (Ger and Belk 1996; Kravets and Sandikci 2014). Access to satellite television and transnational images of advertising and new spaces for shopping and leisure further fueled the development of a globally oriented consumer culture. The changes in the production and consumption domains had their effects on both secular and religious segments of the populations and created new opportunities for wealth accumulation and marketplace participation. For example, in countries such as Turkey, Egypt, Malaysia, and Indonesia to name a few, economic growth along with major socio-political transformations contributed to the development of a conservative but consumption-oriented segment (Gokarıksel and Secor 2009; Nasr 2009; Sandikci and Ger 2002; Wong 2007). As much as secular middle classes developed a taste for globally oriented consumption culture, so did the religious middle classes.

Globalization and marketization have also been linked to the spread of new forms of faith collectivities (e.g., Fernando 2014; Robbins 2004; Wilson and Steger 2013). In the context of Islam, several studies discuss the emergence of new Islamist movements as a key development shaping the political landscape in the last decades (Bayat 2005; Wiktorowicz 2004). New Islamist social movements are seen as strategic activist structures organized around loosely defined networks and groups that promote particular values through proper observance of Islam. As such they parallel the logic of new social movements and seek to create 'networks of shared meaning' (Melucci 1996) through mobilization of various resources such as political parties, religious organizations, NGOs, schools, and social networks (Bayat 2005; Wiktorowicz 2004). Studies indicate that market and consumption play important roles in the growth and spread of these movements (Karatas and Sandikci 2013; Mandaville 2010; Yavuz 2004). In the case of Turkey, for example, Yavuz's (2004) study showed how Islamic groups have benefited from the new 'opportunity spaces' created by economic liberalization. These market-oriented venues to spread ideas and practices, such as the media, financial institutions and businesses, have been instrumental in both propagating the Islamic lifestyles and generating financial resources for the Islamic movements.

Immigration has also been an important factor in the reconfiguration of the relationship between Islam and economy. Beginning in the 1950s, but increasing in the 1980s following the intensification of wars and conflicts in the Middle East and Africa, substantial numbers of Muslims have migrated to Western Europe and North America. The immigration of Muslim labor, students, intellectuals, and refugees brought multiple challenges to the host countries. The addition of the new populations meant new provisions in terms of governance and policy (i.e., social security, education and public services, socioeconomic integration and citizenship) (Modood, Triandafyllidou, and Zapata-Barrero 2006). It also called for provisioning of marketspaces where immigrants could interact with each other as well as the members of the host society. Ethnic grocery stores and local mosques and community schools, which served as identity hubs for socialization and nostalgia for Muslim immigrants, mushroomed. As Muslim populations grew through the second and third generations and the arrival of newcomers, demand for halal services and goods has increased.

The increasing visibility of products and services marked as Islamic in both Muslim-majority and minority contexts caught attention of Western media and consultancy agencies. Since the late 2000s several reports and news stories on the so-called Muslim consumer have appeared. In 2007, A.T. Kearney, a global management consulting firm, published one of the earliest analyses on the topic. The report, titled *Addressing the Muslim Market*, claimed that 'at a time when many other large consumer segments are reaching a saturation point, Muslims are a new outlet from which to build a base for future growth' (2007, 1). According to the A.T. Kearney analysts, Muslims have been 'becoming more integrated into the global economy as consumers, employees, travelers, investors, manufacturers, retailers and traders' and thus presented many opportunities for Western companies (2007, 1). In 2009, John Walter Thompson, a New York-based marketing communications firm, shared the results of a 10-country study through a document titled *Understanding the Islamic Consumer*. In 2010, Ogilvy and Mather, another New York-based global marketing communications agency, created a special unit called Ogilvy Noor to better engage with Muslim consumers worldwide. Same year, Ogilvy Noor announced the findings of a study conducted in partnership with research agency TNS. Titled *Brands, Islam and the New Consumer* (Ogilvy and Mather 2010), the report identified 'the New Muslim Consumer' as a critically important development for brands hoping to build successful relationships with the Islamic world. In the meantime, the *Economist* (2007), *Time* (Power 2009), the *New York Times* (Gooch 2010), and the *Financial Times* (Janmohamed 2012) published feature stories on Muslim consumers. In recent years, several other prominent organizations joined the trend and contributed to the proliferation of the analysis of the Islamic economy: Thomson Reuter's *State of the Global Islamic Economy* (2015), Economist Intelligence Unit's *The Sharia-Conscious Consumer: Driving Demand* (2012), and Dinar Standard's *Global Muslim Lifestyle Travel Market* (2012).

Typically, these publications begin with an emphasis on the current size of the Muslim population and its expected growth rate: 'The global Muslim community stands at almost 1.8 billion people. By 2050, more than half of the world's population will be Muslim' (Ogilvy and Mather 2010). However, this impressive population remains underserved and ignored by Western companies: 'Surprisingly, save for one or two examples, most brands have been slow to directly target their products and services to this market' (O'Neill 2010, 60). The analysts interpret this as a major business oversight and assert that the market is worth tapping into (Gooch 2010; Power 2009). Estimates set the value of the Islamic market around $2 trillion (Economist Intelligence Unit 2012; Thomson Reuters 2015). Given the immense growth rate and sales potential, reports advise companies not to overlook such a lucrative market: 'Since Muslims are the fastest growing segment in the world, any company that is not considering how to serve them is missing a significant opportunity' (Kearney 2007, 18; also see Thomson Reuters 2015).

In general terms, identification of Muslims as consumers resembles the discovery in the US of non-mainstream communities such as gays, Hispanics, immigrants, and blacks as viable market segments (Keating and McLoughlin 2005). As studies indicate, these 'segments' were not preexisting entities that marketers simply appealed to but constructions (e.g., Davila 2001; Sender 2004). An important step in the construction process is establishment of groups as viable and relevant consumer segments. In her analysis of the making of the Hispanic market in the United States, Davila (2001, 1–2) observes that 'long before the current popularization of Latin culture, [marketing and advertising] industry first advanced the idea of a common "Hispanic market" by selling and promoting generalized ideas about "Hispanics" to be readily marketed in corporate America'. Similarly, marketing professionals and media engender discourses that endorse and promote the existence and profitability of Muslims as a genuine and commercially viable segment and aim to sell the idea of 'Muslim consumer'.

However, identifying certain populations as market segments is only an initial stage in the process of constructing them as consumers. As Miller and Rose (1997, 7) argue making up the consumer has never been a simple matter of manipulation or 'invention and imposition of "false needs"'. Rather mobilizing people as consumers entails 'a delicate process of identification of the "real needs" of consumers, of affiliating these needs with particular products, and in turn of linking these with the habits of their utilization' (Miller and Rose 1997, 7). In identifying the 'real needs' of Muslim consumers, marketing analysts and consultants claim confidently that Muslims are a 'unique' segment that require products and services specifically tailored for them. Typically, the reports outline the five pillars of Islam and key Islamic values, such as modesty and gender relations, and argue that faith shapes everyday lives and marketplace behaviors of Muslims in unique and particular ways. Consider for example, the characterization of Muslims offered by an Islamic market consultancy company:

> The Islamic market differentiates itself in the way that Muslims worldwide identify themselves; first as Muslim, then culturally, then by nationality and so on. Islam being a complete way of life doesn't leave any aspect of life untouched. Therefore the Muslims's purchasing decision process is directly influenced by their belief system. Islam embodies an ethical approach that requires individuals and corporations alike to act fairly, honestly, respectfully and responsibly. (Islamic Market Consultancy, n.d.)

According to the analysts, such foundational differences set Muslim consumers apart from all comparable segments that marketers have engaged before and necessitate adoption of an alternative managerial approach:

> The tendency of the marketing and advertising industry [is] to see it [Muslim consumers] as just another interesting segment. In this mindset, it becomes equated with 'greys', or the 'Pink Dollar'; or Latinos in the US. Of course, all these are very valid targets for segmentation strategies, but the Islamic opportunity surely differs qualitatively. We are not looking here at a segment which is qualified by one primary difference, be it age, orientation, language or skin colour, and then whether attitudes and behaviour vary from a norm in accordance with that. Rather, we are looking at an alternative norm, one where the starting point is Islamic identity, and everything else fits into it. (Young 2010)

By identifying Muslims as a vast, untapped, and valuable segment, marketing research and consultancy agencies create and promote an image of Muslims as individuals eager to consume yet underserved by the market. They encourage Western companies to better understand Islamic principles and values and design offerings that meet religious requirements. The portrayal of Muslims as enthusiastic consumers presents a stark contrast to the view of Muslims as marginalized/poor consumers, outside of or against the capitalist market. However, in casting Muslims as consumers, these analyses tend to treat religion as a homogenizing force that univocally and indiscriminately govern marketplace behavior (Jafari and Sandikci 2015; Sandikci 2011). There are two problems in this perspective.

First, it leads to an overemphasis of religion at the expense of other aspects of identity such as gender, social class, age, and their interactions and flattens out sectarian differences in how Islam is experienced and practiced in daily life. Second, it represents Muslim identity as inherently different from consumers in general. The assumption of difference derives from an essentialized view of Islam and inadvertently reproduces the Orientalist dichotomy. While Muslims emerge as viable and capable participants of the Western consumer culture, they still remain different from the mass consumer and are considered to engage with the market in their terms.

Stylization

Identification of populations as potential market segments constitutes an important step in turning people into consumers. Historically, marketing gained importance only when increase in production capacity forced companies to find new ways to encourage individuals to consume more (Baudrillard 1988). Early marketing research techniques helped forecast aggregate demand but did not say much why people would buy a product (Bartels 1988). In the 1950s, with entry of psychologists and sociologists like Ernst Dichter, George Katona, Paul Larzarsfeld, and Pierre Martineau into the marketing research profession, focus has shifted to understanding consumers' behavior, attitudes, and motivations (Cohen 2003). As analyses revealed the diversity of priorities, the notion of the unified mass market came under question. Market segmentation was born in the 1970s as a tool to classify consumers into different clusters based on their demographic, psychographic, and geographic characteristics (Goss 1995). Improvements in segmentation techniques enabled companies to fine-tune their marketing practices and better reach to targeted clusters.

As discussed in the previous section, in identifying Muslims as consumers, marketing analysts propagate the notion of a homogeneous segment economically attractive enough yet differentiated from mainstream consumers by their strong adherence to faith. However, marketing exists to promote and sustain an illusion of difference – constructing and communicating an individualized identity amid mass manufactured objects. In the context of Muslim consumers too, the fiction of a unified market could not hold for long and soon gave way to an emphasis on difference. As for example an analyst writing for Campaign notes while religion is the uniting factor, 'brands need to be careful not to generalize the Muslim community because they are not homogeneous' (O'Neill 2010, 63). Justifying Muslims as viable consumers required establishing them as distinct from consumers in general. Yet, for sustainable marketing success, Muslim consumers needed to be distanced from their marginal position. This entailed a shift in the focus of marketing professionals' attention to subgroups that were deemed to have the highest economic and cultural capital and would be willing to engage in lifestyle consumption.

The concern with lifestyle is a fundamental aspect of the consumer culture. As several theorists have argued, in contemporary societies, consumption's role extends well beyond an instrumental logic and the symbolic value of goods reign over their use value (e.g., Baudrillard 1981; Featherstone 1991). Because the planning, purchase, and display of goods entail a balancing of the instrumental and expressive desires, aesthetic considerations become at least as important as utilitarian ones. Baudrillard argues that in late capitalism commodities are promoted as emblems of a certain desired lifestyle and consumed mostly for what they symbolize. Hence, individuals become defined by the goods they consume rather than the socioeconomic positions they occupy. Similarly, Featherstone (1991, 81) relates the proliferation of goods in the late capitalist societies to the stylization of everyday life, a process that 'foregrounds the importance of style, which is also encouraged by market dynamics with its constant search for new fashions, new styles, new sensations and experiences'. The concern over style expresses itself in a preoccupation with cultivating an original, aesthetically choreographed, up-to-date self through choice and use of proper products and services.

The notion of Muslim lifestyle became popular in the discussions of Muslim middle class. For example, in his analysis of the rise of the new Muslim middle class, Nasr (2009, 14) argued that 'this upwardly mobile class consumes Islam as much as practicing it, demand[ing] the same sorts of life-enhancing goods and services as middle classes everywhere'. A news story published in Time the same year announced that Muslims are hungry for Islamic versions of mainstream pleasures such as fast food and saying 'we want pizzas, we want Big Macs' (Power 2009, 3). The article further stated that:

> During the 1980s and '90s, many Muslims in Egypt, Jordan and other Middle Eastern countries expressed their religious principles by voting Islamic. Today, a growing number are doing so by buying Islamic, connecting to their Muslim roots by what they eat, wear and play on their iPods. Rising Muslim consumerism undermines the specious argument often heard after 9/11: that Muslims hate the Western way of life, with its emphasis on choice and consumerism. The growing Muslim market is a sign of a newly confident Islamic identity — one based not on politics but on personal lifestyles. (Power 2009, 4)

The newly emerging genre of Islamic lifestyle magazines has also been influential in promoting lifestyle as an anchor for identity (e.g., Jones 2010; Lewis 2010). These journals, such as *emel* and *Sisters* in the UK, *Azizah* and *Muslim Girl* in the US and Canada, *Ala* and *Aysha* in Turkey, and *Alef* in Kuwait, target the urban, well-off, modern Muslim women across the world. As Lewis argues, they function as an arena where 'style mediators' reconcile the expectations of different faith communities and the demands of the marketplace. Indeed, a report in Financial Times confirms that 'Muslim women ... increasingly see no conflict between faith and fashion' and 'see fashion precisely as an expression of their faith' and want 'cutting edge, fashion forward lines' (Janmohamed 2012, 3). Similarly, Lian Rosnita Redwan-Beer, the publisher of Aquila Asia, a fashion and lifestyle magazine and website for cosmopolitan Muslim women, states in an interview to the Campaign magazine that the new generation of Muslim consumers are 'curious, culturally exposed, and very interested in others' (O'Neill 2010, 63). As she explains, these women 'love to share knowledge, info, tips, experience and problems' and promote products, services or places that meet their spiritual needs (O'Neill 2010, 63).

The more Muslims are promoted as consumers who are able to skillfully combine the demands of a pious yet modern life, the more companies that help them to do so get attention and publicity. For example, news about mainstream fashion companies 'seeking to profit from the rising demand for Islamic clothing' appear frequently in the media (Kern 2016, 1; also Express Tribune 2016; Jameson 2016). Readers learn that Dolce & Gabanna, Oscar de la Renta, Tommy Hilfiger, Uniqlo and DKNY have released 'modest wear' capsule ranges; H&M used a Muslim model in a hijab in one of its advertisements; Spanish fashion retailers Zara and Mango launched a special collection for Ramadan.

THE MARKETIZATION OF RELIGION

Examples are also abundant in the travel industry. In an article titled *Rise of the Affluent Muslim Traveler*, BBC News Magazine maintains that global urban Muslims are seeking out goods and services that respect and reflect their needs as Muslims, including luxurious holiday resorts and villas that offer halal food, do not serve alcohol, offer prayer rooms and family-friendly activities, and equipped with separate pools and spa facilities for men and women (Akhtar 2012). According to a study conducted by Dinar Standard (2012, 3), several companies have indeed responded to this need:

> Australia's Gold Coast is attracting Muslim tourists by offering a Gold Coast Ramadan Lounge. In Thailand, spa-outlets have introduced the concept of Muslim-friendly spas in a bid to lure tourists from the Middle East. Global Health City, in Chennai, India, has gotten Halal-certified to better serve its growing medical tourists from Muslim countries. Even in Muslim-majority destinations, hotels/resorts such as De Palma Group of Hotels in Malaysia, Al-Jawhara Hotel in Dubai, Amer Group of Resorts in Egypt, Ciragan Palace Kempinski Hotel in Turkey are offering Muslim lifestyle related services by not serving alcohol, separating recreation services/timing for women, providing prayer facilities and more. Airlines and destinations are just beginning to pay attention.

As evident in travel, fashion, and other industries, a significant catalyst in shaping and satisfying the demands of Islamic style consumption are Muslim entrepreneurs. Consultancy reports and news stories frequently portray pious business people from Malaysia to Turkey, India, Kuwait, the UK, USA, and Australia who successfully design, manufacture and market products that cater to the needs of modern Muslim consumers. Among the popular examples are Turkish *Tekbir* and British Aab, modest fashion companies, Syrian Newboy Design Studio, producer of *Fulla* dolls, and Australian Ahiida, marketer of the 'modest' swimsuit *Burqini*, a term derived from merging 'burqa' and 'bikini', and Singapore based halal-friendly travel agent Crescent Rating. An article published recently in Management Today, titled 'Islam means business: Meet the new generation of Muslim entrepreneurs', declares that there is now 'a bewildering array of products in the Muslim consumer market … . You can buy a burkini for the beach in Dubai, visit Islamic sex stores in Amsterdam or customise your Koran in magenta or baby pink online. There's an Islamic version of practically everything' (Gale 2016, 3).

Indeed, nothing seems to escape the attention of Muslim entrepreneurs. Consider for example the British Mocktail Company, provider of non-alcoholic mojito, the Nojito. In an interview given to the BBC News, its founder Shahin Hussain explains how she came up with the idea:

> I'd always known growing up in Britain that the culture of being British and being Muslim sometimes conflicted, particularly at university when a lot of my friends were drinking. And as I grew older I saw no one had filled the gap in the market for non-alcoholic drinks aimed at Muslims. (BBC News 2016, 3)

It is reported that only three months after its launch, the company have already sold 19 000 bottles of Nojito and is planning to release new flavors (BBC News 2016, 3). The success of Mocktail is not an exception. The Muslim Lifestyle Expo conducted in London in April 2016 showcased young Muslim startups. In its coverage of the event, the Guardian states that 'Young Muslim entrepreneurs were responsible for an explosion in small business startups marketing products and services, particularly in the spheres of fashion, cosmetics and personal products, and food' (Sherwood 2016, 2). Speaking to the

Guardian, Shelina Janmohamed, vice president of Ogilvy Noor explains that 'when a young Muslim consumer doesn't find a product that they are looking for on the high street, their instinct is to go and create it themselves' (Sherwood 2016, 2).

While marketing professionals relate the emergence of Muslim entrepreneurs to the mainstream brands' failure to respond to the requirements of the new Muslim lifestyle, academic research identifies development of a new form of 'pious neoliberalism' as a key factor (Adas 2006; Atia 2012; Osella and Osella 2009; Sloane 1999). According to Atia (2011, 2) pious neoliberalism refers to 'the discursive combination of religion and economic rationale in a manner that encourages individuals to be proactive and entrepreneurial in the interest of furthering their relationship with God'. Drawing on a globalized religious discourse and combining it with entrepreneurship, pious neoliberalism cultivates subjects who are driven toward material success in the present life and spiritual success in the afterlife. In her study of the Opus Dei movement in Chile, Olave (2010) reports that, by representing business as a religious vocation, the movement provided moral justification to the establishment of a neoliberal economic model in the country. Similarly, in the context of Islam, the emphasis on prosperity in this and other world has encouraged Muslims to pursue economic success and reframes a proactive engagement with the market as a religiously appropriate endeavor.

The focus on middle-class sensitivities and entrepreneurial skills functions as a rhetorical move to distance Muslims away from the associations with poverty and anti-capitalism as well as the recently prevailing images of 'Islamic' violence and terrorism. However, adoption of a stylized approach to life requires not just financial resources but also cultural capital. In order to 'turn li[fe] into a work of art' (Featherstone 1991, 97), one needs to possess appropriate skills, knowledge, and abilities. Accordingly, attention turns into identifying groups of consumers that are likely to possess the required capital. Analysts propose various classificatory schemes to highlight the most pertinent sub-segments and, in order to render them attractive for companies, use market-friendly labels such as 'Futurists', 'New Age Muslims', 'Mipsterz' (Muslim hipsters), 'GUMmies', (global urban Muslim consumers), and 'Generation M'. For example, Ogilvy Noor divides the Muslim consumer market between 'Traditionalists' and 'Futurists'. While Traditionalists constitute a larger group, 'it is the Futurist group–which combines a modern outlook with a strong religious commitment– that is most interesting to brands' (O'Neill 2010, 63). Futurists, according to Shazia Khan, associate planning director at Ogilvy Noor, are young, goal-orientated and ambitious, and find 'individualistic brands that reflect this zest and drive … appealing' (Goh 2011, 31). They 'combine[s] a modern outlook with a strong religious commitment' and 'wholeheartedly integrate brands into their own lives' (O'Neill 2010, 63).

Similarly, Generation M, or 'Muslim millennials', offers unprecedented opportunities for brands (Campaign 2016; Sherwood 2016). The term Generation M was recently coined by Shelina Janmohamed, the vice president of Ogilvy Noor and discussed in detail in her book *Generation M: Young Muslims Changing the World*. What makes Generation M unique, Janmohamed explains,

> is their cross-cultural background, their love for the internet, and the mastering of social media. It is not an age group that brands should target but a mind-set. The digital technology offers modern Muslims a new tool for navigation, especially amongst the female consumers who are extremely active online, looking for the latest fashion trends and even leading some of the hottest feeds on Instagram. (Janmohamed 2016)

Generation M, Gummies or Mipsters or whatever they are called to 'are not just avid consumers; they are energetic entrepreneurs' who believe that 'being faithful and living a modern life go hand in hand and that there is absolutely no contradiction between the two' (Sherwood 2016).

Overall, marketing and media discourses promote an image of young, globally connected, digitally masterful, fashion-forward, and financially well-off Muslim consumers who embrace brands and pursue a lifestyle that seamlessly blends faith and modernity. The once marginalized groups of people come to be seen as a lifestyle community embedded in the language of consumption. As noted by several scholars, marketing does not merely respond to needs but plays a proactive role in constituting and modifying them (e.g., Dolan 2009; Knights and Sturdy 1997; Miller and Rose 1997). Discourses of the marketing research and consultancy agencies provide a viewpoint from which Muslims can be made knowable and comparable and provide legitimacy for products, from the Nojito to halal nail polish. Regimes of governmentality are about constituting subjects in terms of 'truths' and norms (Beckett 2012). Norms, for example, what it means to be a modern Muslim consumer, frame an identity. By encouraging individuals to identify with these norms, marketing experts contribute to the mobilization and governance of the new Muslim consumer subjectivity.

Conclusion

The literature on religion and economy offers disparate views on the role of the market. Some scholars highlight the damaging effects of the market and perceive consumerism as a threat to religion. Others draw attention to the adoption of the market logic in the religious realm and discuss how religious organizations employ the language and techniques of marketing to attract members, funds, and public support. My goal in this article has been to shift attention from the impact of the market on religion to the cultural practices and processes through which particular forms of religious identities, experiences, and belongings are discursively produced and configured in the market under the conditions of neoliberal political economy. In my analysis, I consider the emergence of the new Muslim consumer as a socio-cultural construction, shaped by an ongoing history of events, forces, and practices. As a construction, the relation between Muslims and the market takes different forms and involves complex mechanisms through which the desires and conduct of individuals are mobilized and governed (Foucault 1982, 1991).

As many scholars point out media, popular culture and the market contribute greatly to the increasing visibility of religion in everyday life (e.g., Casanova 2006; Davie 2010; Granholm and Moberg 2017). However, the proliferation of religiously coded products, services, and practices do not merely represent the expansion of market logic to the realm of religion or the infiltration of religion into the sphere of market. Rather, the current relationship between religion and the market point to a new configuration in which piety and consumption is inseparable and constitutive of a modern religious subjectivity. In other words, as much as the global expansion of neoliberalism is implicated in the marketization of religion, the newly emerging consumption practices create opportunities for imagining and expressing new forms of religious identities, both collectively and privately. Focusing on this symbiotic relationship between religion and market enables uncovering the processes through which the new Muslim consumer gets discursively constructed through the imaginations and practices of the marketers.

Recently scholars have argued for the relevance of discursive approaches for the study of religion (Taira 2013; Wijsen 2013) and suggested that they can be fruitfully utilized in understanding construction of social reality, including what is considered to be religious or not religious. This article traces the development of the Muslim consumer subjectivity through the analysis of the discourses of marketing professionals and the media, and provides further support for the potential of discursive approaches in understanding the complex and multilayered relationship between religion and market. The contemporary neoliberal political economy, which is characterized by the marketization of all domains of life provides a fertile context to explore the (re)configuration of religious identities through mobilization of various discursive practices. Such an approach requires utilization of a multidisciplinary theoretical toolkit that allows for a critical engagement with concepts such as market, consumer, and subjectivity and further unpack the symbiotic relationship between faith and profit.

Disclosure statement

No potential conflict of interest was reported by the author.

References

Adas, Emin Baki. 2006. "The Making of Entrepreneurial Islam and the Islamic Spirit of Capitalism." *Journal for Cultural Research* 10 (2): 113–137.

Akhtar, Navid. 2012. "The Rise of the Affluent Muslim Traveller." *BBC News Magazine*, August 20. http://www.bbc.co.uk/news/magazine-19295861.

Al-Faruqi, Ismail. 1982. *Islamization of Knowledge*. Herndon, VA: International Institute of Islamic Thought.

Al-Sadr, Muhammad Baqir. 1961. *Our Economics*. 4 vols. Tehran: World Organization for Islamic Services.

Appadurai, Arjun. 1996. *Modernity at Large: Cultural Dimensions of Globalization*. Minneapolis: University of Minnesota Press.

Arif, Muhammad. 1985. "Toward a Definition of Islamic Economics: Some Scientific Considerations." *Journal of Research in Islamic Economics* 2: 79–93.

Armbrust, Walter. 1996. *Mass Culture and Modernism in Egypt*. Cambridge: Cambridge University Press.

Arvidsson, Adam. 2001. "From Counterculture to Consumer Culture Vespa and the Italian Youth Market, 1958–78." *Journal of Consumer Culture* 1 (1): 47–71.

Atia, Mona. 2012. "'A Way to Paradise': Pious Neoliberalism, Islam, and Faith-based Development." *Annals of the Association of American Geographers* 102 (4): 808–827.

Barber, Benjamin R. 1995. *Jihad vs. McWorld*. New York, NY: Random House.

Bartels, Robert. 1988. *The History of Marketing Thought*. Columbus, OH: Horizons.

Baudrillard, Jean. 1981. *For A Critique of the Political Economy of Sign*. St. Louis, MO: Telos Press.

Baudrillard, Jean. 1988. "Consumer Society." In *Selected Writings*, edited by Poster Mark, 29–56. Stanford, CA: Stanford University Press.

Bayat, Asef. 2005. "Islamism and Social Movement Theory." *Third World Quarterly* 26 (6): 891–908.

BBC News. 2016. "The Rise of the Muslim Female Entrepreneur." October 28. http://www.bbc.com/news/business37798677.

Beckett, Antony. 2012. "Governing the Consumer: Technologies of Consumption." *Consumption, Markets & Culture* 15 (1): 1–18.

Binkley, Sam. 2006. "The Perilous Freedoms of Consumption: Toward a Theory of the Conduct of Consumer Conduct." *Journal for Cultural Research* 10 (4): 343–362.

Callon, Michel, ed. 1998. *The Laws of the Market*. Oxford: Blackwell and Sociological Review Press.

Campaign. 2016. "Why Brands Should not Overlook the Muslim Consumer." September 12. http://www.campaignlive.co.uk/article/whybrandsnotoverlookmuslimconsumer/1408542.

Casanova, J. 2006. "Religion, European Secular Identities, and European Integration." In *Religion in an Expanding Europe*, edited by T. Byrnes and P. Katzenstein, 65–92. Cambridge: Cambridge University Press.

Chapra, M. Umer. 2000. *The Future of Economics: An Islamic Perspective*. Leicester: The Islamic Foundation.

Ciscel, David H., and Julia A. Heath. 2001. "To Market, to Market: Imperial Capitalism's Destruction of Social Capital and the Family." *Review of Radical Political Economics* 33 (4): 401–414.

Cohen, Lizbeth. 2003. *A Consumer's Republic: The Politics of Mass Consumption in Postwar America*. New York: A. A. Knopf.

Comaroff, Jean, and John L. Comaroff. 2001. *Millennial Capitalism and the Culture of Neoliberalism*. Durham, NC: Duke University Press.

COMCEC. 2014. "Poverty Outlook 2014: Multidimensional Poverty." The Standing Committee for Economic and Commercial Cooperation of the Organization of the Islamic Cooperation. http://www.mod.gov.tr/Lists/RecentPublications/ Attachments/ 66/COMCEC%20Poverty%20Outlook%202014%20-20 Revised%20Edition.pdf.

Davie, Grace. 2010. "Resacralization." In *The New Blackwell Companion to the Sociology of Religion*, edited by Bryan S. Turner, 160–177. Chichester: Blackwell.

Davila, Arlene. 2001. *Latinos Inc.: The Marketing and Making of a People*. Berkeley, CA: University of California Press.

Dinar Standard. 2012. "Global Muslim Lifestyle Travel Market: Landscape and Consumer Needs Study." http://www.dinarstandard.com/travel-study/.

Dolan, Paddy. 2009. "Developing Consumer Subjectivity in Ireland: 1900–80." *Journal of Consumer Culture* 9 (1): 117–141.

Economist. 2007. "Food, Fashion and Faith: Companies are Starting to Reach out to Muslim Consumers in the West." August 2. http://www.economist.com/node/9587818.

Economist. 2016. "Modesty Sells." June 4. http://www.economist.com/news/britain/21699971britishmuslimsaregrowingmarketmodestysells.

Economist Intelligence Unit. 2012. "The Sharia-Conscious Consumer: Driving Demand." https://www.eiuperspectives.economist.com/strategy-leadership/sharia-conscious-consumer.

Engler, Steven. 2016. "Why be Critical? Introducing a Symposium on *Capitalizing Religion*." *Religion* 46 (3): 412–419.

Esposito, John L. 1998. *Islam and Politics*. Syracuse, NY: Syracuse University Press.

The Express Tribune. 2016. "British Brands Eye Growing Muslim Consumer Market." December 16. http://tribune.com.pk/story/1081211/britishbrandseyegrowing muslimconsumermarket/.

Ezra, Elizabeth. 2000. *The Colonial Unconscious: Race and Culture in Interwar France*. New York: Cornell University Press.

Fairclough, Norman. 1992. *Discourse and Social Change*. Cambridge: Polity Press.

FAO. 2014. "Low-Income Food-Deficit Countries (LIFDC): List for 2014." Food and Agriculture Organization of the United Nations. http://www.fao.org/countryprofiles/ lifdc/en/.

Featherstone, Mike. 1991. *Consumer Culture and Postmodernism*. London: Sage.

Fernando, Oshan. 2014. "Religion's 'State Effects': Evangelical Christianity, Political Legitimacy, and State Formation." *Religion* 44 (4): 573–591.

Fischer, Johan. 2009. *Proper Islamic Consumption: Shopping among the Malays in Modern Malaysia*. Copenhagen: NIAS Press.

Fligstein, Neil. 2001. *The Architecture of Markets*. Princeton, NJ: Princeton University Press.

Foucault, Michel. 1982. "The Subject and Power. Afterword." In *Michel Foucault: Beyond Structuralism and Hermeneutics*, edited by Hubert L. Dreyfus and Paul Rabinow, 208–226. Brighton: Harvester.

Foucault, Michel. 1991. "Governmentality." In *The Foucault Effect*, edited by Burchell Graham, Gordon Colin, and Miller Peter, 87–104. Hemel Hempstead: Harvester Wheatsheaf.

Gale, Adam. 2016. "Islam Means Business: Meet the New Generation of Muslim Entrepreneurs." *Management Today*, April 27. http://www.managementtoday.co.uk/islammeansbusinessmeetne wgenerationmuslimentrepreneurs/entrepreneurs/article/1392329.

Gauthier, Francois. 2018. "From Nation – State to Market. The Transformations of Religion in the Global Era, as Illustrated by Islam." *Religion* 48 (3): 382–417. doi:10.1080/0048721X.2018. 1482615.

Gauthier, Francois, and Tuomas Martikainen. 2013. *Religion in Consumer Society: Brands, Consumer and Markets*. Surrey: Ashgate.

Gauthier, Francois, Tuomas Martikainen, and Linda Woodhead. 2013a. "Introduction: Religion in Market Society." In *Religion in the Neoliberal Age: Political Economy and Modes of Governance*, edited by Tuomas Martikainen and Francois Gauthier, 1–18. Farnham: Ashgate.

Gauthier, Francois, Tuomas Martikainen, and Linda Woodhead. 2013b. "Acknowledging a Global Shift: A Primer for Thinking about Religion in Consumer Societies." *Implicit Religion* 16 (3): 261–76.

Ger, Guliz, and Russell W. Belk. 1996. "I'd Like to Buy the World a Coke: Consumptionscapes of the 'Less Affluent World'." *Journal of Consumer Policy* 19 (3): 271–304.

Goh, Gabey. 2011. "Beyond the Call of Duty." *Marketing Interactive*, August, 30–36.

Gokarıksel, Banu, and Anne J. Secor. 2009. "New Transnational Geographies of Islamism, Capitalism and Subjectivity: The Veiling-Fashion Industry in Turkey." *Area* 41 (1): 6–18.

Gooch, Liz. 2010. "Advertisers Seek to Speak to Muslim Consumers." *New York Times*, August 12. http://www.nytimes.com/2010/08/12/business/media/12branding.html.

Goss, Jon. 1995. "'We Know Who You Are and We Know Where You Live': The Instrumental Rationality of Geodemographic Systems." *Economic Geography* 71 (2): 171–198.

Granholm, Kennet, and Marcus Moberg. 2017. "The Concept of the Post-secular and the Contemporary Nexus of Religion, Media, Popular Culture, and Consumer Culture." In *Post-Secular Society*, edited by P. Nynas, M. Lassander, and T. Utriainen, 95–127. New Brunswick, NJ: Transaction.

Granovetter, Mark. 1985. "Economic Action and Social Structure: The Problem of Embeddedness." *American Journal of Sociology* 91 (3): 481–510.

Hackley, Chris. 2002. "The Panoptic Role of Advertising Agencies in the Production of Consumer Culture." *Consumption, Markets and Culture* 5 (3): 211–29.

Haddorff, David W. 2000. "Religion and the Market: Opposition, Absorption, or Ambiguity?" *Review of Social Economy* 58 (4): 483–504.

Harvey, David. 2005. *A Brief History of Neoliberalism*. Oxford: Oxford University Press.

Hasan, Noorhaidi. 2009. "The Making of Public Islam: Piety, Agency, and Commodification On The Landscape of the Indonesian Public Sphere." *Contemporary Islam* 3 (3): 229–250.

Hefner, Robert W. 2010. "Religious Resurgence in Contemporary Asia: Southeast Asian Perspectives on Capitalism, the State, and the New Piety." *The Journal of Asian Studies* 69 (04): 1031–1047.

Huntington, Samuel P. 1997. *The Clash of Civilizations and the Remaking of World Order*. New York: Simon and Schuster.

Iannaccone, Laurence R. 1991. "The Consequences of Religious Market Structure." *Rationality and Society* 3 (2): 156–177.

Islamic Market Consultancy. n.d. "About Us." Accessed June 21, 2016. http://islamicm arketconsultancy.com/aboutus/.

Izberk-Bilgin, Elif. 2015. "Rethinking Religion and Ethnicity at the Nexus of Globalization and Consumer Culture." In *The Routledge Companion to Ethnic Marketing*, edited by A. Jamal, L. Penaloza, and M. Laroche, 135–146. New York: Routledge.

Izberk-Bilgin, Elif, and Cheryl C. Nakata. 2016. "A New Look at Faith-based Marketing: The Global Halal Market." *Business Horizons* 59 (3): 285–292.

Jafari, Aliakbar. 2007. "Two Tales of a City: An Exploratory Study of Cultural Consumption among Iranian Youth." *Iranian Studies* 40 (3): 367–383.

Jafari, Aliakbar, and Ozlem Sandikci. 2015. "'Islamic' Consumers, Markets, and Marketing: A Critique of El-Bassiouny's (2014) "The One-Billion-Plus Marginalization"." *Journal of Business Research* 68 (12): 2676–2682.

Jafari, Aliakbar, and Ozlem Sandikci, eds. 2016. *Islam, Marketing and Consumption: Critical Perspectives on the Intersections*. London: Routledge.

Jafari, Aliakbar, and Ahmet Süerdem. 2012. "An Analysis of Material Consumption Culture in the Muslim World." *Marketing Theory* 12 (1): 59–77.

Jameson, Angela. 2016. "Big British Business Wakes Up to Spending Power of Muslim Female Shopper." *The National*, August 4. http://www.thenational.ae/business/retail/igbritshbusinessw akesuptospendingpowerofmuslimfemaleshopper#full.

Janmohamed, Shelina. 2012. "The Muslim Consumer: Building your Brand for a Fast Growing Segment." *The Financial Times*, January 5. http://blogs.ft.com/beyond-brics/2012/01/05/the-muslim-consumer-building-your-brand-for-a-fast-growing-segment/.

Janmohamed, Shelina. 2016. "Introducing the Millennial Muslim – and the Global Market that is Worth Trillions of Dollars." April 27. https://www.ifdcouncil.org/introducingthemillenn ialmuslimandtheglobalmarketthatisworthtrillionsofdollars/.

Jones, Carla. 2010. "Images of Desire: Creating Virtue and Value in an Indonesian Islamic Lifestyle Magazine." *Journal of Middle East Women's Studies* 6 (3): 91–117.

Karatas, Mustafa, and Ozlem Sandikci. 2013. "Religious Communities and the Marketplace: Learning and Performing Consumption in an Islamic Network." *Marketing Theory* 13 (4): 265–284.

Kearney, A. T. 2007. "Addressing the Muslim Market." http://www.atkearney.com/images/global/ pdf/AddressingMuslimMarket_S.pdf.

Keating, Anderew, and Damien McLoughlin. 2005. "Understanding the Emergence of Markets: A Social Constructionist Perspective on Gay Economy." *Consumption, Markets and Culture* 8 (2): 131–52.

Kern, Soeren. 2016. "Europe: Sharia Compliant Fashion Goes Mainstream." April 13. https://www. gatestoneinstitute.org/7833/shariafashion.

Khan, M. Fahim. 1992. "Theory of Consumer Behaviour in an Islamic Perspective." In *Readings in Microeconomics in Islamic Perspective*, edited by Sayyid Tahir and Aidit Ghazal, 69–80. Malaysia: Longman.

Khan, M. Fahim. 1995. *Essays in Islamic Economics*. London: Islamic Foundation.

Knights, David, and Andrew Sturdy. 1997. "Marketing the Soul: From the Ideology of Consumption to Consumer Subjectivity." In *Financial Institutions and Social Transformations*, edited by David Knights and Tony Tinker, 158–188. Basingstoke: Palgrave Macmillan.

Koenig, Sarah. 2016. "Almighty God and the Almighty Dollar: The Study of Religion and Market Economies in the United States." *Religion Compass* 10 (4): 83–97.

Kravets, Olga, and Ozlem Sandikci. 2014. "Competently Ordinary: New Middle Class Consumers in the Emerging Markets." *Journal of Marketing* 78, July: 125–140.

Kuran, Timur. 2004. *Islam and Mammon: The Economic Predicaments of Islamism*. Princeton, NJ: Princeton University Press.

Lewis, Reina. 2010. "Marketing Muslim Lifestyle: A New Media Genre." *Journal of Middle East Women's Studies* 6 (3): 58–90.

Lewis, Reina. 2015. *Muslim Fashion: Contemporary Style Cultures*. Durham: Duke University Press.

Loy, David R. 1997. "The Religion of the Market." *Journal of the American Academy of Religion* 65 (2): 275–290.

Mandaville, Peter. 2010. *Global Political Islam.* London: Routledge.

Maqsood, Ammara. 2014. "'Buying Modern' Muslim Subjectivity, the West and Patterns of Islamic Consumption in Lahore, Pakistan." *Cultural Studies* 28 (1): 84–107.

McDannell, Colleen. 1995. *Material Christianity: Religion and Popular Culture in America.* New Haven, CT: Yale University Press.

Melucci, Alberto. 1996. *Challenging Codes: Collective Action in the Information Age.* Cambridge: Cambridge University Press.

Miller, Paul, and Nicholas Rose. 1997. "Mobilizing the Consumer." *Theory, Culture & Society* 14 (1): 1–36.

Modood, Tariq, Anna Triandafyllidou, and Ricard Zapata-Barrero. 2006. *Multiculturalism, Muslims and Citizenship: A European Approach.* London: Routledge.

Nasr, Vali. 2009. *Forces of Fortune: The Rise of the New Muslim Middle Class and What it Will Mean for Our World.* New York: Free Press.

Ogilvy and Mather. 2010. "Brands, Islam and the New Muslim Consumer." http://www.ogilvy.com/News/Press-Releases/May-2010-The-Global-Rise-of-the-New-Muslim-Consumer.aspx.

Olave, Angélica Thumala. 2010. "The Richness of Ordinary Life: Religious Justification among Chile's Business Elite." *Religion* 40 (1): 14–26.

O'Neill, Michael. 2010. "Meet the New Muslim Consumer." *Campaign,* October, 60–66, http://www.campaignasia.com/article/meet-the-new-muslim-consumer/234336.

Ong, Aihwa. 2006. *Neoliberalism as Exception: Mutations in Citizenship and Sovereignty.* Durham, NC: Duke University Press Books.

Osella, Filippo, and Caroline Osella. 2009. "Muslim Entrepreneurs in Public Life between India and the Gulf: Making Good and Going Good." *Journal of the Royal Anthropological Institute* 15: S202–221.

Power, Carla. 2009. "Halal: Buying Muslim." *Time,* May 25. http://www.time.com/time/magazine/article/0,9171,1898247,00.html.

Redden, Guy. 2016. "Revisiting the Spiritual Supermarket: Does the Commodification of Spirituality Necessarily Devalue It?" *Culture and Religion* 17 (2): 231–249.

Robbins, Joel. 2004. "The Globalization of Pentecostal and Charismatic Christianity." *Annual Review of Anthropology* 33 (1): 117–143.

Robinson, Francis. 1997. "Religious Change and the Self in Muslim South Asia." *South Asia (nedlands, W A)* 20 (1): 13–27.

Roy, Olivier. 2004. *Globalized Islam: The Search for a New Ummah.* New York: Columbia University Press.

Rudnyckyj, Daromir. 2009. "Spiritual Economies: Islam and Neoliberalism in Contemporary Indonesia." *Cultural Anthropology* 24 (1): 104–141.

Said, Edward. 1978. *Orientalism.* New York: Vintage.

Sandikci, Ozlem. 2011. "Researching Islamic Marketing: Past and Future Perspectives." *Journal of Islamic Marketing* 2 (3): 246–258.

Sandikci, Ozlem. 2017. "Cultural Industries and Marketplace Dynamics." In *The Ashgate Research Companion to Veils and Veiling Practices,* edited by A. Almila and D. Inglis, 197–212. London: Ashgate.

Sandikci, Ozlem, and Guliz Ger. 2002. "In-between Modernities and Postmodernities: Investigating Turkish Consumptionscape." *Advances in Consumer Research* 29: 465–70.

Sandikci, Ozlem, and Guliz Ger. 2007. "Constructing and Representing the Islamic Consumer in Turkey." *Fashion Theory* 11 (2/3): 189–210.

Sandikci, Ozlem, and Guliz Ger. 2010. "Veiling in Style: How does a Stigmatized Practice Become Fashionable?" *Journal of Consumer Research* 37 (1): 15–36.

Schulz, Dorothea E. 2006. "Promises of (Im)mediate Salvation: Islam, Broadcast Media, and the Remaking of Religious Experience in Mali." *American Ethnologist* 33 (2): 210–229.

Sender, Katherine. 2004. *Business, Not Politics: The Making of the Gay Market.* New York: Columbia University Press.

Sherwood, Harriet. 2016. "Muslim Lifestyle Expo in London Highlights Largely Untapped Market." *The Guardian*, April 7. https://www.theguardian.com/world/2016/apr/07/muslimlifestyleexpolo ndonglobalbrandsspendingpower.

Siddiqi, Mohammad N. 1995. "The Guarantee of a Minimal Standard of Living in an Islamic State." In *Islamic Perspectives on Sustainable Development*, edited by Iqbal Muhawar, 74–89. Basingstoke: Palgrave MacMillan.

Slater, Don, and Frank Tonkiss. 2001. *Market Society: Markets and Modern Social Theory*. Cambridge: Polity Press.

Sloane, Patricia. 1999. *Islam, Modernity, and Entrepreneurship Among the Malays*. New York: St. Martin's Press.

Stark, Rodney, and Roger Finke. 2000. *Acts of Faith: Explaining the Human Side of Religion*. Berkeley: University of California Press.

Starrett, Gary. 1995. "The Political Economy of Religious Commodities in Cairo." *American Anthropologist* 97 (1): 51–68.

Taira, Teemu. 2013. "Making Space for Discursive Study in Religious Studies." *Religion* 43 (1): 26–45.

Tarocco, Francesca. 2011. "On the Market: Consumption and Material Culture in Modern Chinese Buddhism." *Religion* 41 (4): 627–644.

Thomson Reuter. 2015. "State of the Global Islamic Economy." www.dinarstandard.com/state-of-the-global-islamic-economy-report-2015/.

Trentmann, Frank, ed. 2006. *The Making of the Consumer: Knowledge, Power and Identity in the Modern World*. Oxford: Berg.

Turner, Brian. 1994. *Orientalism, Postmodernism and Globalism*. London: Routledge.

Van Hove, Hildegard. 1999. "L'émergence D'un 'Marché Spirituel.'" *Social Compass* 46 (2): 161–172.

Wijsen, Frans. 2013. "'There Are Radical Muslims and Normal Muslims': An Analysis of the Discourse on Islamic Extremism." *Religion* 43 (1): 70–88.

Wiktorowicz, Quentin, ed. 2004. *Islamic Activism: A Social Movement Theory Approach*. Bloomington: Indiana University Press.

Wilson, Erin K., and Manfred B. Steger. 2013. "Religious Globalisms in the Post-secular Age." *Globalizations* 10 (3): 481–495.

Wong, Loong. 2007. "Market Cultures, the Middle Classes and Islam: Consuming the Market?" *Consumption Markets & Culture* 10 (4): 451–480.

Yavuz, Hakan. 2004. "Opportunity Spaces, Identity and Islamic Meaning in Turkey." In *Islamic Activism: A Social Movement Theory Approach*, edited by Quentin Wiktorowicz, 270–288. Bloomington: Indiana University Press.

Young, Miles. 2010. "Muslim Futurism and Islamic Branding." Speech at the Inaugural Oxford Global Islamic Branding and Marketing Forum, UK, July 26. http://www.wpp.com/wpp/marketing/marketing/muslim-futurism-and-islamic-branding/.

Zaman, Asad. 2008. "Islamic Economics: A Survey of Literature." Religions and Development Research Programme Working Paper 22-2008, University of Birmingham, UK.

The marketization of church closures

Jes Heise Rasmussen

ABSTRACT

In recent years, the impact of marketization on the religious field has gained increasing attention within sociology of religion. However, one of the recurring issues has been how to define marketization. In this article, I propose a particular theoretical definition focusing on the intertwinement of neoliberalism and New Public Management, and by using Critical Discourse Analysis I find that demands for structural reorganization, i.e., closing churches, in the Diocese of Copenhagen increasingly makes use of the discourse of marketization. I examine the consequences of two municipality reforms from 1970 and 2007 on the Diocese, trying to pinpoint instances of marketization, before analyzing how the issue of church closures becomes the focal point in the structural discussions from 2005 to 2013. By exploring the minutes from the Diocese council, I argue that marketization has become embedded in the institutions within the Church to the point where it has become a cultural dominant.

Introduction

Within the sociology of religion recent studies have brought attention to the interplay between neoliberalism and religion (e.g., Gauthier and Martikainen 2013; Martikainen and Gauthier 2013; Moberg 2016; Usunier and Stolz 2014). This field of inquiry is necessary in order to avoid preconceptions regarding how wider economic and societal changes influence religion (Gauthier and Martikainen 2013, 24). The Finnish sociologist of religion, Marcus Moberg, has previously studied how neoliberal ideology, in the form of a marketization discourse, is a part of the contemporary Nordic Folk Churches. Hence, Moberg raises an important question which outlines future research:

> [I]t is worth asking whether it is now possible to identify the establishment and perpetuation of a new 'cultural dominant' (i.e., marketization discourse) that is beginning to have an increasingly formative effect on the very character of church life, organization, and practices on the whole. (Moberg 2016, 255)

I will not presume that this article can provide a definite answer, but it may contribute with a small piece in a very large puzzle. In his analysis, Moberg draws upon theory of critical discourse analysis as put forth by the British linguist, Norman Fairclough. While the method of critical discourse analysis is applicable to the sources presented in this article, it is not, as

THE MARKETIZATION OF RELIGION   115

such, an ideal example of Critical Discourse Analysis. This would require establishing the orders of discourse associated with each text analyzed, which for reason of brevity, is not possible.[1] However, I will highlight changes outside and inside the Evangelical Lutheran Church in Denmark. By accentuating changes it is possible to pinpoint the establishment of a new 'cultural dominant', and in doing so, continuing a long-held tradition within the field of sociology going back to the French sociologist, Emilie Durkheim.

In Durkheim's 'Les Règles de la Méthode Sociologique' from 1895, the founder of French sociology proposed that sociology is the study of social facts, defined as the following:

> A social fact is any way of acting, whether fixed or not, capable of exerting over the individual an external constraint; or: which is general over the whole of a given society whilst having an existence of its own, independent of its individual manifestations. (Durkheim 1982, 59)

The definition has been criticized for being overly focused on the external limits placed on individuals in society, thereby overlooking that every structure also enables certain modes of agency (Giddens 1984, 169). This critique should not be ignored, but taken into account. Structural restrains are never just that, they are also opportunities for certain modes of action and thought. However, with due care taken, and attention given to theoretical developments such as critical discourse analysis, this should not deter the continuous sociological inquiry into the varied structures that play a part in defining the everyday world of religious institutions.

In this article, I will give an account on how the Evangelical Lutheran Church in Denmark has come under pressure to change not of its own accord, but because of wider societal changes linked to the rise of neoliberalism. By identifying the agents involved, both individuals and institutions, it becomes possible to track the increasing presence of marketization discourse inside and outside of the Church.

The analysis is presented in two sections. I will show how local government reforms have affected the Church, and I will illustrate the gradual impact of marketization by analyzing sources from the Ministry of Ecclesiastical Affairs and the Diocese of Copenhagen. The chosen sources are from the 1970s, the 1990s and the 2000s with that in common, that they are all linked to the overall theme of church closures in Copenhagen.

Before the analysis, I will briefly outline the introduction of neoliberalism in Denmark and the link to New Public Management. Establishing a connection between the political ideology and public management is helpful, as it provides the tools necessary for pinpointing instances of marketization discourse.

Neoliberalism and new public management

In the 1970s, a number of OECD member states experienced a decline in economic growth, high unemployment and inflation partly as a consequence of rising oil prices (Boston 2011, 19). The political discourse of neoliberalism presented a new way forward. The solution to the financial problems was an austere fiscal policy and a reduction of the public sector through cutbacks, privatization and increased competition:

> [S]tate enterprises should be privatized; commercial and non-commercial activities should be separated, while the former subject to normal market disciplines; wherever feasible and

---

[1]Fairclough defines an order of discourse for a social domain or institution as: 'the totality of its discursive practices, and the relationships (of complementarity, inclusion/exclusion, opposition) between them' (Fairclough 1993, 135).

appropriate, public agencies should be subject to competitive pressures and responsive to customer preferences. (Boston 2011, 19)

In the quote, the political scientist, Jonathan Boston, describes the strategies prompted by neoliberal ideology. These strategies changed public administration and would later be linked with the term New Public Management (Boston 2011, 19). This enables us to infer that New Public Management is an operationalization of the neoliberal ideology seen in the 1980s and 1990s (Boston 2011, 17–18; McChesney 1998, 7).

The early stages of marketization and New Public Management within the Danish public sector began with a modernization reform launched by the Ministry of finance in 1983 (Hansen 2011, 116; Knudsen 2007, 257; Pedersen 2011, 211). The main elements introduced by the reform was an emphasis on decentralization, increasing consumer choices, revising funding mechanisms, improving customer service, human resource development and a better utilization of new technology (Finansministeriet 1983).

The concept of New Public Management was coined by the political scientist, Christopher Hood in 1989. In the late 1970s and the 1980s, Hood had observed a change in public administration:

Thatcher in the United Kingdom [...] have done for public administration what the Luftwaffe and the RAF did for British and German town planning in the 1940s – that is, provided the conditions for a drastic rethink. (Hood 1989, 346)

By associating the change with the conservative prime minister in Britain, Margaret Thatcher, a leading political figure promoting neoliberal policies, Hood created a link between a political ideology and the everyday management of the public sector (Peck and Tickell 2007, 28–29).

In his attempt to define common features of the new management Hood outlined seven doctrinal components:

(1) Hands on professional management.
(2) Explicit standards and measures of performance.
(3) Greater emphasis on output controls.
(4) Shift to disaggregation of units in the public sector.
(5) Shift to greater competition in the public sector.
(6) Stress on private-sector styles of management practice.
(7) Stress on greater discipline and parsimony in resource use (Hood 1991, 4–5).

According to Hood, not all the doctrinal components are used in every case. It should be regarded as a political tool box, subject to changes from country to country. However, this strengthens the argument, that New Public Management is a general term for management tools used to promote marketization of the public administration. The seven components will be used in the second part of the analysis dealing with church closures, but the first analysis will highlight the changing relationship between the Danish Evangelical-Lutheran Church and the local governments.

The local government reform in 1970

On 1 April 1970, the largest local government reform in Denmark was implemented. Until then Denmark had consisted of approximately 1300 municipalities and 86 boroughs divided into 25 counties. The reform brought an end to the division between municipalities and boroughs, reducing the number of municipalities to 277 and the counties to 14. Initially, the municipalities shared their geographical boundaries with the parishes, but the reform changed the geographical overlap between the municipalities and the parishes (Christoffersen 1998, 177). This was a watershed moment for the Evangelical Lutheran Church in Denmark. The municipal layout was built on the parish structure, ensuring that the basic religious and secular administrative units were a geographical mirror image of each other up until the reform.[2] As such, the reform was not only a remodeling of the local governments but also instead a clear indicator of the changing relationship between the religious and the secular spheres.

Leading up to the reform in 1970, the Ministry of the Interior established a commission in 1958 tasked with presenting recommendations regarding the new structure for the municipalities and a new municipal administration act (Indenrigsministeriet 1966, 1). In 1964, the Ministry of Ecclesiastical Affairs established a commission, whose tasks were defined as following:

> Considering, whether in tune with the rapidly changing structure of society, there would be grounds for carrying out certain changes regarding the ecclesiastical domain, and if so, in that case put forward suggestions about this. (Kirkeministeriet 1971, 11)

The commission set down by the Ministry of Ecclesiastical Affairs was given explicit instructions to follow and coordinate with proposals put forth by the municipal commission, and to work towards ecclesiastical structures with larger administrative units than the current parishes (Kirkeministeriet 1971, 13). In short, the proposed solutions should correspond to the changes happening in the municipal structure. The secretary of the Ecclesiastical commission, the Danish sociologist of religion, Per Salomonsen, confirmed this by stating that the main reason for the ecclesiastical commission was the municipal restructuring (Reeh 2001,187–189). From this perspective, the cause for change was not grounded within the religious domain, but a response to a political vision initiated within a very different domain. The Canadian sociologist of Religion, Francois Gauthier, has proposed that the change from a 'National-Statist to a Global-Market regime of religion' plays a major role in the changing religious landscape (Gauthier, forthcoming). In the case of the Ecclesiastical commission, the Church is required to change along with the needs of the state and the population, which indicates that this was a time where the National-Statist regime was still the defining context.

The Ecclesiastical commission proposed that a new larger administrative unit should replace the existing parish structure and be named deaneries. Deaneries where already present in the structure of the Church, but these entities should correspond geographically with the municipal structure implemented in 1970, and be given new powers and responsibilities (Kirkeministeriet 1971, 104). However, the recommendation regarding a restructuring was not implemented. At the time the Minister of Ecclesiastical Affairs, Arne Fog Pedersen, from liberal party, Venstre, forming the government at the time, were against any reform of the parish structure or the Church in general and the lack of support was also widespread in the Christian community (Reeh 2001, 170, 2012,17). Some of the

---

[2]There were minor exceptions to the overlap between the parishes and the municipalities, mainly in the larger cities such as Copenhagen which included a large number of parishes within the geographical boundary of the municipality.

commission's recommendations set the agenda for the Church's future development, including the introduction of parish assistants, part-time and special priests and the establishment of the Council on International Relations of the Evangelical Lutheran Church in Denmark (Reeh 2012, 18).

From the perspective of critical discourse analysis, the promotion of a new administrative unit was a discursive practice. In the struggle for relative hegemony within the larger political and churchly domains, the restructuring discourse failed to bring about real change. The reason given for a reshuffling of the bureaucracy mainly has to do with efficiency, even though this is often a part of a marketization discourse, the notion of a market, competition, output controls and so on are lacking in the report. This efficiency is meant within a bureaucratic framework, i.e., delivery of services to the population, not in terms of cost-effectiveness. Interpreting the recommendations as a clear example of a marketization discourse would be a mistake.

The local government reform in 2007

The political pressure on the Church to remodel its parish structure to reflect the municipal system did not disappear after 1970. Instead the request was reintroduced in 2005, in the exact same way as the first time, in connection with a reform of the local governments. The plans for the reform was made public in 2005 and implemented in 2007, resulting in the creation of 98 municipalities covering the whole of Denmark.

The Minister of Ecclesiastical Affairs, Bertel Haarder, from the liberal party, Venstre, saw the municipal reform as way for the Church to address the exact same issues, at the ones seen in 1970:

> The municipal reform is a good opportunity for the Evangelical Lutheran Church to consider its structure and organization. Obviously, changes in the structure or organization should not be made just for the sake of the changes themselves. Neither should changes be made simply because the municipal boundaries are being changed.
>
> But by adjusting the boundaries of the deaneries to correspond with the new municipal boundaries, the deaneries will be similar to the area where the members of the Evangelical Lutheran Church with their church tax pays for the costs of churches, cemeteries and so on. When you also review and possibly adjust tasks delegated to the dean and the deanery council, among other things tasks relating to the parish councils in each parish, then the structure and the organization of the Evangelical Lutheran Church can hopefully be even better than today in supporting the Church's main mission: to preach the Gospel. (Kirkeministeriet 2005)

The quoted passage above is from a press release by the Ministry of Ecclesiastical Affairs announcing a new task force who had been given the task of proposing a new structure and organization for the Church.

The task force recommended that the boundaries of the deaneries should be realigned to match the new municipalities and this time the politicians adopted the proposal into law (Kirkeministeriet 2007). Where the reform in 1970 dissolved the geographical overlap between the municipalities and the parishes, the reform of 2007 reconstructed a spatial alignment between religious and secular administrative entities, but this time between municipalities and deaneries. This is an example of how a restructuring discourse identified in 1971 was rearticulated by the Ministry of Ecclesiatical Affairs in 2005, and

THE MARKETIZATION OF RELIGION 119

how the influence of the discourse has gained enough momentum within the Danish Parliament to enforce a change. Having shown how the restructuring discourse has been actualized in 2007 the focus will now shift to the case of church closures in Copenhagen and the emergence of a marketization discourse.

The marketization of church closures

According to a memo from the Ministry of Ecclesiastical Affairs, fourteen parish churches were closed since the founding of the Evangelical Lutheran Church in 1849.[3] Today nine are used for secular activities, while five are used for religious purposes (Rasmussen and Warburg 2016). In the same period, a total of 571 new churches have been built, bringing the total number of churches to 2340 (Danmarks Statistik 2016, 171). Since the year 2000, eight churches have closed and ten have been built, making it quite clear, that closing a church is a rare occurrence. However, debates on closures have been on-going, and the importance of these debates by far exceeds the relative small number of actual church closures. Disregarding the importance of closures because of their rareness would result in overlooking the question a stake: Is marketization a contributing factor to the latest church closures in the Diocese of Copenhagen?

In 1976, a ministerial task force was appointed to scrutinize the status of the Church in Copenhagen and the report from 1979 by the task force painted a bleak picture of the situation. A growing proportion of the population was leaving the city, instead moving into the surrounding municipalities. This left a larger proportion of students and elderly in the city which affected the income from church taxes negatively. Baptisms were also in decline, partly caused by the change in demography, but also because the remaining Copenhageners were actively opting out of baptizing their children (Kirkeministeriet 1979, 2). Three areas were highlighted as especially challenging for the future: declining membership, due to depopulation and migration, maintenance of church buildings and finally, salaries (5). In order to deal with these challenges the church had to accommodate itself to the new environment.

In the report, the authors make use of, what would later be known as, New Public Management components, when discussing the changes needed. They advocated a need for professional management, more flexibility in employment and a continuous focus on savings. In addition to these recommendations, they pointed out, that a closure of eight churches in Copenhagen would create the greatest savings (14). However, after a discussion with the affected parish councils, they recommended merging the eight small parishes into larger parishes, thereby creating larger administrative units. A restructuring would allow for the eight churches to remain open, but under different circumstances. It was suggest, that seven of the eight churches should no longer have their own parish council or church register. A general reduction in clerks, deacons, organists and choir amounting to 26 positions was also proposed suggested. No priests would be made redundant by this, but 14 unoccupied positions would be discontinued (25). The parish councils agreed that a reduction in staff excluding the priests was an option, but they were opposed to any changes regarding the parish councils or church registers. Instead they recommended that the church tax

---

[3]The year marked the transition from absolutism to constitutional monarchy. The constitution establishes the state church from the absolutist era as the Evangelical Lutheran Church of Denmark.

should be raised and the state should pay the costs of restoring and maintaining the historical churches. It underlines the difference of opinion between the appointed task force and the parish councils, whereas the first makes use of arguments drawing upon a marketization discourse, while the latter sees more state funding as a viable solution.

Towards the church as a religious business

In 1996, the Bishop of Copenhagen, Erik Norman Svendsen established a think tank with a specific task. They had to present proposals for a more effective structure and 'a better use of available resources for church services, teaching and diaconal work' in the Diocese of Copenhagen (Tænketanken 1997, 2). The think tank released two reports, the first in 1997 and the last in 1998. The reports are interconnected and draw heavily on the discourse of marketization. In the report from 1997, the authors are concerned with defining the religious needs of the population of Copenhagen. Implicitly, the church is represented as a supplier of religious goods with one key question: Who are our members, and what do they want? They tried to give an answer by dividing the population into five categories: The Close Congregation, the Distant Congregation, the Searching Congregation, the Caring Congregation and the Non-Congregation. Each congregation was then assigned different attributes regarding their religious needs which are subdivided into ten separate dimensions: Preaching , pastoral care, community, experience , redemption, structural circumstances, the church's voice, church dogma, the church's teaching and Christianity at home (10). The result was five categories that define the wants and needs of both members and potential members. What is even more striking is the fact, that the church described how the needs were being fulfilled at the moment and what was lacking.

In the report from 1998, there is a focus on the supply-chain and how structural reforms might help to better the services provided. Professional personnel administration, a merger of parishes, a strengthening of the deanery and more private-sector management practices are asked for. When the report describes the situation in the Church it does so by borrowing concepts from the private sector:

> [A] significant part of the problems in the life of the Church can be traced to an unclear organizational and management structure and not least a rigid and inappropriate personnel structure that counteracts progress and innovation in the Diocese. (Tænketanken 1998, 6)

If the words *Church* and *Diocese* was removed from the quote above, one would be hard pressed to identify the organization in question as the Evangelical Lutheran Church in Denmark. This is not a coincidence, but a strategy used repeatedly in the report. The church is framed as a counter-image to private-sector styles of management and structure:

> On paper, the parish councils have a lot of power, but it is rarely used to any great extent. This results in major untapped opportunities and resources. Better cooperation could help increase everyone's well-being and influence. No other business would tolerate that degree of failure to analyse and acknowledge problems that is characteristic of the church in the city. (Tænketanken 1998, 7)

The church is portrayed as the antithesis of an effective business, but is, at the same time also framed as a business. By doing so, the discourse of marketization is integrated into the representation of the church, making it inherently clear to the reader, that the church is, in fact, a religious business, but a business nonetheless.

THE MARKETIZATION OF RELIGION 121

The possibility of church closures is only mentioned briefly in the last report in relation to the issue of parish mergers. When a parish becomes too small in numerical terms it should be merged with a neighboring parish and in that case a church might be closed, but this is not discussed in depth (Tænketanken, 14). Instead of closing churches, the report discussed the possibility of strengthening the collaboration between the parishes, thereby pooling resources, both economic and human. This would make it possible to give a number of churches a special profile, oriented towards attracting students or migrant congregations (15). Again, this is an indication of marketization, since the idea seems to be, that the church should differentiate its output in the hopes of attracting new members or more active existing members, instead of supplying the same services everywhere to everyone.

The Diocese council

The interrelation between text and context is crucial when assessing the impact of marketization. Fairclough makes a distinction between discourse as the text itself and the discursive practice of producing, distributing and reading the text. He also includes the social practice which simultaneously is influencing and being influenced by the written discourse (Fairclough 1992, 73). By analyzing minutes from the Diocese council in Copenhagen, it becomes apparent, that the interplay between the discourse of marketization and the social practice, instituted by the new council, was crucial in developing an organizational structure that could maintain and extend the push for church closures.

In 2003, the Bishop, Erik Norman Svendsen, decided that the time had come to establish a Diocese council. This organizational innovation was made possible by a ministerial dispensation from the legislation governing the Diocese committees (Kirkeministeriet 2012, 3). The Bishop reasoned that he needed a stronger democratic mandate in the discussion regarding the structure of the Church in Copenhagen (Kirkeministeriet 2008, 32). When the council convened for the first time in 2005 it consisted of 21 members: 11 lay members chosen from the parish councils, 1 from each deanery in the Diocese; 5 priests; 3 deans, 1 of which was the dean of Vor Frue Kirke, the Copenhagen cathedral; a representative from the state administration and finally the Bishop.[4] The analysis of the agenda and minutes from the first council meeting on 2 May 2005 shows that the Bishop, in his address to rest of the council, rearticulated the central argument from the reports made by the Think Tank in 1997 and 1998. Erik Norman Svendsen insisted on the need to restructure the parishes, churches and positions, as well as the likelihood of church closures due to the decline in church membership and the need for more effective economic management (Københavns Stiftsråd 2005). The main difference between the reports from the late 1990s and the Bishop's address in 2005 is not the arguments themselves, but the context, the social practice, in which the discourse is situated. The relationship between text and context changed with the establishment of the Diocese council. With the endorsement from the rest of the council, the restructuring agenda was no longer solely a project linked to the Bishop: it became a larger agenda supported by a new churchly institution with a democratic mandate.

---

[4]The size of the council has changed over time, partly due to the merger of deaneries in Copenhagen and the fact that the state representative no longer has a seat in the council. In 2017, the council consisted of 15 members: 9 lay members; 3 priests, 2 deans, 1 being the dean of Vor Frue Kirke and the bishop.

In a proposal to the Ministry in 2008, the Diocese council recommended a large-scale restructuring. A total of 24 parishes would be affected by parish mergers, making ten parish churches redundant (Københavns Stiftsråd 2008a).[5] In the proposal, it is stated that while the council advises that ten churches should be taken out of use as parish churches, it would be up to the local parish councils to consider in what capacity the churches should be used in the future (Københavns Stiftsråd 2008a, 2). The Minister of Ecclesiastical Affairs, Birthe Rønn Hornbech, from the liberal party, Venstre, were not sympathetic to the idea of a restructuring resulting in a downsizing of parish churches and that part of the proposal was rejected, while a number of mergers were approved (Københavns Stiftsråd 2009). This resulted in a partly implemented strategy, where the Church was allowed to reorganize the administrative structure on a micro level, by creating larger parishes. From a marketization point of view, heralded by the council, this would enable the Church to be more effective by cutting down on administration and free up resources for religious activities. However, since all churches had to continue operating as they were, the cost-cutting was limited.

Shortly after the proposal fell through, Erik Norman Svendsen announced his resignation and Peter Skov-Jakobsen succeeded him on 1 September 2009 (Københavns Stiftsråd 2008b). The new Bishop had been a member of the Diocese council since its inception in 2005 and the council continued to follow through with a policy that advocated the need for church closures in the name of economic necessity. This indicates that the discourse of marketization was not limited to the former bishop, but had been adopted by the council and the successor.

As a last example of the discourse of marketization, I will focus on the report titled 'Analysis of data from the Evangelical Lutheran Church' commissioned by the Diocese council in 2011. The purpose was to present all available data on the churches in Copenhagen in such a way that a direct comparison between the parishes became possible. The report was written by a Copenhagen-based company specializing in organizational and societal analysis. In the preface, the authors establishes the importance of the work:

> This data material is unique, for the first time, it enables us to gain an overall view of the church statistics in the Diocese of Copenhagen, but also because it allows for the study of the ecclesiastical activities in relation to the accounting figures for all parishes in the Diocese. (Rådgivende Sociologer 2011, 3)

The report lists a number of variables from 2006 to 2010, namely, finances, the number of church services held, baptisms, confirmation, weddings, funerals, as well as changes in church membership in each of the parishes. On the basis of this, the authors constructed indexes such as 'Church Life' (Rådgivende sociologer 2011, 24). The authors note that they do not distinguish between the different forms of church activities and their importance when determining whether a parish is experiencing a decline or increase in 'Church Life'.

---

[5]The proposal lists the suggested changes regarding each deanery, all of which are effected by parish mergers. In addition, the following deaneries are advised to consider closing a number of parish churches. Vesterbro: four parishes should be merged and Absalons, Gethsemane and Bavnehøj church should no longer be used as parish churches. In Bispebjerg-Brønshøj, two parishes should be merged making Ansgar church redundant. Holmens deanery should merge two parishes and find other uses for Sankt Pauls church. Vor Frue deanery should merge two parishes and no longer use Sankt Andreas and Fredens Kirke as parish churches. After merging three parishes Nørrebro deanery is advised to finder other uses for Samuels church and Brorsons or Blågårds Church. The deanery of Østerbro is advised to merge three parishes and close Luther Church.

THE MARKETIZATION OF RELIGION

Nor do they wish to take a stance on the necessity of adjustments in the parish structure (2011, 11). While this adheres to the German sociologist Max Weber's ideals of objectivity in the social sciences, the methodological and analytical approach presented in the report made way for the discourse of marketization (Weber 1904, 25). It created a situation where religious institutions were in direct competition for religious customers, with key indicators for efficiency being assessed, combined with the risk of closure. This resulted in a surrogate market that aligns well with Hood's second and fifth components in the definition of New Public Management, namely: 'explicit standards and measures of performance' and 'shift to greater competition in the public sector'.

The chairman of the council since 2005, Inge Lise Pedersen, does not attribute the report any special significance in the selection process. It merely substantiated the view that was already held by the council.[6] However, there are differing opinions outside the council. When interviewing members from parish councils involved in the process there is a wide consensus that the data collection and the use of it, as seen in the report, instigated a new social practice within the Diocese.[7] Informants both from parishes that experienced closures and those that did not, explained that the truthful reporting of church attendance were a challenge when everyone knew what was at stake. Obvious exaggerations were out of the question, but in some instances adjustments were made where it was possible. This also created a situation, where parish council members began visiting other churches for Sunday service in order to check up on the competition. The parishes knew they were being judged in relation to their peers and were, as such, in a state of competition.

In 2012, after the report was made publicly available, the Bishop initially recommended that 17 churches should be closed. After repeated discussion in the Diocese this was later revised to 14 in 2013 (Skov-Jacobsen 2013a, 2013b, 2013c, 2013d, 2013e, 2013f, 2013g, 2013h, 2013i, 2013j, 2013k, 2013l, 2013m, 2013n). Later in the same year, the Ministry of Culture, Marianne Jelved, from the liberal party, Radikale Venstre, approved the closure of six parish churches in larger parishes with multiple churches. The main reason that more closures were not approved was due to the threat of legal actions from a number of the parishes. The parish councils argued that the Ministry was acting in direct violation of the legislation, but court proceedings were avoided by staying clear of the troublesome parishes (Rasmussen, forthcoming; Rasmussen and Warburg 2016, 46).[8]

Conclusion

I have examined how the Evangelical Lutheran Church in Copenhagen has been under long-lasting political pressure to reorganize the Church structure and close churches. The discourse of marketization has played an increasingly prominent and visible role. By looking at the municipality reforms in 1970 and 2007, it was evident that the discourse of marketization was largely absent from the debate in the 1970s. While there were

---

[6]Interview with Inge Lise Pedersen on 4 July 2017.

[7]Four group interviews with four or more participants and eight individual interviews were conducted between March 2015 and April 2017. Since the field of study is rather small total anonymity was given to all informants.

[8]The decision was handed to the Minister of Culture, since the Minister of Ecclesiastical Affairs, Manu Sareen, from the same party, had declared himself unfit to make the decision. In 2012, Sareen had remarked that he was inclined to follow the recommendations from the Diocese, this led to accusations from the opposition that the minister was biased (Kirkeministeriet 2013).

arguments that drew upon components that would later be understood as New Public Management, they were not able to enforce change on a structural level resulting in the closure of churches. This changed quite significantly with the latest municipality reform in 2007, in which a national reorganization of municipalities and deaneries were implemented with arguments drawing heavily on marketization discourse. Turning to the analysis regarding the Diocese of Copenhagen and the decision to close six churches in 2013, I have argued that New Public Management and marketization discourse is used in the arguments put forth by the Diocese council and that the parish councils operate within a field under the influence of that very discourse. The discourse of marketization is by no means the only discourse influencing the social practice within the Diocese of Copenhagen, but it holds an increasingly influential position which, for the time being, seems to be accepted, reluctantly or willingly depending on the position in the field. Certain rituals have undergone change on a local scale due to the stress of performance measurements and direct competition, the question remains how far the changes will go and in what direction. However, it seems safe to say, that the notion of marketization as something apart from the Diocese of Copenhagen must be rejected. It is embedded within the governing structures on multiple levels and has become a cultural dominant where proponents and opponents alike acknowledge the new state of affairs. Whether this holds true for the Evangelical Lutheran Church on a national level remains to be examined.

Disclosure statement

No potential conflict of interest was reported by the author.

References

Boston, J. 2011. "Basic NPM Ideas and their Development." In *The Ashgate Research Companion to New Public Management*, edited by T. Christensen and P. Lægreid, 17–32. Farnham: Ashgate.
Christoffersen, L. 1998. *Kirkeret mellem stat, marked og civilsamfund*. København: Jurist- og Økonomforbundets Forlag.
Danmarks Statistik. 2016. *Statistisk årbog 2016*. København: Danmarks Statistik.
Durkheim, E. 1982. *The Rules of the Sociological Method*. New York: Free Press.
Fairclough, N. 1992. *Discourse and Social Change*. Cambridge: Polity Press.
Fairclough, N. 1993. "Critical Discourse Analysis and the Marketization of Public Discourse: The Universities." *Discourse & Society* 4: 133–168.
Finansministeriet. 1983. *Redegørelse til folketinget om regeringens program for modernisering af den offentlige sektor*. København: Finansministeriet.
Gauthier, F. Forthcoming. "From Nation-State to Market. The Transformations of Religion in the Global Era, as Illustrated by Islam." *Religion* 48 (3): 382–417. doi:10.1080/0048721X.2018. 1482615
Gauthier, F., and T. Martikainen, eds. 2013. *Religion in Consumer Society*. Farnham: Ashgate.
Giddens, A. 1984. *The Constitution of Society*. Cambridge: Polity Press.
Hansen, H. F. 2011. "NPM in Scandinavia." In *The Ashgate Research Companion to New Public Management*, edited by T. Christensen and P. Lægreid, 113–130. Farnham: Ashgate.

Hood, C. 1989. "Public Administration and Public Policy: Intellectual Challenges for the 1990s." *Australian Journal of Public Administration* 48 (4): 346–358.

Hood, C. 1991. "A Public Management for All Seasons." *Public Administration* 69 (1): 3–19.

Indenrigsministeriet. 1966. *Kommuner og kommunestyre: Betænkning nr.420 af 17/5/1966.* København: Indenrigsministeriet.

Kirkeministeriet. 1971. *Folkekirken i det moderne samfund: Betænkning nr.610 af 3/3/1971.* København: Kirkeministeriet.

Kirkeministeriet. 1979. *Indstilling fra arbejdsgruppe af 13. Maj 1976 angående de kirkelige forhold i København.* København: Kirkeministeriet.

Kirkeministeriet. 2005. *Arbejdsgruppe skal foreslå ændringer i folkekirkens inddeling efter kommunalreformen.* København: Kirkeministeriet.

Kirkeministeriet. 2007. *Bekendtgørelse om landets inddeling i stifter, provstier og sogne: BEK nr. 24 af 09/01/2007.* København: Kirkeministeriet.

Kirkeministeriet. 2008. *Betænkning 1495 Evaluering af forsøg med stiftsråd.* København: Kirkeministeriet.

Kirkeministeriet. 2012. *Rapport for evaluering af permanente stiftsråd.* København: Kirkeministeriet.

Kirkeministeriet. 2013. *Ansvaret for sager om kirkelukninger overføres fra ministeren for ligestilling og kirke til kulturministeren.* København: Kirkeministeriet.

Knudsen, T. 2007. *Fra folkestyre til markedsdemokrati: Dansk demokratihistorie efter 1973.* København: Akademisk Forlag.

Københavns Stiftsråd. 2005. "Referat af møde i stiftsrådet mandag den 2. maj 2005 kl. 16.30 – 20.00 i Trinitatis sognegård." Københavns Stift. Accessed April 2017. https://kirkenikbh.dk/om-stiftet/stiftsraad-og-udvalg/stiftsraadets-moedereferater.

Københavns Stiftsråd. 2009. "Referat af stiftsrådets møde den 2.februar 2009 i Helligåndshuset." Københavns Stift. Accessed April 2017. https://kirkenikbh.dk/om-stiftet/stiftsraad-og-udvalg/stiftsraadets-moedereferater.

Københavns Stiftsråd. 2008a. *Stiftsrådets forslag til sogne- og pastoratændringer i Københavns stift.* København/Copenhagen: Københavns Stift.

Københavns Stiftsråd. 2008b. "Referat af stiftsrådets møde den 17. november 2008 i Helligåndshuset." Københavns Stift. Accessed April 2017. https://kirkenikbh.dk/om-stiftet/stiftsraad-og-udvalg/stiftsraadets-moedereferater.

Martikainen, T., and F. Gauthier, eds. 2013. *Religion in the Neoliberal Age.* Farnham: Ashgate.

McChesney, R. 1998. "Introduction." In *Profit over People: Neoliberalism and Global Order*, edited by N. Chomsky, 7–16. New York: Seven Stories Press.

Moberg, M. 2016. "Exploring the Spread of Marketization Discourse in the Nordic Folk Church Context." In *Making Religion: Theory and Practice in the Discursive Study of Religion*, edited by F. Wijsen and K. v. Stuckrad, 239–259. Leiden: Brill.

Peck, J., and A. Tickell. 2007. "Conceptualizing Neoliberalism, Thinking Thatcherism." In *Contesting Neoliberalism: Urban Frontiers*, edited by H. Leitner, P. Peck, and E. Sheppard, 26–50. New York: Guilford Press.

Pedersen, O. K. 2011. *Konkurrencestaten.* København: Hans Reitzels Forlag.

Rådgivende Sociologer. 2011. *Analyse af folkekirkedata. En analyse af data indsamlet vedrørende de københavnske folkekirker.* København: Københavns Stift.

Rasmussen, J. Forthcoming. "Fra folkekirke til konkurrencekirke." In *Religion i det offentlige rum*, edited by B. A. Jacobsen, S. A. E. Larsen, og H. R. Christensen. Aarhus: Aarhus Universitetsforlag.

Rasmussen, J., and M. Warburg. 2016. "Kirkelukninger og kulturarv." *Religion. Tidsskriftet for Religionslærerforeningen for Gymnasiet og HF* 2: 42–53.

Reeh, T. R. L. 2001. *Vorherre har været igennem EDB-anlægget, samfundsvidenskabernes indflydelse på kirkesynet i Danmark i anden halvdel af det 20. århundrede.* København/Copenhagen: Københavns Universitet.

Reeh, T. R. L. 2012. " … i pagt med tidens udvikling og den rivende ændring af samfundets struktur." *Dansk Teologisk Tidsskrift* 5 (1): 2–19.

Skov-Jacobsen, P. 2013a. *Indstilling til Ministeren for Ligestilling og Kirke vedrørende Sankt Pauls Kirke.* København: Københavns Stift.

Skov-Jacobsen, P. 2013b. *Indstilling til Ministeren for Ligestilling og Kirke vedrørende Tagensbo Kirke.* København: Københavns Stift.

Skov-Jacobsen, P. 2013c. *Indstilling til Ministeren for Ligestilling og Kirke vedrørende Ansgar Kirke.* København: Københavns Stift.

Skov-Jacobsen, P. 2013d. *Indstilling til Ministeren for Ligestilling og Kirke vedrørende Aalholm Kirke.* København: Københavns Stift.

Skov-Jacobsen, P. 2013e. *Indstilling til Ministeren for Ligestilling og Kirke vedrørende Sankt Lukas Kirke.* Københavns Stift.

Skov-Jacobsen, P. 2013f. *Indstilling til Ministeren for Ligestilling og Kirke vedrørende Solbjerg Kirke.* København: Københavns Stift.

Skov-Jacobsen, P. 2013g. *Indstilling til Ministeren for Ligestilling og Kirke vedrørende Samuel Kirke.* København: Københavns Stift.

Skov-Jacobsen, P. 2013h. *Indstilling til Ministeren for Ligestilling og Kirke vedrørende Blågårds Kirke.* København: Københavns Stift.

Skov-Jacobsen, P. 2013i. *Indstilling til Ministeren for Ligestilling og Kirke vedrørende Utterslev Kirke.* København: Københavns Stift.

Skov-Jacobsen, P. 2013j. *Indstilling til Ministeren for Ligestilling og Kirke vedrørende Bavnehøj Kirke.* København: Københavns Stift.

Skov-Jacobsen, P. 2013k. *Indstilling til Ministeren for Ligestilling og Kirke vedrørende Absalon Kirke.* København: Københavns Stift.

Skov-Jacobsen, P. 2013l. *Indstilling til Ministeren for Ligestilling og Kirke vedrørende Gethsemane Kirke.* København: Københavns Stift.

Skov-Jacobsen, P. 2013m. *Indstilling til Ministeren for Ligestilling og Kirke vedrørende Sankt Andreas Kirke.* København: Københavns Stift.

Skov-Jacobsen, P. 2013n. *Indstilling til Ministeren for Ligestilling og Kirke vedrørende Fredens Kirke.* København: Københavns Stift.

Tænketanken. 1997. *Delrapport fra tænketanken.* København: Københavns Stift.

Tænketanken. 1998. *Delrapport fra tænketanken.* København: Københavns Stift.

Usunier, J.-C., and J. Jörg Stolz, eds. 2014. *Religions as Brands: New Perspectives on the Marketization of Religion and Spirituality.* Farnham: Ashgate.

Weber, M. 1904. "Die 'Objektivität' sozialwissenschaftlicher und sozialpolitischer Erkenntnis." *Archiv für Sozialwissenschaft und Sozialpolitik* 19: 22–87.

Index

Note: *Italic* page numbers refer to figures and page numbers followed by "n" denote endnotes.

Addressing the Muslim Market (A.T. Kearney) 101
Advisory Commission on Religious Freedom 83
Advisory Council on Religious Diversity 88
'Analysis of data from the Evangelical Lutheran Church' 122
Antonsich, Marco 79
Aquila Asia 104
Astor, Avi 83
Atia, Mona 106

Barber, B. 97
Baudrillard, J. 103
Bauman, Zygmunt 41, 80
Bayat, Asef 47
Becker, Gary 24
Ben Ali 45
Berger, Peter 1, 23, 24, 26, 30
Berlin, Christmas fairs in 12–16
Beyer, Peter 32, 50
Boston, Jonathan 116
Bouchard-Taylor commission 86
Brand Islam (Shirazi) 28
Brands, Islam and the New Consumer 101
Brands of Faith (Einstein) 26, 64, 65
British religious market 67
Bruce, Steve 25
Burchardt, Marian 3n1, 4, 29

Caillé, Alain 31
Callon, Michel 68
Campaign magazine 103, 104
Canada: economic competitiveness 90; legal governmentality 81–82
capitalism 4, 24, 62, 77; consumer 29, 44, 45, 69, 96; ideology of global 80, 90, 97; Islam and 98, 99; of Keynesian political economy 59; transnational neoliberal 78, 82
capitalist economy 95, 97
Carrette, Jeremy 1, 28
Carrier, James G. 59
Casanova, José 41

'Catalanization' 87–88
Catalonia: to ban Islamic full-face veiling 85, 88; ethnographic fieldwork in 88; global capitalism 90; globalized capitalism 4; nation-building project 78–79, 89; religious diversity in 86, 89; secularism in 78
Catholicism 83, 89
Central Product Classification (CPC) 68
'Charter of Quebec Values' 78, 84, *87*
Charter of Secularism 84–86
Christmas fair, in Danish churches abroad 3, 11–12; Berlin 12–16; as congregational community venture 8, 9, 15–18; *Gemeinschaft* 18–19; legal and organisational position of 7–8; organisational embedment of 12–13; Paris 12, 13, 14n1, 15, 16; profitability of 8, 12, 14, 15, 18; resource mobilisation at 8–11, 13–15; South France 11–12, 15–17; valuation of 15–18; voluntary work 3, 12, 13; willingness-to-accept 16–17; willingness-to-pay 16
church closures, marketization of 3, 119; in Copenhagen 118–119; critical discourse analysis 114–115; Diocese council 121–123, 122n5; national-statist regime 33–34; New Public Management 115–116, 119, 123–124
Complementary and Alternative Medicine 62
'*conflit des deux France*' 34
consumer culture 40–41, 62
consumerism 4, 29, 30–32, 38–40, 42, 51, 60–61, 97
'consumers of religion' 69
consumer subjectivity 93–95, 108
consumption, anthropology of 27–28, 39
contemporary individualism 41
contemporary neoliberal political economy 94, 107, 108
contemporary religion 1, 31, 42, 61
Copenhagen: church closures in 115, 118–119; Diocese council 121–123, 122n5; Evangelical Lutheran Church in 115, 119, 119n3, 123, 124
CPC *see* Central Product Classification (CPC)

128 INDEX

critical discourse analysis 114–115, 118, 122
cultural diversity 77–80, 89
cultural political economy 94

Danish churches abroad, Christmas fair
    3, 11–12; as congregational community
    venture 8, 9, 15–18; *Gemeinschaft* 10, 11, 14,
    18–19; *Gesellschaft* 10–12, 14, 15; legal and
    organisational position of 7–8; organisational
    embedment of 12–13; resource mobilisation at
    8–11, 13–15; in South France 11, 12; Sunday
    mass 3; voluntary work 3, 12, 13; willingness-
    to-accept 16–17; willingness-to-pay 16
Danish emigrants 7
Danish Seamen's church 8, 18
Davie, Grace 66, 67
Davila, Arlene 102
deaneries 117, 118
deep rootedness concept 84
Deng Xiaoping 38
Denmark: Evangelical Lutheran Church in 115,
    117; local government reform in 116–119,
    117n2; neoliberalism in 115; Venstre 117, 118,
    122, 123
Dichter, Ernst 103
Dinar Standard 101, 105
Diocese council 121–123, 123n8, 124
Diocese of Copenhagen 115, 119, 120–124,
    121n4
discourse of marketization 120–124
discrimination laws and policies 79
diversity 89; governmentality of religious
    85, 86; migration-driven 78, 82, 84, 90;
    multiculturalism-type 79; political force of 79;
    see also cultural diversity; religious diversity
DKNY 104
Dolce & Gabbana 93, 104
Douglas, Mary 27, 51
Durkheim, Émile 10, 25, 51, 115

Ecclesiastical commission 117
economic liberalism 4, 38, 59
'economics of religion' 26, 51, 58, 67
economic theory: liberal 95; neoclassical 22–23,
    27, 30, 51, 94; promises and deceptions of
    24–27
economization 68–69
Einstein, Mara 26, 64, 65
Eisenstadt, Shmuel 34, 35
*Enquiry into the Nature and Causes of the Riches
    of Nations* (Smith) 38
Europe: Christian churches in 61; economic
    force in 89; global-market regime 40;
    multiculturalism 81; national-statist regime
    32–34; religious field in 64, 66, 67, 77n1
Evangelical Lutheran Church 115, 119, 119n3,
    123, 124

Fairclough, Norman 114, 115n1, 121
Featherstone, Mike 104
Florida, Richard 77
'Fordist' economy 59
Foucault, Michel 4, 80, 94; notion of
    governmentality 76, 80
Franco's rule 83
freedom of religion 82
free-market ideology 4, 29, 30, 38, 51

GATS *see* General Agreement on Trade
    Services (GATS)
Gauchet, Marcel 41
Gauthier, François 3, 3n1, 4, 60, 70, 94, 117
Gemeinschaft 3, 10, 11, 14, 18–19, 23, 26–28
Gemeinschaft and Gesellschaft (Tönnies) 10
General Agreement on Trade Services (GATS) 68
Generation M 106–107
*Generation M: Young Muslims Changing the
    World* (Janmohamed) 106
Gesellschaft 3, 10–12, 14, 15, 23, 27, 28
global capitalism 80, 90, 97
global-market regime 4, 37–40, 51; embedment
    in Human Rights 37; Europe 40; globalisation
    of 40–43; religion transformation in 43–44;
    secularisation paradigm 37–44
Global Muslim Lifestyle Travel Market (Dinar
    Standard) 101
governance: definition of 38; Muslim consumer
    subjectivity 100, 107
governmentality 38, 84, 89–90, 94, 107; Foucault's
    notion of 76, 80; of religious diversity 85, 86
guerres de religions 32

Haarder, Bertel 118
Hacking, Ian 81
Haenni, Patrick 44, 44n2, 45, 49
Hispanic market 101–102
H&M 93, 104
Homo oeconomicus 2
Hood, Christopher 116, 123
Hornbech, Birthe Rønn 122
Howell, Julia D. 36, 46, 47
human capital 77, 77n1
Hussain, Shahin 105

Imperial Encounters (Veer) 34
individualism 40–42
Indonesia, Islam in 36, 44n2, 45–46n3, 45–48
Iqtidar, Humeira 47
Iranian revolution 44, 45
Isherwood, Baron 27
Islam: as anti-Western force 98, 99; and economy
    93–94, 100; fundamentalism 97–98; global
    transformations of 4, 5; in Indonesia 36, 44n2,
    45–46n3, 45–48; key values 102; lifestyle
    magazines 104; market 93, 102; national-statist

INDEX

regime 36–37; neoliberal politicisation of 49; rise of market 44–49; Western view of 97
Islamic/halal economics 96, 98, 101
Islamic radicalism 37, 48
Islamisation project 36–37
Islamism 48, 96
Islamist social movements 100
Islamization of knowledge (Al-Faruqi) 98
'Islam Means Business: Meet the New Generation of Muslim Entrepreneurs' (Gale) 105
ISSR Conference 2, 3

Jafari, Aliakbar 3
Janmohamed, Shelina 106
Jelved, Marianne 123
Jihadism of ISIS 48
Jihad vs. McWorld (Barber) 97
John Walter Thompson 101

Kant (philosopher) 40
Katona, George 103
Kearney, A. T. 101
Keen, Steve 25, 51
Khaled, Amr 45, 46
Khan, Shazia 106
King, Richard 1, 28
knowledge economy 60, 77
Koch, Anne 3
Koenig, Matthias 37
Kuhn, Thomas S. 31
Kuran 99

Larzarsfeld, Paul 103
'Law on Centers of Worship' *[ley sobre los centros de culto]* 78
Lee, Wei-Na 62
legal governmentality: Canada 81–82
Legal governmentality: Spain 82–84
Lentin, Alana 79
'Les Règles de la Méthode Sociologique' (Durkheim) 115
Lewis, Reina 104
liberal economic theory 1, 4, 24, 95
liberal governance 94
Liquid modernity (Bauman) 41

Maclaren, Pauline 3
McCarthy, John 9
market and consumer society: religious change in 58–59; for religious field 66–67; for social life 63–66; *see also* religious market
market competition, in religious field 64
market economics 23–24
market exchange 28–29, 70, 94
'the Market Idea' 59–60, 71
'Market Islam' *(islam de marché)* 44, 44n2, 45, 48, 49

market segmentation 22–23, 101–103
market societies 3, 4; culture of 40; double-sided complex of 28–30; neoliberal 58, 76; religious change in 68
Marmor-Lavie, Galit 62
Martikainen, Tuomas 4, 94
Martineau, Pierre 103
Marx, K. 95
Matejskova, Tatiana 79
Mauss, Marcel 2, 33
methodological nationalism 31, 42–43, 49
migration-driven diversity 78, 82, 84, 90
Miller, Paul 94, 102
Millo, Yuval 68
Ministry of Ecclesiastical Affairs 117, 118
Ministry of the Interior 117
Moberg, Marcus 3, 3n1, 4, 114
modern Islamist movements 37, 47, 48
modernization 95, 97, 98
modern political form 33, 35
Muhammadiyah Islamist movement 36, 37, 47–48
multiculturalism 80; Europe 81; legal governmentality 81, 82; -type diversity 79–81, 90
'multiple modernities' (Eisenstadt) 34
'multiple secularities' 31, 34, 42, 49
Muniesa, Fabian 68
Muslim Association of Spain 83
Muslim consumers 93; economics 93–94; exclusion of 96–99; identification of 99–103; immigration 100–101; marginalization of 97; market 95–96; as modern consumers 4, 95; sociological approaches 95–96; stylization of 103–107; subjectivity 93–95, 108; Traditionalists *vs.* Futurists 106; and Western consumer culture 97–99, 103
'Muslim millennials' 106

Nasr, Vali 104
National Catholicism 83
national-statist regime 3, 4, 32; Churches 33–34; embedment of society in 32–34, 37, 50; Europe 32–34; globalisation of 34–35, 34n1; Indonesian Islam 36, 45–46n3, 45–48; Islam 36–37; religion transformation in 35–36; secularisation paradigm 30, 32, 34
Nelson, Robert H. 25
neoclassical economic theory 2, 4, 23, 25–27, 30, 51, 95
neoliberal globalization 96, 99; *see also* pious neoliberalism
neoliberal ideology 59–60, 114, 116
neoliberalism 4, 29, 30, 38–39, 49, 77, 78, 90, 115–116
neoliberal political economy 94, 107, 108
neo-nationalist movements 43

New Age spirituality 45–47
'the New Muslim Consumer' 101
New Public Management (NPM) 5, 115–116, 119, 123–124
Nietzsche (philosopher) 40
Njoto-Feillard, Gwenaël 46, 47

Ogilvy and Mather 101
Ogilvy Noor 101, 106
Olave, Angélica Thumala 106
open market system 63
'open secularism' 83
Orientalism (Said) 97
Orientalism, Postmodernism and Globalism (Turner) 97
Oscar de la Renta 104

Paris, Christmas fairs in 12, 13, 14n1, 15, 16
parish councils 119–124, 122n5
parish mergers 121, 122, 122n5
Parsons, Talcott 10
Parti Quebecois (PQ) 78, 85
Passas, Nikos 61
Peace of Westphalia 32
Pedersen, Arne Fog 117
Pedersen, Inge Lise 123
Pentecostalism 37, 42, 94
pious neoliberalism 106
Polanyi, Karl 29
Possamai, Adam 3
'post-Westphalian' 50
PQ *see* Parti Quebecois (PQ)
'private firms' 2
Prophet Mohammed 43, 45
psychological sciences 94

Quebec: ban religious symbols in 86; 'Charter of Quebec Values' 78, 84, *87*; Charter of Secularism in 84–86; globalized capitalism 4; nationalism 85; religious diversity in 86; secularism part of 78, 85
Quranic injunctions 98

Rasmussen, Jes Heise 3n1, 5, 29
Rational Choice Theory (RCT) 1, 2, 4, 24–26, 51, 61, 95
RCT *see* Rational Choice Theory (RCT)
Reagan, Ronald 38
reasonable accommodation 85, 86
Redwan-Beer, Lian Rosnita 104
regional government 87
're-islamisation' 4
religion: consumerism on 4; ideational dimensions of 69–70; legal governmentality of 81–84; marketization of 22–24, 50, 51, 69–71; in market regime 44 (*see also* global-market regime; national-statist regime); modernisation of 33–35, 70; neoliberalism on 4, 29, 30, 38–39, 49,

77, 78, 90, 115–116; neo-nationalist movements 43; notions of 2, 77; political activism 47, 83; as social spheres 22, 28 (*see also* social spheres); sociological study of 58; sociology of 9, 25, 49, 71, 77, 114; state regulation of 39; transformation 26, 29–31, 35–36, 43–44; visibility 29–31, 43, 44, 46, 48, 99, 107; Western-centric sociology of 71; in Western countries 35 (*see also* Western countries); in Western immigrant societies 77, 78
religious business, church as 120–121
religious change: consumerism 5; neoliberalism 5
religious consumers 65, 68–69
religious diversity 76, 80–81; contemporary regimes of 80; cultural difference 77–80, 89; globalization pressures 78; governmentality of 85, 86; political and cultural pressures 78; political force of 79; promotion of 87–90; in Quebec 86; reasonable accommodation 85, 86; recognition of 77n1; in sociology of religion 77
'Religious Diversity in Open Societies: Criteria for Decision-Making' 88
religious economy 64, 69
religious identities 79
religious institutions 31, 37, 39, 43, 123
religious market 63, 68–69, 95, 107; as de facto empirical entity 63–66
religious products 68–69
resource mobilisation, Danish churches: activities 8–11, 14–15; in quantitative terms 13–15
Reuter, Thomson 101
Rinallo, Diego 3
Rise of the Affluent Muslim Traveler (Akhtar) 105
Rodatz, Mathias 79
Roof, Wade Clark 1, 24, 30, 64, 65
Rosanvallon, Pierre 38
Rose, Nicholas 94, 102
Rudnyckyj, Daromir 44n2, 46

The Sacred Canopy (Berger) 23, 24
Said, E. 97
Salomonsen, Per 117
Sandikci, Özlem 3, 3n1, 4
Sareen, Manu 123n8
Scott, Linda 3
secularisation paradigm 24, 30–32, 46n3, 49; global-market regime 37–44; national-statist regime 30, 32, 34 (*see also* national-statist regime)
secularism 78; in Catalonia 78; of Quebec 78, 85; *see also* Charter of Secularism; 'open secularism'
Sennett, Richard 60
Shirazi, Faegheh 28
Shogren, J. F. 17
'sincerity of belief 82, 84
Singapore, Danish Seamen's church in 8, 18
Skov-Jakobsen, Peter 122

INDEX

Slater, Don 59
Smith, Adam 38
social spheres 22, 33, 70, 95; de-differentiation of 41, 42; differentiation of 31, 41, 43, 50; interpenetration of 30; religion as 28
socio-cultural construction: marketing in 94, 96, 107
South France, Christmas fairs in 11, 12, 15–17
Spain: economic competitiveness 78–79; economic crisis 88; legal governmentality 82–84
Spanish bureaucracies 84
Spanish Constitution of 1978 82–83
Spiritual Marketplace (Roof) 64
State of the Global Islamic Economy (Reuter) 101
Stolz, Jörg 3, 26
Stout, Patricia A. 62
Sufism 46–47
Suharto 46, 47
Sukarno 36, 47
Sunday services 8, 9, 13, 16, 18, 123
Supply-Side economics 63–64, 69
Svendsen, Erik Norman 120–122

Taira, Teemu 62
tasawwuf 46
Taylor, Charles 40
Thatcher, Margaret 38, 116
Thrift, Nigel 70
Titley, Gavan 79
Tommy Hilfiger 93, 104
Tonkiss, Fran 59
Tönnies, Ferdinand 10, 23
traditional religion 32, 35, 38, 95
Treaty of Westphalia (1648) 32
Trentmann, Frank 69
Turkey, Islamic groups in 100
Turner, B. 97

Ulama 46
Understanding the Islamic Consumer 101
Uniqlo 93, 104

United Kingdom, Muslim retail market in 93
United States: Christian churches in 61; Hispanic market in 101–102; liberal economic theory 95; market competition 64; religious landscape of 64, 66–67; sociological study of religion in 63
Usunier, Jean-Claude 3, 26, 66, 68, 69

Veer, Peter van der 34
Venstre 117, 118, 122, 123

Warburg, Margit 3, 3n1, 23
Warner, Stephen R. 63
Watson, Bill. (C. W.) 46
Weber, Max 28, 45, 95, 123
Western Christianity 35
Western consumer culture 97–99, 103
Western countries: consumer culture 59, 97–99, 103; global economy 101; global-market regime 37, 38, 40, 41; modernisation in 35; Muslim diasporas in 48, 97, 98, 102; 'post-secular' hypothesis on 48; religious diversity 77; sociology of religion 71
Western Europe: multiculturalism 81; Muslims in 9, 100
Western immigrant societies 77, 78
'Western world' 33
Westphalia 32, 50
willingness-to-accept 16–17
willingness-to-pay 16–17
Woodhead, Linda 94
The World of Goods (Douglas and Isherwood) 27
World Trade Organisation (WTO) 68
WTO *see* World Trade Organisation (WTO)

Yavuz, Hakan 100
Yücel, Clémence Scalbert 79

zakat (obligatory almsgiving) 98
Zald, Mayer 9
Zara 93, 104
Žižek, Slavoj 80